THE COLLECTED WORKS OF CHÖKYI NYIMA RINPOCHE

Volume 1

RANGJUNG YESHE BOOKS • www.rangjung.com

PADMASAMBHAVA: *Treasures from Juniper Ridge* • *Advice from the Lotus-Born* • *Dakini Teachings* • *Following in Your Footsteps: The Lotus-Born Guru in Nepal* • *Following in Your Footsteps: The Lotus-Born Guru in India*

PADMASAMBHAVA AND JAMGÖN KONGTRÜL: *The Light of Wisdom, Vol. 1, Vol. 2, Vol. 3, Secret, Vol. 4 & Vol. 5*

PADMASAMBHAVA, CHOKGYUR LINGPA, JAMYANG KHYENTSE WANGPO, TULKU URGYEN RINPOCHE, ORGYEN TOBGYAL RINPOCHE, & OTHERS *Dispeller of Obstacles* • *The Tara Compendium* • *Powerful Transformation* • *Dakini Activity*

YESHE TSOGYAL: *The Lotus-Born*

DAKPO TASHI NAMGYAL: *Clarifying the Natural State*

TSELE NATSOK RANGDRÖL: *Mirror of Mindfulness* • *Heart Lamp* • *Empowerment and Samaya*

CHOKGYUR LINGPA: *Ocean of Amrita* • *The Great Gate* • *Skillful Grace* • *Great Accomplishment* • *Guru Heart Practices*

TRAKTUNG DUDJOM LINGPA: *A Clear Mirror*

JAMGÖN MIPHAM RINPOCHE: *Gateway to Knowledge, Vol. 1, Vol. 2, Vol. 3, & Vol. 4*

TULKU URGYEN RINPOCHE: *Blazing Splendor* • *Rainbow Painting* • *As It Is, Vol. 1 & Vol. 2* • *Vajra Speech* • *Repeating the Words of the Buddha* • *Dzogchen Deity Practice* • *Vajra Heart Revisited*

ADEU RINPOCHE: *Freedom in Bondage*

KHENCHEN THRANGU RINPOCHE: *Crystal Clear*

CHÖKYI NYIMA RINPOCHE: *Bardo Guidebook* • *Collected Works of Chökyi Nyima Rinpoche, Vol. 1 & Vol. 2*

TULKU THONDUP: *Enlightened Living*

ORGYEN TOBGYAL RINPOCHE: *Life & Teachings of Chokgyur Lingpa* • *Straight Talk* • *Sublime Lady of Immortality*

DZIGAR KONGTRÜL RINPOCHE: *Uncommon Happiness*

TSOKNYI RINPOCHE: *Fearless Simplicity* • *Carefree Dignity*

MARCIA BINDER SCHMIDT: *Dzogchen Primer* • *Dzogchen Essentials* • *Quintessential Dzogchen* • *Confessions of a Gypsy Yogini* • *Precious Songs of Awakening Compilation*

ERIK PEMA KUNSANG: *Wellsprings of the Great Perfection* • *A Tibetan Buddhist Companion* • *The Rangjung Yeshe Tibetan-English Dictionary of Buddhist Culture* & *Perfect Clarity*

The Collected Works of Chökyi Nyima Rinpoche

Volume 1

The Union of Mahamudra and Dzogchen

Bardo Guidebook

Translated from the Tibetan by Erik Pema Kunsang
Edited by Marcia B. Schmidt

Rangjung Yeshe Publications
55 Mitchell Blvd, Suite 20
San Rafael, CA 94903 USA

www.rangjung.com
www.lotustreasure.com

Copyright © 2020 Rangjung Yeshe Publications

All rights reserved. No part of this book may be reproduced in any form or by any means, electronic or mechanical—including photocopying, recording, and duplicating by means of any information storage and retrieval system—without written permission from the publisher.

1 3 5 7 9 8 6 4 2

First paperback edition published in 2021
Printed in the United States of America
Distributed to the book trade by:
Perseus Books/Ingram

Publication data: ISBN13: 978-1-7328717-8-6 (pbk)

Title: *The Collected Works of Chökyi Nyima Rinpoche, Volume 1*
Chökyi Nyima Rinpoche, Karma Chagmey the First.

The Union of Mahamudra and Dzogchen. Translated from the Tibetan by Erik Pema Kunsang (Erik Hein Schmidt). Root text is a translation of:
'phags pa thugs rje chen po'i dmar khrid phyag rdzogs zung 'jug gi nyams len snying po bsdus pa bzhugs so.
1. Mahamudra — Dzogchen. 2. Avalokiteshvara.
Foreword by Kybje Tulku Urgyen Rinpoche (1920–96).

The Bardo Guidebook. Translated from the Tibetan by Erik Pema Kunsang (Erik Hein Schmidt).
1. Death and dying. 2. Bardo. 3. Vajrayana philosophy Buddhism.
4. Buddhism Tibet. I. Title.

FIRST EDITION

Photo credit: Chris Zvitkovits

The Union of Mahamudra and Dzogchen

*A Commentary on The Quintessence of Spiritual Practice,
The Direct Instructions of the Great Compassionate One*

Karma Chagmey Rinpoche

Clarification by
Chökyi Nyima Rinpoche

CONTENTS

Proclamation by His Holiness the 16th Karmapa	1
Translator's Preface	3
Introductory Teachings	7
Summarizing the Profound Teachings	21
Taking Advantage of the Human Body Which Is Difficult to Find	47
Thinking of Impermanence, Cause and Effect	63
The Meditation Session	89
Training Directly in Development and Completion	125
Clearing Obstacles for Experience to Occur	161
The Song of Enhancement	215
Taking Death as Path	231
Five Songs by Chökyi Nyima Rinpoche	245

HIS HOLINESS
THE GYALWA KARMAPA

DHARMA CHAKRA CENTRE
RUMTEK
GANGTOK
SIKKIM

Proclamation to all faithful people whose eyes are wide open to the Dharma

This is to certify that I have recognized Drongtrül Chökyi Nyima Rinpoche as the seventh incarnation of the Dharma sovereign of Drong-ngur Tubten Shedrub Dargye Ling Monastery. From the age of thirteen, he has studied here at my seat, Rumtek Monastery, reflecting upon an ocean of scriptures. Like filling a vase to the brim, I have personally bestowed upon him empowerments, reading transmissions, and oral instructions.

In accordance with my command, the eminent Tulku Urgyen Rinpoche, my root guru, has established a new institute for the Buddhadharma in the country of Nepal. For that reason, with an auspicious enthronement, I have reinstated Chökyi Nyima Rinpoche in his traditional position of a superior incarnate lama of the Kagyü lineage.

Having empowered him as an upholder of the Buddhadharma, he shall be capable of benefitting living beings and spreading the teachings. This he shall do by safekeeping and sustaining the Dharma and by means of exposition, debate and composition, in that monastery as well as in all countries worldwide. It is my deepest aspiration that this may be accomplished.

This was written by the sixteenth in the line of incarnations of the glorious Karmapas on the tenth of September 1974, at the great monastery of Rumtek in Sikkim (India).

Translator's Preface

Chökyi Nyima Rinpoche was born near Lhasa in central Tibet in 1951. When 18 months old, he was recognized by His Holiness the Gyalwang Karmapa as the seventh incarnation of the great yogi Gar Drubchen, an emanation of Nagarjuna. Shortly thereafter, he moved to his predecessor's monastery, Drong Gön Tubten Dargye Ling, at Nakchuka north of Lhasa. Rinpoche left Tibet before the 1959 communist takeover.

Since 1959, he has received personal guidance and transmission from many of the foremost Buddhist teachers of this century headed by His Holiness the Gyalwang Karmapa, H.H. Dudjom Rinpoche, H.H. Dilgo Khyentse Rinpoche, his father, H.E. Tulku Urgyen Rinpoche, Most Venerable Kalu Rinpoche, Khenchen Thrangu Rinpoche, Kunu Rinpoche, Khenpo Rinchen and Khenpo Dazer.

In 1974, he moved to Boudhanath, near Kathmandu, and helped his father build the Ka-Nying Shedrup Ling Monastery. Later he was made abbot by H.H. Karmapa, taking responsibility for the physical and spiritual well-being of the community of monks. Fulfilling the wish of his teachers, he has over two decades generously given his time and energy to teaching people from all corners of the world.

The 1985 seminar, presented at Rangjung Yeshe Institute in the monastery, was based on a text entitled *The Union of Mahamudra and Dzogchen, The Direct Instructions of the Great Compassionate One*, written by Karma Chagmey the First (1605–70). This text offers clear and concise teachings on the practices of Mahamudra and Dzogchen, which can be applied immediately, even by beginners.

The following biographical data about Karma Chagmey the First is extracted from Ven. Khetsun Sangpo's *Biographical Dictionary of Tibet and Tibetan Buddhism*, Vol. VII.

• • •

Karma Chagmey was taught to meditate at the age of five by his own father. From that time on he strove to always remain in undistracted mindfulness.

At the age of twelve he received empowerment from Situ Rinpoche and thereafter stayed in recitation retreat. From his father he received all the instructions on sadhana according to the Nyingma system. When later he presented his understanding to Trungpa Kunga Namgyal (1555–1628), he was given the pointing-out instruction. As advised by Trungpa Rinpoche, he entered the monastery of Sadam.

At one point he visited Tsurphu and met the tenth Karmapa and also the Sixth Sharmapa, Chökyi Wangchuk (1584–1630), who allowed him to remain there. At Tsurphu, he studied the Five Treatises of Maitreya and the Hevajra Tantra as well as the Third Karmapa's explanation of Vajrayana practice, *Sabmo Nangdön, the Profound Inner Meaning*. During this time, he concentrated on the sadhana of White Manjushri and became renowned as being invincible in debate. Once when he made supplications at the tomb of the Sixth Sharmapa, the wisdom of Mahamudra dawned in his mind. Later on, at Nedo, he spent a long time in retreat. In a vision of Sharmapa Chökyi Wangchuk, he was entrusted with the teachings of Mahamudra. Moreover, he was given the prediction that by devoting his life completely to practice, he would be able to tremendously help those essential teachings.

He had numerous visions of his *yidam;* the protectors of the Dharma offered themselves to him as servants. All the signs and experiences accompanying his progress through the paths and bhumis appeared and he was endowed with the splendor of clairvoyance and miraculous powers. During his lifetime he reached the level of realization in Mahamudra called 'greater one taste.' There were many people who realized the natural state simply through receiving empowerment, instructions or a letter of advice from him.

At the age of 64 Karma Chagmey passed away and went to the Realm of Lotus Light, the pure land of Padmasambhava. At the cremation ceremony, rainbow lights appeared, and a gentle rain drizzled. In his ashes were found several naturally formed images and numerous relic-pills.

· · ·

Karma Chagmey had tremendous impact on the Kagyü and Nyingma lineages. He authored more than 55 volumes. His writings were in a simple language which common people could also understand. The most famous of his writings is *Chagmey Richö, Chagmey's Mountain Practice;* a collection of advice to meditators. During the three centuries since his passing away, countless meditator-hermits and lay practitioners learned his *Direct Instructions of the Great Compassionate One* by heart and would use it as a guideline for their spiritual practice.

Tulku Urgyen Rinpoche suggested that the Union would be suitable for foreign students at the yearly Dharma assembly. In preparation, a translation of Karma Chagmey's root text was made with the difficult points clarified by Chökyi Nyima Rinpoche himself. During the seminar, Chökyi Nyima Rinpoche gave 20 talks which were later transcribed, edited and presented herein as a book. I am deeply grateful to the Rinpoches for making this opportunity possible and am honored to share these teachings with interested practitioners.

A living master's oral teachings are especially precious because they represent the quintessence of all the scriptures he has studied and the teachings he has received which otherwise lie beyond the reach of ordinary people. Even more precious is Rinpoche's insight and skill in adapting his teaching to a present day audience.

From beginning to end, this work was the outcome of a group effort. I would like to thank the editorial assistants: Judith Amtzis and S. Lhamo, and the staff: Maria Pelaez, Ben Rosensweig, Phinjo Sherpa, Karen Ariens, and Carol Faust, as well as all our other friends who generously contributed their time and energy.

Erik Pema Kunsang

Introductory Teachings

Explanation of the Title

The teachings in this book are based on the text entitled *The Union of Mahamudra and Dzogchen: The Direct Instructions of the Compassionate One,* by Karma Chagmey Rinpoche the First.

The term 'Direct Instructions' indicates that these teachings are for people who intend to put them directly into practice. Of all the direct instructions, such as Mahamudra and Dzogchen, this instruction is the essence of how to practice. Just as the essence of milk is butter, this instruction is the very quintessence of all the pure teachings condensed into their essential points.

The 'Great Compassionate One' is the bodhisattva Avalokiteshvara. The bodhisattva path has been traversed by all the buddhas of the past, who, by perfecting the virtues of the bodhisattvas, the six *paramitas,* attained complete enlightenment. All the buddhas of the future will also progress on the path of the bodhisattva. Those presently on the way to attaining enlightenment practice the bodhisattva path in the same way. The Great Compassionate One, Avalokiteshvara, is the embodiment of compassion and loving kindness.

The 'Union of Mahamudra and Dzogchen' means that no separation exists between the two. Both Mahamudra and Dzogchen contain three subsections. In Mahamudra the sections are called *Sutra, Tantra,* and *Essence Mahamudra*. In Dzogchen they are called *Mind, Space,* and *Instruction Sections*. In the ultimate view of these two schools, there is no difference.

The correct view is free from extremes. It is the state beyond concepts, transcending mental fabrications. It is inexpressible, inconceivable, and indescribable. If one has any attachment or clinging, one does not have the right view: the true view is without fixation. Thus, from the point of the view, no contradiction exists between Mahamudra and Dzogchen; they are inseparable, in union.

This book includes teachings on the *general outer preliminaries* of the *four mind-changings:* the precious human body, impermanence and death, cause and effect regarding actions, and the sufferings of samsara. Also included are *the special inner preliminaries,* as well as the main practice of the stages of *development* and *completion,* in the sense that instructions are given on how to visualize ourselves in the form of the deity Avalokiteshvara. The final section presents teachings on the view of Mahamudra and Dzogchen.

These root verses of Karma Chagmey also concern the nature of mind, the natural state, the self-existing wakefulness within ourselves. They explain this natural state, how it works, what its characteristics are, and how it can be known. In addition, Karma Chagmey describes the benefits of recognizing it, the disadvantages of not knowing about it, and how it is acknowledged through the pointing-out instruction of a qualified master. Once we recognize the nature of mind, is that simply enough, or must we then practice some kind of path? How do we practice? What mistakes or errors can we make? If we do take a side-track, how can this be corrected? These are the subjects of these teachings and the questions this book tries to answer.

THE AUTHOR

The author of the root text upon which this commentary is based, the Tibetan siddha Karma Chagmey also known as Raga Asya, was a great master, who, through study, attained vast learning regarding the Dharma. Next, through reflection, he clarified all his doubts and uncertainties; and finally, through practice, he attained spiritual realization. He spent most of his time meditating in secluded mountain caves.

The first Karma Chagmey was a great practitioner who spent his whole life in different mountain retreats, attaining great realization. He was a very simple man, with few plans and worldly activities. When he composed something, it was because someone asked for a teaching. He would say: "Okay. Where is paper and a pen?" He would write the teaching down, hand it over and that was that. After his death, no one person had a complete collection of all his teachings, as his writings were in the hands of different people. Some teachings were collected later, but it's doubtful that everything was found. Karma Chagmey's complete works don't exist. Karma Chagmey was nonsectarian, highly realized, a learned *yogi* and an incredible teacher. His special ability was to focus on exactly what was beneficial for his students without going into many elaborations. Like Paltrül Rinpoche's teachings, Karma Chagmey's advice are short and to the point. It would be beneficial to study those teachings, to reflect on them, and put them into practice.

Karma Chagmey taught disciples who had fervent devotion, deep interest in the teachings and great diligence in practice. He taught without the slightest expectation of attaining fame, prestige, or a high position, but solely out of genuine kindness and compassion for others.

Karma Chagmey was a contemporary of Sharmapa Chökyi Wangchuk who lived in the beginning of the seventeenth century. Karma Chagmey traveled as a pilgrim and beggar in Tibet, and eventually arrived at Tsurphu monastery, the seat of the Karmapas. The Karmapa had, at that time, passed away, and the Sharmapa was his successor. According to his biography, since Karma Chagmey joined the monastery as a mere beggar, the other monks thought he was useless and gave him a difficult time. Subsequently, when he practiced the *Six Doctrines of Naropa* and Mahamudra in solitary caves, he quickly attained great realization. Later, people said there was no one like Karma Chagmey in all of Tibet.

HOW THE DHARMA IS TAUGHT

A teaching may be given in various ways. A fully enlightened buddha expounds the Dharma in one way; an exalted being, abiding on one of the bodhisattva levels, in another; someone who has attained the realization of an *arhat,* in a third; and a learned *pandita* in yet another. A simple meditator in a mountain retreat teaches with few elaborations; while a high lama, a great master sitting on a throne, teaches the important points of the Dharma in a concise and impressive way. Finally, there is a manner of giving meditation instruction in a direct, simple fashion.

A fully enlightened buddha expounds the Dharma through the threefold miraculous action of his body, speech, and mind. A fully enlightened buddha has purified not only the *obscuration of disturbing emotions,* but also the more subtle *obscuration of habitual tendencies* and the *cognitive obscuration.* Like a fully blossomed flower, he has completely developed all the qualities of abandonment and realization.

When a buddha teaches, he emanates boundless rays of light from his body, forehead, and tongue, which automatically summon all who are qualified to hear the teaching. Not only human beings, but also nonhumans, spiritual, and celestial beings naturally gather in an assembly before him. He has the power to automatically ripen those who have not yet matured, and to free those who have not yet been liberated.

Regarding a buddha's speech, his voice is unlike that of an ordinary being. Usually, those who sit close to a teacher can easily hear him, but those far in the back have difficulty hearing what is being said. However, when a buddha teaches, one can sit anywhere and still hear the words very clearly and precisely. When a fully enlightened buddha teaches, we needn't even understand the language of the teaching; each person will perceive the words in his own native language.

A fully enlightened buddha does not speak like an ordinary person — coughing, making mistakes, or filling in gaps with superfluous words. Even an arhat still speaks this way, confusing the head and tail of a sentence or using unclear words, but a buddha has perfect command of his faculty of speech.

A buddha's mind, which possesses the wisdom that clearly sees past, present, and future, perceives perfectly the different capacities and potentials of each person present, not only for that particular life but for countless past lifetimes. Therefore, he can give teachings which are perfectly appropriate for each individual's propensities. An arhat, on the other hand, is not yet able to do this.

An old story is told about a certain householder. An arhat at first considered teaching him, but concluded that the teachings would not benefit him, and so decided to remain silent. Because he could not see far enough back into the householder's past, the arhat made a poor decision. The Buddha, who was aware of the situation, objected, saying: "That man has potential for enlightenment, and he should be given the teachings, after which he will be swiftly liberated." Thus, a buddha is said to teach through the threefold miraculous actions of body, speech, and mind.

A bodhisattva teaches by means of the *six paramitas* or transcendental actions. A bodhisattva is able to actualize these actions, whereas we, as beginners, can enact only a semblance.

To give or to attend a lecture is the *paramita* of giving. True generosity is free from any hope of reward or gratitude. The paramita of discipline is to proceed in the proper and correct manner. The paramita of patience is to endure whatever difficulties or hardships we encounter. The paramita of diligence is to be tireless or to exert oneself continuously. The paramita of concentration is to remain undistracted and the paramita of knowledge is to embrace the teaching with awareness. The speaker and the listener both should possess these qualities.

An arhat teaches by means of three purities: the purity of the person who is being taught; the purity of the teacher being free from desire for honor and gain; and the purity of the teaching itself being a true remedy for disturbing emotions. How are these three purities actualized? Just as we check to see if a cup is too small or too large when pouring liquid into it, not overfilling a small cup or pouring too little into a large cup, an arhat, possessing the power of clairvoyance, knows the minds of others, and will therefore know whether or not a teaching is suitable for another person at that particular time. Secondly, because he has totally extinguished all his disturbing emotions, the arhat himself is pure. Thirdly, the teachings should also be pure. Causing no negative emotions to arise, they should be methods for discarding the disturbing emotions.

Five qualities must be present when a learned pandita expounds the Dharma. First, the teachings should be based upon the words of a fully enlightened buddha or of a completely qualified master from the past. This must be the basis for his teaching. Secondly, he should elaborate by explaining it with his own commentary and should identify very clearly who authored the teaching. Thirdly, he should state to whom the teaching was given. Was it given to bodhisattvas, *shravakas,* or ordinary beings? Next, he should describe the kind of teaching that it is. Is it a philosophy, such as the *Middle Way*? Additionally, he should be able to identify exactly the different quotations appearing in the text. Finally, he should explain the category of Dharma to which the teaching belongs: *Vinaya, Abhidharma,* or *Sutra.*

There are several other styles of teaching as well. A great master might have a particular style of giving concise but impressive teachings on the key points of the Dharma, while a meditator in the mountains will teach in a very simple and unelaborate way. Finally, a realized meditation master teaches by giving direct instruction for practice. This root text belongs to the last category, that of direct instructions.

HOW TO LISTEN TO THE DHARMA

Listening to a Dharma teaching with the motivation of attaining enlightenment oneself is called an inferior motivation. However, listening with the intention of putting the advice into practice in order to ultimately guide all sentient beings to enlightenment is called the superior motivation or *bodhichitta*. The acts of listening to and studying Dharma teachings should be embraced with this superior motivation.

It is most important to keep a pure attitude, thinking: "I will listen to the teachings and study in order to generate compassion, intelligence, and diligence. Through this, may I become able to benefit myself and others." The correct way to study and practice is with this pure motivation. But, if one has other intentions, is motivated by a desire to aggrandize oneself, to become influential, or to prevent others from becoming more knowledgeable, even though we study a pure teaching, our learning will result in something impure.

Of the different kinds of disturbing emotions, the two most difficult to identify within ourselves are pride and jealousy. These two will prevent good qualities from arising. A proverb states: "Eloquent sayings can also be found in the mouth of a child." One can learn from anyone, and shouldn't belittle those who are unlearned, thinking: "They don't know anything. Knowing much more, I'm more important." It is also said: "The iron ball of arrogance never gets wet inside, even when submerged in water." A proud and arrogant mind cannot assimilate any good qualities.

According to the very profound Vajrayana, one should listen to a teaching while keeping the purity of the *five perfections:* the perfections of teacher, teachings, retinue, place, and time.

A Hinayana practitioner should keep the notion of himself as someone suffering from a disease, of the teacher as a doctor, of the Dharma as the medicine, and of the practice as the cure. These are called the *four pure notions*. Many things are to be kept in mind, but the different attitudes can be condensed into the single thought: "I will listen to the teachings to benefit myself and all other sentient beings."

WHAT TO AVOID

When receiving teachings, a few things should be avoided. One should be free from the three defects of the vessel, the six stains, and the five ways of misapprehending.

The first defect of a vessel is that of inattention. The ears and mind are the vessel, and the teachings, the precious nectar. One listens with one's ears, but if one's mind is focused upon a sight, such as a vase of flowers or a painting on the wall, and is absorbed in the faculty of seeing, the mind does not hear. Although physically present in a Dharma assembly, if one is inattentive to what is being said, one is like a vessel turned upside down, which cannot retain the liquid poured into it. Therefore, being attentive is very important.

The second defect is that of not remembering, like a vessel leaking from the bottom. No matter how much is poured into the vessel, it will never become full. In this situation, one hears something, and then forgets; hearing something else, this too is soon forgotten. If someone asks after a few hours: "What was the talk about today?" one cannot answer. Thus, you must remember and retain what is being said.

The third defect is that of a poisoned vessel spoiling whatever is poured into it. If one harbors the wrong motivation, the Dharma teaching will be spoiled as if placed in a vessel containing poison. For example, if we fail to clean our teacup properly, the fresh tea poured into it will later be entirely spoiled. Tasting it, we will say, "That's unfit to drink." Likewise, when we undertake a study of the Dharma, which is pure and perfect, with a sense of competing with our Dharma friends, with the wish to show off in front of others, or with the desire to seek honor, respect, or a better position in work, then the Dharma will be tainted by our impure motivation, just like a pure liquid poured into a dirty cup.

There are also six stains, of which arrogance is the first. If, inflated with conceit, one feels that one already knows, then learning is very difficult. Arrogance acts like a block, an obscuration. Thinking we already know, we won't ask questions of others; not inquiring, we won't learn anything. Try to avoid this stain.

The second stain is called disinterest. Although one is present, lacking genuine interest, one feels bored. Try to be fresh and ready to receive what is forthcoming.

The third stain, lack of endeavor, means that one is not actively engaging in the teaching, the practice, and so forth.

Distraction is the fourth stain. Sometimes one sits and fiddles with a pen thinking of other things, and the teaching sounds like "blah, blah, blah…" The words aren't even heard distinctly. This is called distraction.

The fifth stain is being withdrawn; one is in a state between sleeping and waking, sitting with open eyes, yet hearing nothing. Being withdrawn means remaining in a dull, stupid state.

The sixth stain is weariness, meaning that one feels a little uncomfortable. The seat might be too hard, or one may feel a little too cold or too hot, hungry or thirsty. This slight discomfort becomes magnified and feels like such a tremendous problem that we want the session to end as soon as possible.

In addition, there are the five ways of misapprehending. The first of these is called 'getting the words, but not the meaning.' For instance, sometimes we might hear a brief enticing story or a very funny one; we laugh, and then try to remember it and repeat it to a friend. We remember that it was funny, but the main points of the story, or in this case the teaching, the crucial points, we forget.

The second is called 'getting the meaning, but not the words.' We have some idea about what is meant by emptiness, and some of the more profound points, but we lack the words that express the teaching. It is necessary to become articulate in order to be able to explain to others.

The next three are quite simple: 'getting the meaning wrong,' 'getting the order wrong,' and 'misinterpreting the examples.'

Since we are here studying the teachings, if we can keep clear of these three defects, six stains, and five ways of misapprehending, we will very quickly progress in our studies, our contemplation, and our practice.

PROPER MOTIVATION AND CONDUCT

It is very important to keep pure motivation and proper conduct while listening to the teachings, while studying and contemplating them, and while applying them in practice.

A story about a Kadampa *geshe* named Ben illustrates this point. While staying in retreat, Ben heard one morning that his disciples and benefactors had decided to visit. He arranged his shrine very neatly in anticipation of their arrival, cleaning everything so that they would be impressed and think that he was really a first-class practitioner. He hoped that they might make larger donations. But then, reflecting upon his motivation, he saw that it was not completely pure, that it was merely an ambitious attempt to impress others and gain something for himself. So, taking a handful of ashes, he threw them all over the shrine until it became a real mess.

Later, when Phadampa Sangye went to Tibet and heard the story, he said: "In all the monasteries and the temples of Tibet, the shrines are arranged very neatly with impressive offerings, but none is as impressive as the offering on the shrine of Geshe Ben." Since throwing ashes and dirt on one's shrine is considered very bad conduct, that was quite an unconventional thing to say. Among Tibetans, if anyone does such a thing, others would consider his actions to be completely improper, but actually, Phadampa Sangye was talking about Geshe Ben's pure motivation underlying that action. He meant that in order for one to gather the accumulations and purify the obscurations, one's shrine should always be kept clean and tidy; but, if this is done only out of a motivation for personal gain and honor, then throwing ashes is better.

If you study, reflect, or practice with an attitude of pride or competition, hoping to become great, then there will be little benefit whatever you do. Hence, whether studying, contemplating, or meditating, we shouldn't allow ourselves to be governed by hypocrisy or competitiveness.

There is a story about a man with little intelligence, but great faith. While walking down the road one day, he saw a *tsa-tsa,* a small religious image, like a stupa made of clay, lying on the ground, and he thought: "How terrible! You shouldn't be lying there in the dust. You'll get cold and wet. I must put you in some safe place." Being a simple-minded person, he regarded the image as though it were a person. He looked right, left, and all around for something to cover it with. Finally, noticing an old shoe lying on the road, he said: "Now, you stay nicely under here, so you won't get wet!" He tucked it under the shoe. In Tibetan culture, to point one's feet at another person, to step over another person, to put shoes or anything that we step upon near or above a sacred image is considered a grave offense, but since this fellow acted out of pure motivation, there was no fault on his part.

Another meditator used to place two heaps of pebbles, one set of black and one set of white, by his side while meditating. Each time he had a good thought, he would place a white pebble in one pile, and each time he had a bad thought, he would add a black pebble to the other pile. At the end of the day, he would count the pebbles to see which color was predominant. If he found seventy black pebbles and only twenty white ones, he would rebuke himself, saying: "You have been really bad today. You haven't maintained good thoughts so you only get half a meal to eat and you can sleep only half the night." He continued on in this way. If there were only black pebbles, he would say "You really are a lousy meditator. No food for you today and no sleep, either. If you continue like this, how can you ever attain enlightenment?" But, if it happened that there were more white pebbles in the pile, then he would say to himself: "Oh, you've been really good today. Tonight you can have an especially good meal and a good sleep. Be happy now." In this way, he trained his mind through this constant checking. The point is that it is important to check your motivation, and to transform it to the correct one.

We may dress up nicely and appear very well-groomed, but if our minds and attitudes are unhealthy, then looking good won't really matter much. This principle is not only for actual practice. When we study or learn something new and reflect upon it, or even when teaching others, we should maintain a pure motivation. It is important to keep the correct attitude, to be honest and straight-forward, to have a good heart and a pure outlook, not only in matters concerning the Dharma, but in our ordinary actions in daily life as well. In this way, whatever we do will be beneficial. Otherwise, though we may appear to be acting in a wholesome way, if our basic intention is tainted by pride, competitiveness, or desire for personal gain or profit, then our actions will generate negative results.

Like Geshe Ben, we must be free from deceit and hypocrisy. If you know something, then you know that much; you should never pretend to know more. If you pretend to have great experience in practice without having done much meditation or if you pretend to be very learned and skilled in the teachings without having studied much, it is hypocritical and deceives others. In a dharmic sense this is dangerous, because if you pretend to be a teacher or a qualified master, others may follow. However, if you are like a person who is blind, lacking the eye of wisdom, then you might jump over a precipice into an abyss with all of your followers. Therefore, it is always a great defect and danger to be hypocritical and pretentious, particularly as a teacher or a student of the Buddhadharma.

In the West you have comic books, and, in Tibet we have similar story books. One such book contains a story about a very proud and aggressive lion. He thought he was the most powerful beast in the world, but one day a mouse came and told him, teasingly: "You know, there's another lion much stronger and fiercer than you are." The lion immediately wanted to find this rival, thinking he would challenge him to a fight, win, and become renowned as the most ferocious lion in all the land.

The lion asked the whereabouts of his foe, and the little mouse led him to a very deep well, pointed down, and said, "The other lion is down there. Just look!" The lion looked into the well, and sure enough, he saw the face of a lion glaring up at him from the bottom. The lion roared at it and the other echoed a reply. The first lion became so terribly angry that he leaped straight down into the face of his 'enemy' and drowned.

A sense of competitiveness, or wondering, "How can someone possibly be better than me?" is detrimental to spiritual practice, and not only harms others, but can also destroy oneself. Therefore, in short, maintain pure motivation.

THE MEANING OF DHARMA

Traditionally, the word *Dharma,* a Sanskrit word, has ten different meanings. Of the ten primary meanings, the one most often associated with this word is what is known as the true Dharma, the ultimate truth, or the nature of things as they are. Without depending upon words and concepts, one cannot realize the ultimate truth; and without this realization, one cannot attain liberation.

One needs a method or means for understanding ultimate truth. In that sense, the Dharma can be thought of as an antidote, a remedy or a cure to promote some kind of positive change or transformation. The word Dharma conveys this meaning: that which is the method for realizing the ultimate truth.

HOW TO ASSIMILATE THE DHARMA

At this point, entering the Dharma, we are engaged in developing three aspects of knowledge: knowledge resulting from learning, knowledge resulting from reflection, and knowledge resulting from meditation. When learning Dharma or listening to a Dharma teaching, we should listen like a mountain deer listening to the sound of a flute — completely absorbed and undistracted. We should concentrate on what is being said without letting our attention wander elsewhere, listening closely and attentively to each word.

When contemplating the teachings, we should be like northern Tibetans shearing a sheep, or like a barber cutting the hair of a customer, or like a carpet-weaver making a carpet. These people must pay constant attention to their work and be aware of whether or not their fingers are making a mistake. Similarly, when contemplating and reflecting on the correct meaning of the teachings, we should be alert and mindful, not jumping at random from one thing to the next.

When meditating on the teachings, we should be like a mute tasting molasses: there is quite a taste, but the mute cannot describe it. This means that with great joy, great interest and great endeavor, we should delight in putting the teachings into practice through meditation.

To practice the Dharma doesn't mean just meditating, but it means engaging in whatever virtuous actions are possible. When practicing the Dharma, we should be like a hungry yak eating grass. One bite alone will not fill his stomach and satisfy him, but as he's chewing one mouthful, he is already eyeing the next patch of grass, ready to go for that. Similarly, if one does just a little bit of practice, and thinks, "Now, that's sufficient," and jumps to something else, one will never be very successful. Rather, be like the hungry yak. As soon as you have heard a teaching, immediately think about it. After that, immediately put it into practice and apply it.

The result of learning and reflection and meditation is like the sun in a cloudless sky. We should practice without separating the three. Practice without learning is like climbing a mountain without arms; learning without practice is like being lost on a vast plain. If we only study and think about the teachings, while failing to put them into practice, we will only develop excessive pride and become bloated with arrogance. Yet, it is difficult to achieve realization if we just practice without studying the teachings and thinking about them. We need some techniques to depend upon, as well as having some idea about what we are doing. Therefore, never separate learning, reflection, and meditation, so that we will be like the sun unobstructed by clouds. This is how it should be, and how it will be.

1
The Song of Summarizing the Profound Teachings

Namo Mahakarunikaye

Emaho!
The sutras, tantras, and philosophical scriptures are extensive and great in number.
However, life is short and intelligence limited, so it is hard to cover them completely.
You may know a lot, but if you don't put it into practice,
It's like dying of thirst on the bank of a great lake.
Likewise, it sometimes happens that a common corpse is found in the bed of a great scholar.

Namo means 'I pay homage;' *Mahakarunikaye* means 'to the Great Compassionate One.' An incredible amount of Buddhist literature has been preserved, such as the sutras of Mahayana, the tantras of Vajrayana, and all the various texts of philosophy, including the thirteen major philosophical texts, the different sciences and so forth. All are contained in a vast number of written works. The Kangyur includes the direct teachings of the Buddha, and the Tengyur contains the treatises and commentaries by panditas.

A human life span is brief, and full of dangers. By eating well, taking medicine, and by a variety of other methods we try to keep ourselves healthy and to extend our lives; yet, sometimes these efforts have the opposite effect. Illnesses are common. In any case, life is impermanent and won't last forever.

Our intelligence is also quite limited; we lack both the capacity and the time to make a thorough study of the vast amount of teachings, and it is difficult to fully study and understand them. Even were we to study quite a lot and become very learned, merely knowing the theories without assimilating them through reflection and actual practice would be like dying of thirst on the bank of a great freshwater lake. What a complete waste to die like that!

In the next line, the word 'scholar' means someone learned in the different sciences and so forth. In the Buddhist sense, it refers particularly to someone learned in the inner sciences: the philosophy of Buddhism, the practices, and so on. Traditionally, studying is said to cause the learned person to become gentle and disciplined, while the sign of success in practice is to have fewer and fewer disturbing emotions. That is how it should be. It could happen however, that instead of becoming a learned scholar and truly assimilating the teachings, our arrogance and pride increase steadily.

At the time of death, wonderful signs such as relic pills remaining in the cremation ashes will indicate the passing away of a truly realized being. In other cases, the body may remain in the meditation posture for a long period of time without decomposing. Rainbow lights and various other signs sometimes manifest. But, if during our lifetime the accumulation of studies did not help our mind or tame our disturbing emotions, we will die just like an ordinary person. Wouldn't this be sad?

At the time of death, there are many ways to discover whether or not a person was a good practitioner. The body left behind by an ordinary being will become stiff in a very short time. If the flesh is manipulated, it will be like chewing gum. If pulled out, it will remain stretched, unlike the skin of a living person. However, if someone has attained a certain level of practice, the body will remain pliant, the flesh supple, and the mouth and eyes will have a particular expression. These are only a few examples of the many types of signs.

Tibetans have a saying: "The butter hide is not cured by butter." This sounds strange to Westerners, but to cure cow hide, we must rub it with oil and manipulate it until it becomes quite flexible. Afterwards, it will never become hard and stiff again. In Tibet, the particular skin used to store butter becomes, after some time, completely stiff, like iron. This is the analogy for a Dharma follower who fails to take the teachings to heart. The whole point of Dharma practice is to increase our love for others, our compassion, and our understanding of emptiness, while decreasing our negative emotions. If, instead, we become more inflexible, a common corpse may be found in the bed of a scholar.

> The scriptures of the sutras and tantras and the words of the learned and accomplished ones of India and Tibet
> All have great blessings but are difficult for ordinary people to grasp.
> Though they are indispensable for teaching in a monastic college,
> For one-pointed practice they are of little use.
> This 'pointing-out instruction for an old lady' is more beneficial for your mind than all of the others.

About 100 volumes of what the Buddha himself taught, the extensive sutras and the profound tantras, are in print. The commentaries on these, written by the panditas and great masters of the past, also have commentaries. Some commentaries on the sutras, the tantras, and the different sciences and philosophies, have themselves innumerable commentaries. In this way, a tremendous amount of literature exists which was composed by the masters of India and Tibet.

It is best is if we can study all of these and get a complete understanding through learning, personal experience, and practice. The scriptures have great beneficial effects and blessings. If we are to become a learned or exalted teacher in a monastic college, we should possess the nine attributes of a learned person. We should, for example, be skilled in composition, debate, and exposition, as well as in study, reflection, and practice. We should possess wisdom and a noble character, and have a pure and excellent attitude. In order to become a great teacher able to expound all these different philosophies, or in order to study in a Buddhist college, learning all of these things is indispensable. But for a householder with a family and without time to devote his entire life to these studies, a vast theoretical understanding is not important. On the contrary, experience through practice is more beneficial. In such a case, it is unimportant to go through this vastly detailed learning, but rather it is more crucial to condense all the teachings into a very short and precise one. If we were to stay alone in a cave and practice one-pointedly, then all this vast learning would be unnecessary.

Therefore, the 'pointing-out instruction for an old lady' means that all the teachings have been condensed into just a few essential lines of text which contain the vital point, the key point regarding the nature of the mind. If we can take such an instruction to heart, it is more beneficial for our mind than all of the scriptures.

> All the innumerable and profound teachings, such as
>   Mahamudra and Dzogchen,
> Which are decisive and unmistaken in each root text,
> Are indispensable when teaching disciples who will hold
>   the Dharma-lineages.
> But for personal practice, for the sake of the future,
> It is more profound to condense them all into one.

Our main teacher, Buddha Shakyamuni, expounded the different levels of teachings which are generally called the *nine vehicles*. Of these, Mahamudra and Dzogchen contain the pinnacle, or the highest and most profound view. It is said that among all the birds, the *garuda* is the most eminent; likewise, among all the viewpoints, Mahamudra and Dzogchen are most supreme.

These teachings have reached us today through a direct lineage. The Mahamudra teachings come through the *Kagyü lineage:* Tilopa, Naropa, Marpa, Milarepa, and so on, directly down to the practitioners of today. The Dzogchen teachings were passed down through Garab Dorje, Manjushrimitra, Shri Singha, and Guru Rinpoche, to our own root teacher. These teachings are transmitted when a qualified and competent master meets with a qualified student.

There are various methods of *transmission:* from mind to mind directly, through indication or gesture, and by words. In the past, for transmission, it was sufficient for the master and disciple to simply rest their minds together in the composure of innate wakefulness. Another teacher might say merely, "Look into your mind!" or might point a finger at the sky. Through that, the disciple would recognize the ultimate nature, also known as *ordinary mind*.

The student would recognize the nature of his own mind through one of these instructions. However, we are not at that stage presently, and therefore must depend upon words and explanations. It is said that without the use of words and concepts, we cannot understand the ultimate truth; and without understanding ultimate truth, we will not attain liberation. Here, at this point in time, we need to rely upon words in order to recognize that which is beyond words, the ultimate truth or ordinary mind.

> To grasp precisely and unmistakenly the various traditions
>   of the Dharma
> Is necessary for upholding the doctrinal teachings.
> But if you are concerned with the welfare of your future,
> It is more profound to train in being nonsectarian, seeing
>   all of them as being pure.

When elaborating on the teachings of these various profound viewpoints, the teacher must expound them exactly according to the traditional methods. In this way the student will achieve an understanding which exactly duplicates the teacher's realization — a perfect replica. Like clay poured into a mold and stamped out, the image will be exactly like the mold. When teaching Madhyamika, we should teach exactly according to the Madhyamika system; when teaching Mahamudra, it should be exactly according to the Mahamudra system and likewise, for the four philosophical schools: the Vaibhashika, Sautrantika, Mind Only, and Madhyamika.

The Vaibhashika school has its own viewpoint, its own practice, mode of conduct, and result. The *Shravaka* teaching itself is divided into eighteen schools, each of which should be kept precisely according to its own point of view, its own practice, and its own result. If we attempt to mix it with other viewpoints, everything will become distorted and we will be unable to ensure that the teachings continue.

Each of the views should be maintained individually. When holding one viewpoint and debating with another, as the views become successively more profound, the highest viewpoint should be able to win the debate. For instance, the Mind Only is more profound than the Sautrantika. In this way, we can progress with successively deeper understanding through the nine vehicles, and if we uphold the Buddha's teachings, we will know precisely and separately how to teach the different views of each. The first three vehicles are for shravakas, pratyekabuddhas, and bodhisattvas. The three outer tantric vehicles are the Kriya, Upa, and Yoga. Finally, there are the three inner tantric vehicles which are Maha, Anu, and Ati. If we know precisely the different details of these, without confusing them, then we will be able to uphold the Buddha's teachings.

In this context, we should, for our own benefit, first study and reflect upon the teachings, and then put them into practice through meditation. For the sake of others, we should be able to expound upon, compose, and refute objections to the teachings. We should be able to expound Shravaka teachings according to the Shravaka system without confusing it with the Pratyekabuddha teachings. We should be able to expound the Pratyekabuddha teachings without confusing them with the Mahayana teachings. When teaching the Mahayana, even though the viewpoints of the *Mind Only school* are very subtle and almost the same as the Madhyamika system, we should still be able to discuss them individually. In this way, we will be able to teach correctly and uphold the Dharma lineages properly. Thus, it is good to study if possible, but if we are only practicing to gain understanding and to facilitate our own enlightenment, such extensive study is not necessary.

When the text advises us to practice for the sake of the future, it doesn't mean only for the next life, but for all times: this present life, the intermediate state after death, and for all future lives, until attaining perfect enlightenment. It is more profound to practice with this understanding, condensing all the teachings into one. This does not mean that we should mix it all together in one big melting pot so that the viewpoint from the Shravaka school is, for example, mixed with the simplicity of Mahamudra. It means that the teachings are all given in order to tame our own mind, to uproot the *three poisons*. Knowing this and practicing from this viewpoint is the meaning of 'condensing all teachings into one.' The significance of condensing them all into one is that we should practice the *three yanas* — the Hinayana, Mahayana, and Vajrayana — without any contradiction or conflict between them.

Regarding the vehicle for shravakas, or Hinayana, the main point is the practice of nonattachment, peace and renunciation. Emphasis is placed on acknowledging that we experience samsaric existence due to ego-clinging and craving for personal gain. Therefore we try to cut down desire, attachment, and the wish to harm other beings. Having discarded ego-clinging, a Shravaka practitioner pursues the attainment of *nirvana,* the state of permanent peace. The main emphasis is on abandoning attachment. There is no contradiction here with respect to the higher vehicles because in both Mahayana and Vajrayana we also abandon the disturbing emotion of attachment.

In Mahayana, we regard the principal disturbing emotion as aversion, which manifests as anger and aggression. This aversion prevents us from benefiting others — the main point of Mahayana practice. In the Mahayana vehicle we practice purifying aggression while aspiring to help others through cultivating love and compassion. This does not contradict the other vehicles, since we also try to eliminate the disturbing emotion of anger in those vehicles.

In Vajrayana, the secret vehicle, ignorance is regarded as the principal problem. Ignorance is considered the most subtle negative emotion and, like a stubborn stain embedded in the weave of a cloth, is the most difficult to clear away. Because ignorance is the basis for all the disturbing emotions, various methods are applied in order to eliminate this basic stupidity. Ignorance is dispelled through the teachings variously known as Mahamudra or Dzogchen. Mahamudra and Dzogchen are such renowned and impressive fundamental teachings because they can completely uproot ignorance, the basic obscuration. Ignorance is cleared away by basic *wakefulness* which is totally free from any kind of fabrication. Basic wakefulness or *thatness* is devoid of mental constructs.

If we practice so that we eliminate all the negative emotions resulting from attachment, aggression, and ignorance, then there are no contradictions among the three vehicles. This is the meaning of 'condensing them all into one,' and is the view of Mahamudra and Dzogchen.

A traditional Tibetan doctor will say there are four hundred and four sicknesses, and that each has a specific medication as its remedy. In fact, all these illnesses actually result from disturbances in the humors of bile, wind, and phlegm. These disturbances themselves stem from the three poisons of attachment, aversion, and ignorance. Tibetan doctors also take into account certain negative influences, such as the evil forces called *gyalpo, mamo,* and *tsen,* which are also manifestations of the same three poisons. If we examine and recognize the true nature of these three poisons, we find that they are actually the *three kayas*.

Because there are many negative emotions and, correspondingly, many teachings or remedies, the higher the view, the more effective it will be. Just as we seek medicine which is able to cure all different sicknesses simultaneously, the higher the view, the more likely that it alone can clear away all of our negative emotions. The unique quality of both Mahamudra and Dzogchen is said to be such a universal remedy.

A basic definition of Mahamudra is as follows. The word 'maha,' great, means there is nothing superior to it. 'Mudra,' seal, means sealed by the great original wakefulness that is emptiness and compassion indivisible.

When we say Dzogchen, *Mahasandhi,* Maha Ati, or the *Great Perfection,* 'perfection' means that all the phenomena of samsara and nirvana are perfect or complete within the space of primordially pure awareness. Here, the word 'great' means that there is no greater method or means for clearing away all the disturbing emotions.

There are many philosophical viewpoints and many different

systems of teachings, but actually there is nothing which is not included within Mahamudra and Dzogchen. Just as all things are contained within space, likewise, all the other viewpoints and systems are included within these two. Since these two are essentially the same, condensing everything into a single practice is most profound.

There are four main traditions of Dharma, *Kagyü, Nyingma, Sakya,* and *Gelug.* A holder of one of these lineages must understand these teachings precisely and unmistakenly, without mixing them with others. For example, a holder of the Kagyü lineage should meticulously keep the tradition of Kagyü teachings which he has received, including how the *empowerments* are conferred, how the teachings are given, etc. Likewise, a Sakya lineage holder should preserve the Sakya teachings exactly according to the Sakya tradition. However, if one is not going to be a lineage-holder but is only practicing in order to attain enlightenment or to benefit one's future lives, it is more important to be nonsectarian and not cling to being strictly Kagyü or Nyingma. We should simply practice without partiality, seeing everything as pure.

> It is necessary to focus your mind on one single and sufficient master,
> If you are to be his chief disciple.
> But if you wish to have the virtues of experience and realization dawn within you,
> It is more profound to combine all the teachers you have met into one,
> And to visualize him as the Buddha resting on your crown and to supplicate him.

This verse indicates that as the chief disciple of a particular master, we should focus our mind exclusively on him. Staying with just one teacher is sufficient, even though we may have had connections with other teachers in past lives. However, if one desires to achieve *experience and realization* quickly, assimilating all the teachers into one is more profound. Lacking the *pure perception* which enables us to supplicate our master in an ordinary form, we can instead imagine him as a deity, the form of a buddha, and supplicate him as the embodiment of all the teachers that we have met. This will generate greater faith, and we will quickly gain experience and realization; in addition, obscurations and habitual patterns can swiftly be cleared away.

Some present-day practitioners seem to have a particular problem experienced by others in the past. A practitioner might stay in one area of the country, have contact with one teacher, receive teachings, empowerments, and initiations, and develop a very close relationship with a great deal of trust and affection. Then if he travels to another region, he might meet another teacher and again form a close relationship and feel great trust. Due to the blessings of this new teacher, he might receive new practices and progress on the path and might then wonder: "Have I completely abandoned my previous teacher? What should I do? If I return, what about my current master? It would be like throwing him away." Thus, our mind becomes very disturbed and we cannot choose. With the ability to combine all teachers into one, there will be no conflict about choosing one particular master over another.

> The different recitations for various development stage practices
> Of numerous yidam deities in the sections of tantra
> Are indispensable if you are to give empowerments as a great master.
> But as a means for purifying your own obscurations and attaining accomplishment,
> It is more profound to practice one deity and mantra which includes them all.

Years ago, the only two methods for getting around in Tibet were on horseback or on foot, and travel took a long time. Today, if we had to reach America on foot, it's doubtful whether we would arrive in this lifetime. However, many easy and convenient methods of travel have developed in the West, such as cars, trains, and planes, so that we arrive at our destination rapidly and with little trouble. In the same way, Vajrayana is characterized as having many skillful means and only minor hardship, such as yidam practice. Since the highest or most subtle view is to be realized through this vehicle, it is a direct presentation of the teachings for persons who possess the highest or sharpest faculties.

In yidam practice, we visualize a deity and recite its mantra. Though all the details of these practices of visualization and mantra recitation might seem quite pointless or superfluous, they are actually great skillful means and are necessary for many reasons. Ultimately, the colorfully ornamented deities with many arms and attributes have no true and concrete existence. However, engaging in these practices, we can dissolve the habitual tendency to solidify things, like our belief in a concrete physical body, the sound of our own voice, and so forth. If we visualize the yidam's body, recite the mantra as the yidam's speech, and practice the *samadhi* of the yidam's mind, these effective techniques are the skillful means for purifying our habitual patterns which solidify reality.

A supreme deity is the yidam to whom we are connected through past lives and past aspirations. This deity is revealed during an empowerment when we toss a flower into a mandala and it lands on a particular deity's image. When practicing this deity, we will very easily and quickly attain accomplishment of its body, speech, and mind. Accomplishing the yidam's mind is most important.

Since the yidam deity embodies complete enlightenment, the qualities of *abandonment and realization,* by practicing a yidam such as Manjushri or Avalokiteshvara, we will very quickly give rise to those qualities, just as an image is produced from a mold. We will also quickly receive the blessings. A blessing can refer to many things, but in this context, it means the realization of original wakefulness. Visualizing the form of the deity as our own body dissolves the tendency to solidify reality. Likewise, the techniques of reciting the yidam's mantra and practicing the samadhi of the yidam's mind, quickly bring about the attainment of enlightenment. The technique is not ultimate in itself however, because in the absolute sense, nothing whatsoever, including the body of a yidam or its speech, truly exists. There is no external thing such as a yidam. Real *buddhafields* also have no concrete existence. Ultimately, these things are all unreal, being simply the single and unbiased expanse of *dharmakaya*.

There are many tantric practices, which are classified as being higher or lower, but all these methods are given exclusively to enable us to tame our disturbing emotions. The different tantras teach different modes of practice. The Nyingma system includes the six tantras of Kriya, Upa, and Yoga as well as Maha, Anu, and Ati. The *New Schools*, the *Sarma system*, teach the four tantras of *Kriya, Charya, Yoga*, and *Anuttara*. Each has various methods and special features. Some systems focus mainly on visualizations, while others focus on the *Six Doctrines of Naropa*, which are the practices utilizing the inner elements of the *channels, energies*, and *essences* called *nadi, prana*, and *bindu*. Totally purifying and mastering these, they become the three kayas, at which point our body turns into the form of the deity itself. Like taking a jumbo jet, we can arrive at enlightenment very swiftly through these practices.

There are different recitations for each of the various development stage practices of the numerous yidam deities of tantra. Various traditions and systems emphasize different aspects, according to their schools. Some practice mainly the yidam deities connected with the Six Doctrines of Naropa, and as in the *tummo* practice, focus on the nadi, prana, and bindu aspects. If these practices are done incorrectly, we can become very uncomfortable physically, but if practiced properly, great benefit results. Such practices exist not only in the Tibetan tradition, but in other cultures as well, where they may be called *tai-chi, kung-fu,* etc. These practices are used to control our inner energies and essences in order to attain a particular result. In the tummo practice, for example, if we practice correctly, we will develop what is called the blissful heat and experience the *four joys*.

In short, there are various practices of both the development and completion stages, as well as others involving the practices of nadi, prana, and bindu. A worldly person, through training in kung-fu or tai-chi can gain mastery over phenomena, especially by controlling the bindu, and feel great bliss and so forth. There is also a Vajrayana practice where, after understanding emptiness, one practices with a *mudra,* either actual or imagined, and through the experience of the four joys, quickly reaches the full realization of Mahamudra, the unity of bliss and emptiness.

Gaining personal experience through the study and practice of all these different sections of tantra is imperative if we aspire to become a great teacher truly able to help others. Concerning the Six Yogas of Naropa, for example, we should know all the details and gain certainty about them. Through our own practice as well, we should gain a certain amount of experience and realization; otherwise, we will not be able to clearly explain it to others. Practicing Dzogchen methods, such as *Trekchö* and *Tögal,* we should proceed through the *four visions* and gain confidence in them in order to be qualified to guide others. However, if we are practicing only to purify our own obscurations and to attain enlightenment, then simply concentrating on one deity and one mantra which contains all of them is most profound.

The different yidam practices of the development stage are strictly for purifying our misdeeds and obscurations, and for bringing about the accomplishment of the qualities of abandonment and realization. They have no other purpose. There are basically three kinds of obscurations: the obscuration of disturbing emotions, the cognitive obscuration, and the obscuration of tendencies or habitual patterns.

The obscuration of disturbing emotions is quite gross or coarse compared to the cognitive obscuration. The obscuration of habitual tendencies is the most subtle and the most difficult to clear away. For example, a glass bottle may have contained a strong smelling substance. Although the bottle has been cleaned, when we put it to our nose, we notice a lingering odor.

Having purified these three kinds of obscurations, we attain accomplishment. The word for accomplishment in Sanskrit is *siddhi* which means the attainment of various powers — such as flying, being able to walk through solid matter, or knowing the minds of others. These are known as common or relative siddhis. The supreme, ultimate siddhi is the realization of the ultimate view of dharmakaya equality, 'thatness beyond mental constructs,' the buddha mind exactly 'as it is.' To quickly attain this supreme accomplishment, it is more profound to practice and concentrate on just one single deity. For example, if we practice the Great Compassionate One, Avalokiteshvara, the natural form of the unity of great compassion and emptiness, and recite the mantra of the six syllables, OM MANI PADME HUNG, we will purify the six disturbing emotions and close the gates to rebirth within the *six realms*.

> The innumerable practices of the completion stage, with
>   and without reference point,
> Are indispensable for expounding the innumerable
>   meditation manuals.
> But as a means for the virtues of experience and
>   realization to dawn within you
> It is more profound to sustain the essence, which is the
>   embodiment of them all.

Each of the different tantric sections emphasizes its own special teachings and attributes. There are various practices both with and without reference points and mental constructs; some are very simple, some quite elaborate. If we are going to teach these, it is important to know all the details, because each individual needs a specific teaching.

Everyone has a different disposition and what benefits one person will not necessarily benefit another. Just as in a garden with many different flowers, some need a lot of water while others quickly rot with too much, some grow best in sunlight, others need shade, some bloom with moonlight and others with sunlight. People are the same way. With many different propensities, people require different teachings to help them more readily attain liberation. A student who needs merely a simple and direct instruction to attain enlightenment is not greatly benefited if the master starts to give a very lengthy discourse.

For example, to take a person qualified to work as a high official and make him sweep floors is a waste. Taking a floor-sweeper and installing him in high office is also useless. Thus, if we are to guide others, we need to know the fine details of all the different teachings about the completion stage. A tour guide must know all the streets and sightseeing spots in his city in order to guide visitors. But, an ordinary person, wishing only to reach his destination, need only know the most direct route. The innumerable guide books and instructions on the completion stage are indispensable if we are to expound the teachings to others. Simply for oneself to attain experience and realization, it is more important to practice the embodiment of all the teachings and to sustain the essence. In other words, it is more important to recognize the nature of mind than it is to practice many deities and recitations.

There is much to discuss about the phrase, 'sustain the essence.' The word 'essence' here refers to the enlightened essence, the buddha mind within all sentient beings. 'To sustain' means to recognize the essence and maintain that recognition without losing its continuity. In Mahamudra, there are different stages in the teachings, such as the three stages of each of the four yogas, making twelve stages. Dzogchen has the Trekchö teachings. There are many details, but what it really boils down to is maintaining the recognition of the enlightened essence.

Mahamudra is divided into *four yogas* called one-pointedness, simplicity, one taste, and nonmeditation. These terms are very important, especially for people who have already received some teachings. One-pointedness means remaining undistractedly in the state of meditation for as long as we intend. Simplicity means recognizing that the nature of ordinary mind, (in Tibetan: *thamal gyi shepa,*) is completely baseless and groundless. One-taste means that the fixation on the dualistic experiences of samsara and nirvana has been liberated within awareness. Nonmeditation is the relinquishment of all opinions, concepts, and tendencies. Opinion here means that we hold on to an intellectual understanding of the enlightened essence as being a certain way.

The most profound way to sustain the essence is through either the Mahamudra teachings of the twelve yogas, by recognizing the essence and developing this recognition through the practice of the Six Doctrines of Naropa; or, through the Dzogchen system. In Dzogchen, we first recognize the primordially pure essence, by means of the view known as Trekchö, Cutting Through, and then we train through Tögal, the practice of 'spontaneous presence,' progressing through the four visions. When reaching the stage called 'exhaustion of phenomena beyond concepts,' we can, within this very lifetime and in this very body, attain the mind of a fully enlightened buddha. These profound oral instructions still exist and are given in order to enable us to 'sustain the essence.'

> There are many ways of demonstrating the view,
> Such as cutting through fabrications from outside and
>   from within.
> But, just as smoke vanishes when the flames in a fireplace
>   are extinguished,
> It is more profound to cut through the root of mind.

The view of nonconceptual knowledge can be demonstrated either by cutting fabrication from outside or from within. 'To cut from the outside' means that we begin by changing our behavior patterns, such as walking in a certain way or talking in a certain way. We try to transform bad thoughts into wholesome ones. Finally, after trying to change everything, we reach the correct view of how to sustain the essence of nonconceptual wakefulness.

A second approach is 'to cut fabrication from within.' The teacher directly points out the mind essence so that the student recognizes it, without mentioning anything about certain conduct we have to adopt, or about 'good' and 'bad' thoughts to be cultivated or abandoned. Demonstrating the mind essence directly is like taking something when it is red-hot or totally fresh.

These are two of the many different methods of demonstrating the view. When we find smoking embers in a fireplace and pour water on them, the smoke will automatically vanish. If, in this way, we can cut through the root of mind and resolve our doubts regarding its nature, then this is the most profound method. Mind is the most essential because it is that which experiences all pleasure and pain. The smoldering embers in this example are the source of the smoke, in the same way that the mind is the very root of samsara and nirvana. Going directly to the source and severing the root is the most profound method.

> Although there are numerous meditation techniques, both
> with and without concepts,
> It is more profound to practice the unity of luminosity
> and emptiness,
> The development stage completed by mere recollection.

Numerous meditation techniques exist, both with and without concepts. However, it is more profound to practice the unity of appearance and emptiness regarding whatever we see; the unity of sound and emptiness of whatever we hear; and the unity of luminosity and emptiness of whatever we cognize. This is the development stage completed by mere recollection.

> Although there are numerous kinds of behavior, high and
> low, coarse and precise,
> It is more profound to exert yourself as much as you can
> in practicing virtue and abandoning evil deeds.

'Precise behavior' means being very deliberate and extremely careful in everything we do. For example, a monk is advised to walk like a tortoise, slowly and carefully, and to see exactly what he is doing and thinking before acting, both when walking and when sitting down. He should check first and think "Is this a good place for me to sit?" If someone else is there, he should ask first, "May I sit here?" Otherwise his behavior may offend. Before speaking, he should think "Will what I want to say now disturb others? Will it cause jealousy, attachment, or anger?" After thinking like this, he should then speak slowly and precisely. Two hundred and fifty three such precepts exist for monks, three hundred and sixty two for nuns.

From another point of view, we can act without taking anything into consideration, without accepting or rejecting anything whatsoever; since 'good' and 'bad' actions are merely concepts, as are 'good' and 'bad' words. We can act thus once we have fully realized the ultimate truth of *dharmata,* of thatness. At that point, just as the sky is unharmed by slashing it with a knife, we will not be tainted by karmic actions. At present, however, we are just beginners who have yet to attain enlightenment, so practicing what is virtuous, and abandoning what is evil and unwholesome, as much as possible, is more profound.

> Although numerous things have been taught about attainment, the time of reaching fruition,
> It is more profound to possess the definite certainty of attainment
> After having unmistakenly practiced the view, meditation, and action.

This verse teaches that, although numerous ways of attainment are taught about the moment of reaching fruition, there is not just one 'fruition' but a certain result to be attained for each practice. There is the *serenity of cessation* attained by an arhat, as well as the various samadhis, and different temporary experiences such as bliss, clarity, and nonthought, which can be gained through meditation practice. However, it is important not to cling to any of these experiences or to regard them as being the final result, but instead to practice, unmistakenly, the view, meditation, and action.

The correct view is embraced by the unity of emptiness and compassion. Meditation can be either with or without form, but should be embraced by undefiled, nondualistic wakefulness. Finally, the action should completely accord with the way a bodhisattva acts through the six paramitas. If, after practicing like this, we feel confident of attainment, without a shadow of doubt, this is most profound. If, on the other hand, we regard temporary experiences, such as feeling that everything has vanished, leaving only empty space or feeling totally blissed-out with no desire to eat or drink, totally fixated on the taste of samadhi, and so forth as being the ultimate, this is a great defect.

When practicing the six paramitas, each should be preceded by a clear consideration of the object, such as the object offered in the case of generosity, using discriminating knowledge regarding who should receive a certain item. For instance, we don't give knives or poison to an infant. In like manner, discrimination should precede the remaining paramitas of discipline, patience, diligence, concentration and knowledge. Each of these six is further divided into three. They are quite important to know, and can be found elsewhere.

> Although bodhisattvas who have accomplished the levels
> Are not obscured even by serious wrongdoing or misdeeds
>   done for the sake of the teachings,
> Since someone like us has to fear the lower realms,
> It is more profound to shun, without involvement,
>   wrongdoing and severe faults.

According to the shravaka teachings, we should never perform any negative actions of body or speech. In no cases are negative actions of mind allowed. The negative actions of the body are killing, stealing, and sexual misconduct; the negative actions of speech are lying, harsh words, divisive talk, slander, and idle gossip. Since the Hinayana teachings emphasize cleansing oneself of faults more than benefiting others, a Hinayana practitioner would never, under any circumstance, commit any of these misdeeds.

Mahayana and Vajrayana both grant that we are sometimes allowed to perform negative actions if for the general benefit of others. According to Mahayana, one first equalizes oneself with others, then exchanges oneself with others, and finally regards others as more important than oneself. From this viewpoint, we seek to benefit others in any way possible. Thus, performing one of the seven misdeeds of body and speech is sometimes permissible if it is solely for the benefit of others, with no self-interest involved, and with no expectation of reward, such as hoping to be regarded as a great bodhisattva.

To give an example; knowing that someone intends to kill a hundred people, a bodhisattva, in order to save these lives, will first try to dissuade the murderer from committing the crime. If this proves impossible, the bodhisattva may have to kill him. He will then gain the negative action of killing one person, but will also gain the good karma of saving the lives of a hundred others. Moreover, the potential murderer will then not suffer the negative karma of having killed a hundred people. The bodhisattva, considering the other person more important than himself, is willing to undertake the negative action to benefit others and also to save the hundred lives. This is permitted if the act is embraced by a pure motivation totally free of self-interest.

In the case of stealing, in a place where many people are starving to death, if there is a rich person who refuses to give any aid, a bodhisattva should first try to persuade him to donate some of his wealth to save the lives of the others. If this fails, the bodhisattva might have to steal, not all of the rich person's possessions, but just enough to keep the others alive. Again, this conduct must be without any self-interest whatsoever, and with no expectation of reward.

Regarding sexual misconduct, if someone claims that he or she will either commit suicide or go completely crazy if we refuse to engage in sexual relations with them, a bodhisattva might have to do this, but should do so without any self-interest. The same holds true for the negative actions of speech, such as lying, slander, harsh words and idle gossip.

The three negative actions of mind are covetousness, ill will and wrong views. A bodhisattva would never engage in these because they can never benefit anyone. However, a great bodhisattva who has attained the first *bhumi* can engage in negative actions of body and speech because he will be able to do so without becoming entangled. A good swimmer can enjoy himself in huge waves at the beach, while a beginner will have great difficulty. For himself, the great bodhisattva will perfect the accumulation of wisdom and merit as a unity, while at the same time, benefiting others. An ordinary person, a beginner on the path, without real certainty about what will happen after death, must fear the negative consequences of evil actions: rebirth in the lower realms. For a beginner then, it is more profound to refrain, as much as possible, from negative actions.

> Moreover, without self-interest and for the general benefit of beings,
> It is profound to seal your practices, such as offering and giving, copying teachings and reciting texts,
> With a dedication free from conceptualizing the three spheres.

When making offerings, being generous and giving, and copying the teachings and reciting them, without conceptualizing the three spheres of — subject, object, and action — we should dedicate the merit to the welfare of all sentient beings.

QUESTIONS AND ANSWERS

STUDENT: How can one say of Mahamudra that everything is sealed with emptiness and compassion?

RINPOCHE: Since all phenomena are not separate from the seal of indivisible emptiness and compassion, when Mahamudra is realized, all phenomena of samsara, nirvana, and the path totally dissolve into, or merge with, the single sphere of dharmakaya. At that time, all concepts about the different realms which we normally experience: a perceiver, that which is perceived, and the act of perceiving, completely collapse. No concept exists of any of the realms, of 'I' or 'other.' At the same time, our perception of all the impure experiences of other beings is not obstructed. There are no personal deluded conceptions, but there is unobstructed, unimpeded perception of the nature of things, of all that exists, and of other sentient beings in their deluded states. This is accompanied by compassion, not merely in a conceptual way, but by nonconceptual compassion. We know that although all beings have buddha nature — the potential for enlightenment, they are not enlightened but deluded; and, that a way exists for all beings to be liberated. This wisdom is accompanied by an effortless nonconceptual compassion that acts for the sake of benefiting sentient beings. This compassion is one of the buddha qualities.

Anyone with a mind has *buddha nature*. An ordinary person who has not practiced has, nonetheless, a nature endowed with knowledge, compassion, and power. Without this nature or potential, there would be nothing to develop. At present, we have some capacity for learning; that is our potential for wisdom. Even an evil person has someone he cares for, a wife, parents, or children; that is our potential for compassion. A lion or tiger living solely by killing and eating other beings still shows affection for its own offspring. Lastly, even a child has some power or ability corresponding to his own age level. The potential for these three aspects of knowledge, compassion, and power exists in all beings even though they are not enlightened. When the seal of fixation is broken by the wakefulness of indivisible compassion and emptiness, these three potentials are completely manifest at the state of complete enlightenment. At that time, they are called the wisdom of knowledge, the compassion of loving kindness, and enlightened activity.

STUDENT: If all sentient beings have buddha nature, why is it that the scriptures state that some sentient beings are unfit to receive the teachings? What does that actually mean?

RINPOCHE: It's not that there are people who are totally unsuitable to receive Dharma teachings, but some particular teachings are unsuitable or do not fit the character of that particular person. For instance, the Mahayana type of person should have the Mahayana teachings. No one is totally unsuited to receive the Buddha's teachings.

STUDENT: What is the meaning of *instantaneous recollection*?

RINPOCHE: In the development stage, there are different ways of visualizing a deity. 'Mere recollection' means we have, in an instant, the complete vivid presence. For example, after having practiced Avalokiteshvara for some time, we don't focus on one detail after another, but visualize the whole figure at once with all the details complete.

STUDENT: What is meant by Trekchö and Tögal in the Dzogchen practice?

RINPOCHE: In the system of Dzogchen, the view is called Trekchö, *Cutting Through,* the meditation is called Tögal, Direct Crossing. 'Cutting Through' means to be introduced to, to have pointed out, the original wakefulness which is inherent to oneself. The first syllable, 'trek' means thoroughly, or completely, not just a little bit or halfway. *Chö* means cut or destroyed. For example, when the net or cover of the confused perception of dualistic fixation is, in an instant, completely and thoroughly cut through, the original wakefulness that dwells in oneself is instantly and vividly present. If the clouds of the sky were instantly dispersed, the sun would be directly present, shining immediately. When a thick curtain covering a window is pulled back, in one instant, we immediately see outside.

Tögal, Direct Crossing, is the training after we have already recognized the view of Trekchö. It is a meditation with various methods to enhance our practice. We train through experiences and through visions, using either daylight or darkness in the training. At the outset, many things appear. Finally, they all vanish.

In the practice of Tögal, we use the support of the sunlight, moonlight, or various other things. Experiences and visions occur corresponding to our inner realization of the view of Trekchö. We must receive these teachings orally from a qualified master. Without proper guidance, we might go astray.

STUDENT: Rinpoche said that *yidams* don't exist in the absolute sense. Do they exist in the relative sense?

RINPOCHE: At the time of fruition, there is no such thing as a truly existent deity or god, but deities do appear in our experience at the time of the path. Some yidam deities are beneficial to practice, bringing about the quick accomplishment of siddhis and letting us rapidly receive the blessings. Employing these techniques brings great effects, but when we reach the stage called exhaustion of phenomena beyond concepts, there are no extremes such as existence or nonexistence. Everything has merged into great oneness and there is no such thing as a truly existent yidam. There is nothing to be achieved and no one to achieve it. The ultimate yidam is completely beyond expressions of speech and mental formulations.

STUDENT: A lot of people here don't understand the term 'yidam,' so can you explain further?

RINPOCHE: You explain that, Erik.

ERIK: Literally, 'yidam' means mental commitment, something to keep in mind, to keep in our practice continuously. Generally, a yidam is a male or female buddha whom we visualize, whose mantra we recite, and in whose state of mind we try to remain.

Rinpoche: There are different aspects of yidam: inner yidam, outer yidam, and ultimate yidam, but we are never separate from the yidam if we never stray from ordinary mind, innate wakefulness free from mental constructs.

As long as we are still training on the path, we need a method, and yidam practice has great benefit. There is someone to supplicate, blessings to receive, compassion to develop, and so on. These all exist as the power of compassion and blessings; practicing a yidam is very beneficial. Ultimately though, we move beyond these things. In essence, yidam means that never being apart from the continuity of the correct view is sufficient. There's more to learn about this.

STUDENT: In the example of a bodhisattva committing murder, would that bodhisattva reap the bad karma from this murder?

RINPOCHE: Yes, it will harm him. By killing another, he will become obscured. He won't fall back from the path, but it is harmful. He knows this, but does it anyway. That's quite amazing.

STUDENT: Rinpoche, would you agree with the view that a normal practitioner should practice with just one yidam throughout his life and not practice various yidams?

RINPOCHE: It's difficult to say. Some people can easily and without any conflict practice several yidams simultaneously with great benefit. Some have difficulty practicing even one. In general, maybe it's best to stick just to one. Some people feel extremely disposed to one single deity, even from a very young age. Some people, without having heard about yidams before, will spontaneously feel strong admiration when presented with either Avalokiteshvara, Manjushri, or Vajrapani. Probably one of these is the best yidam for them to practice. In the past, great masters with clear knowledge of the dispositions of their students could state directly, "Your yidam is so and so," and that would be sufficient. Also, Naropa said to Marpa, "The yidam is not somewhere else; it is oneself," then he revealed himself as the yidam.

There is also a great purpose for practicing the yidam. Though considered a great master, Mipham Rinpoche was not particularly intelligent when he was young. However, after practicing Manjushri for a long time, he became totally unimpeded in composing and expounding the teachings, in memory, debate, and so forth. He attributed that to his yidam who had appeared to him in a vision, giving him direct blessings and teachings. Later, as a sign of practice, the syllable dhih became visible on his tongue.

When the first Jamgön Kongtrül wrote his many texts, he didn't have to look up and copy passages from scores of scriptures, piecing them all together; he could just compose freely and directly. Many people saw a small image of Manjushri, in rainbow light, sometimes appeared behind him emitting a beam of orange-colored light from his Dharma-expounding mudra which connected to Jamgön Kongtrül's pen. Many masters such as Marpa and Naropa composed songs about being accepted and blessed by their yidams, like Hevajra, Chakrasamvara, Vajra Varahi and so forth. So, it is said that if we are blessed or accepted by the yidam deity, many qualities such as realization and understanding can manifest.

STUDENT: The Mahayana teachings say that it's best to give all praise and good things to others, and to take all bad things and blame on oneself, but not being a bodhisattva, how can we do that purely, without any improper motivation?

RINPOCHE: This practice is called *tong-len, giving* and *taking,* and is chiefly a Mahayana practice. This is the method to apply it: We visualize ourselves as the Great Compassionate One, the white buddha Avalokiteshvara, and imagine that rays of light, which are our merit, our knowledge, compassion, virtuous karmas, fame, and fortune and so forth, stream from our body in all directions. They stream forth and radiate out like rays of light and descend like snowflakes, showering down upon sentient beings and dissolving into them. Thus, all of our positive energy is distributed to all other beings. Next, we imagine that all of their sufferings, negative karmas, obscurations, and so forth are absorbed into ourselves. Finally, we imagine that we have perfected the accumulation of merit, and that our body, in the form of Avalokiteshvara, has become even more radiant, dazzling and immaculate than before. It is actually quite easy.

2
The Song of Taking Advantage of The Human Body That is Difficult to Find

> Kyemaho!
> There are many aeons, but it is rare that the sacred teachings flourish.
> There are many realms, but it is rare that a buddha appears.
> Although a buddha appears, it is rare that the teaching will remain.
> Among the six kinds of beings, it is rare to obtain a human form.

'Aeon' refers to a span of time, such as the four major aeons: the aeon when the world system is created, the aeon when the world system remains, the aeon when the world system is being destroyed, and the aeon when the world system is void or emptied, when nothing whatsoever remains. Right now, we are experiencing the second great aeon when the world system is remaining.

Of these four aeons, not every aeon is filled with buddhas who give teachings which is, in fact, an extremely rare occasion. The present aeon, however, is called the 'excellent' or 'good aeon' because a thousand buddhas will appear and teach, a very rare event.

There are many realms, refers to both buddha realms and samsaric realms. In just our own section of the universe, there are said to be one billion worlds, but the buddhas do not appear in every one. Even in worlds where buddhas appeared, if they appeared long ago, the teachings could have disappeared with the passage of time. Had Buddha Shakyamuni's teachings not been preserved through great masters who realized and transmitted the teachings through unbroken lineages down to the present, we would have nothing left. Even though a buddha has appeared, the continuance of the teachings is quite exceptional, and therefore is a rare event.

We presently live in the second great aeon when the world system exists, but later it will be destroyed. The traditional prophecy is that it will be destroyed by seven suns or fires and once by water. There may be no contradiction in equating the fires with atomic bombs. Who knows? But, at any rate, the world system will eventually be destroyed.

Among the six kinds of beings, it is rare to obtain a human form. 'Being' means a sentient being who transmigrates and has a mind that can think. There are six classes of beings: human beings, animals, hungry ghosts, hell-beings, demigods and gods. Among these, the superior being, in terms of ability to practice the Dharma, is a human being possessing this unique opportunity. Being human is rare and wonderful.

It is important to be a human because the sentient beings in the *lower realms* of the hells, hungry ghosts, and animals lack intelligence and suffer a great deal. For instance, the hell-beings suffer from heat and cold while the hungry ghosts suffer from hunger and thirst. Due to the intensity of suffering in these realms, the beings there have neither the opportunity, the inclination, nor the intelligence to practice the Dharma or to receive the teachings. In the higher realms, like the god realms, everything is too perfect. Always distracted by entertainment, wealth, and various enjoyments, these beings never find a chance to practice Dharma. Swayed by negative emotions of envy and jealousy, the demigods spend their time competing and engaging in warfare and consequently have no time for practice. In the human realm however, nothing is really too good or too bad. Suffering and enjoyment are mixed. Suffering is rarely too intense; pleasant circumstances are never so good nor so long-lasting as to completely carry one away. For this reason, the human form is held to be the best circumstance for practicing the Dharma. Among the six classes of beings, attaining a human form is the most excellent.

> Among the four continents, it is rare to be born on the
> Jambu continent.
> Within the Jambu continent, it is rare that the sacred
> Dharma flourishes.
> Although one is born here, it is rare to have all one's
> senses intact.
> Although one may have all one's senses, it is rare to have
> any thought of the perfect Dharma.

This world is traditionally held to consist of four continents situated in the four directions of *Mount Sumeru*. Birth on the southern continent, the land of the Jambu continent, where the Dharma flourishes, is rare. Though this is a rare opportunity, that's where we are right now. However, even on the Jambu continent, only occasionally do the Dharma teachings appear. Of all the people in this world, very few are sincerely interested in practicing spirituality. We can easily observe how rarely people take interest in Dharma and that the teachings are certainly not abundant.

Though one may be born as a human being in this world, to have all one's senses intact is also rare. Here, 'senses' refers to the five ordinary sense organs plus the mental faculty. Lacking these faculties, it is difficult to understand what is being communicated. If one cannot hear, one can't receive the teachings, and so on. The most important sense is, of course, the mental faculty, the intellect. Without this, one would be an imbecile.

Yet, even having all the senses and being a complete human being, it is still unusual to even think about Dharma practice. Instead, people occupy themselves trying to fulfill all kinds of worldly plans and ambitions, many of which will never be realized. Many people act like small children jumping from one project to another, leaving lots of loose ends and spending all their time in this state of dissipation.

> Although one wishes to practice, it is rare to find a
> qualified teacher.

> Even though one may meet a teacher, it is rare to receive instructions on practice.
> Even though one may receive them, it is rare to be ripened through the empowerments.
> Although these two may come together, it is rare to recognize one's essence.

If one feels dissatisfied with the superficial experiences and attainments of this world, then one will want to get involved with something real and ultimately true. One will wish to practice spirituality, Dharma, or whatever you want to call it. In that case, one needs to find a *qualified teacher,* someone whose eye of wisdom is fully opened and who is capable of guiding others. Since we ourselves are blinded by ignorance, following an unqualified teacher is like "the blind leading the blind," which can only end in disaster.

A teacher may be very eloquent and behave impressively like a politician, but if he doesn't truly and genuinely possess the correct motivation, one will be cheated in the end. Because of the great danger of being led astray down the wrong path, the student should scrutinize the teacher to see if he is truly qualified. There are different ways to evaluate whether a teacher has the correct qualifications or not. Both the sutras and the tantras have specific methods, but the essential point is that the teacher should have truly developed the altruistic good heart. If he truly possesses bodhichitta, he will never deceive others. Though he may appear to become temporarily angry or speak and act oddly, if he has genuine bodhichitta and selflessness, he will never truly forsake or deceive anyone. Therefore, finding a truly qualified teacher is imperative.

Physically meeting a teacher and spending time visiting with him is not enough. One must receive the instructions on practice in accordance with one's own degree of experience. This is extremely important. For example, if one has a specific illness like gallstones, there are many medicines one can take, such as vitamins or ginseng, but these won't help much because they are general, superficial medications. One needs something that will hit exactly the vital point of one's illness. Only if one takes medicine which can dissolve one's gallstones, will one be cured, but otherwise not.

According to the Vajrayana teachings, although one receives beneficial and suitable instructions on practice, one must still receive the *four empowerments* in order to ripen one's nature and to give rise to the original wakefulness that is the nature of realization. These are known as the vase empowerment, the secret empowerment, the wisdom knowledge empowerment, and the precious word empowerment. After having gained a certain experience and understanding according to each empowerment, one is finally introduced to wakefulness devoid of constructs, to 'thatness.' This introduction is the true sense of receiving empowerment. Here, 'ripening' does not merely mean getting bonked on the head with a ritual object. The real and true empowerment is gaining full experience and understanding.

Many people receive empowerments, but few are ripened or matured through them. These days, the empowerments given seem to be a little different from the ones given in the old days. You may have heard stories about Tilopa and Naropa, great masters in the Kagyü lineage. Even prior to meeting his teacher Tilopa, Naropa was already quite an accomplished and realized person. However there still was something lacking. One day, he had a vision of his yidam who prophesied that he still needed to develop the full power of realization. In order to do so, he was to meet the siddha Tilopa who lived in a certain place.

Naropa left in search of Tilopa, went to the prescribed area and asked around. No one had ever heard of a siddha named Tilopa. They knew only the beggar Tilopa. Naropa was directed to a ruin of a house from which smoke was coming. He walked over and saw a dirty-looking beggar sitting with a tray of fish, some alive, some dead. He was taking the fish, one after the other, whether alive or dead, tossing them into the fire, snapping his fingers, and then eating them.

At this moment, Naropa must have had some kind of experience, for otherwise Tilopa's actions of killing animals and then eating them would have been considered very evil. Naropa however felt great faith and asked, "Are you the siddha called Tilopa?" Tilopa replied, "I'm no siddha, just a beggar who does evil things." Nevertheless, Naropa prostrated and was accepted as Tilopa's disciple. To kill sentient beings without accumulating negative karma, and to actually benefit sentient beings instead, one must have the power to resurrect the dead, as well as the accomplishment of being able to guide them to liberation. Having the faith that Tilopa was such an accomplished master, Naropa followed him. Tilopa gave him a very difficult time, putting him through twelve major and twenty-four minor trials. You can read about them in Naropa's biography.

One day when they were walking together, they saw some field workers eating. Naropa, who had become Tilopa's servant, begged a bowl of soup for Tilopa. Tilopa ate the soup, pretending that it was the most delicious food he had ever eaten. Extremely pleased, Naropa thought, "I've been serving Tilopa for such a long time, but I have never been able to really please him before. I think I'll go back and get him more of this soup."

When he went back for the soup, there were no people around and Naropa thought, "If I wait for someone to come, I can't be sure they'll give me some. Maybe I should steal it." As he was helping himself to the pot of soup someone of course came by and said, "You're no good! First, we give you some food out of kindness, but it wasn't enough. Now, you come back to steal!" He was beaten nearly to death and lay there, broken, for several days before Tilopa happened by and asked, "Anything wrong? Are you having a hard time?" Naropa replied, "Having a hard time? I'm almost dead!" Tilopa blessed him and he became well immediately, and they walked on. This wasn't the last trial Naropa had to endure.

They continued in this way for many years, until finally one day Naropa asked Tilopa a question. In reply, Tilopa took off his sandal and smacked Naropa across the forehead with it. Naropa blacked out for a short while and when he regained his senses, his realization was equal to Tilopa's. That was a true empowerment. These days forget about a shoe! We get vases of gold and silver plating on our head for empowerment, but the realization doesn't seem to take place in quite the same way. A shoe might be better. In brief, many receive empowerment, but few are ripened.

Naropa was an Indian master, but numerous accounts tell of Tibetan masters who received empowerment in unusual ways as well. One story is about a very recent master by the name Neten Chokling Rinpoche who lived at Bir in Himachal Pradesh. He has passed away, but as a young man, he was very intelligent and studious, he became quite proud and satisfied with his own knowledge. He thought, "Now, I'll go and debate at the monasteries in Lhasa and defeat all the geshes there." He readied himself to leave.

At that time, he was studying with the reincarnation of *Jamyang Khyentse Wangpo* called *Chökyi Lodrö* who was living in the Tibetan province of *Kham*. Chokling Rinpoche asked permission to leave for Lhasa, and Chökyi Lodrö said, "Yes, but wait a little while." A few days later, Chökyi Lodrö was giving an empowerment and the young Chokling was sitting in the row with the others tulkus. Chokling had an upset stomach that day. When Chökyi Lodrö passed him in the row and placed the empowerment vase on the crown of his head, simultaneously he kicked Chokling in the gut. Due to the gas in Chokling Rinpoche's stomach, he let out a tremendously loud fart. In a temple before high lamas that is considered totally improper. Chokling was overcome by extreme embarrassment and fear. In that very instant, his master Chökyi Lodrö shouted, "That's it!"

Because Chokling Rinpoche's mind was, in that moment, totally stripped of thoughts, he recognized mind essence. When I had the occasion to meet Chokling Rinpoche, he told this story about himself and remarked that from that moment on, he never had any change in his realization. That's another story of true empowerment, the pointing out of mind essence.

Still another story tells about a master in Tibet who was visited by a person from quite far away. At that time the master was living in an encampment of tents. The master himself would seldom give teachings to new people. One would have to study with his students, later with his more advanced students, and only then would one be able to occasionally come face to face with the master.

This stranger was able to see the master immediately, on the very first interview. None of the other disciples paid much attention to him, and afterwards he never again had a private audience with the master. He became a herdsman tending the horses and cattle, chopping wood, fetching water, and so forth. The other students said, "Look, you're just a newcomer. You don't know anything. Just do your *preliminary practices* and prostrations."

Some years went by and one day he slipped and fell off a cliff. When the others discovered him, he regained consciousness and had completely changed. They thought he had gone crazy from hitting his head. Figuring that the master didn't know about this obscure herdsman, the students reported that this fellow who had been around for a few years, without knowing any Dharma or doing much practice, had fallen down and become crazy. The master laughed and said, "Yes, he's crazy and so am I. We are the same. Equally crazy. There's no difference."

The man had actually attained great realization during that time without even having a close personal relationship with the master. At their first and only meeting, the master must have pointed out the mind essence and this newcomer must have recognized it immediately. It boils down to this: it doesn't matter how much time one spends in the close company of a great master, but it does depend upon whether or not one practices what one has had pointed out and correctly recognized. One can easily stay far away and still develop quickly in practice if one has had the essence pointed out. On the other hand, one can spend a great deal of time in close proximity to a master and get nowhere.

> All these rarities you have now obtained.
> This is not an easy thing — it is the result of aspirations
>   from former lives.
> So now, turn your back on samsara.

> If you are unable to do that, you will certainly be nothing more
> Than someone returning empty-handed from an island of precious jewels.
> There is only the slightest possibility that such conditions will come together in the future.

Although one may meet a master and receive teachings, it is rare to recognize one's essence if the right conditions don't come together. But all these rare circumstances one has now obtained do not come about because of one's intelligence, they result from having *gathered accumulations* and *purified obscurations,* and having made aspirations in many past lives.

When this great opportunity presents itself, one should not waste it. Just as a person with good vision will not leap into an abyss, one should likewise turn one's back on samsara and practice. Failing to do this, at the time of death, one will be like a person returning empty-handed from an island filled with precious jewels. The possibility that one will again have the chance to meet the teachings and the master, have the freedom to practice, be able to receive empowerment and to be ripened is quite unlikely — it is a uniquely rare occasion.

> In particular, the Secret Mantra, the unexcelled Vajrayana,
> Will not be taught by the thousand buddhas beginning with Maitreya,
> So, there is no other hope of receiving it.

The teachings of Vajrayana, or *Secret Mantra,* in particular, will not be taught by all the buddhas, but only by the present Buddha Shakyamuni. None of the future buddhas of this kalpa will teach the vehicle of Secret Mantra so one cannot even hope to receive it in a future life. In short, we have only this opportunity to receive instructions, so take them to heart, and practice.

> You have now obtained this precious human form, which
>   is difficult to find.
> If you don't make use of this, it will be abandoned and
>   discarded in no time,
> Only to be eaten by birds and dogs or cremated by fire.
> So, take advantage of this now, otherwise it is pointless.

Right now, though we have, through great difficulty, acquired the *precious human body,* death can come at any moment. If we don't make use of what we have acquired, we will leave this body behind to be either burned or buried or eaten by wild animals, and all will have been quite pointless.

> Purely keep the vows and samayas you have taken.
> Keep the one-day precepts on the new moon, full moon,
>   and on the eighth day, etc.
> To make use of your hands, make one hundred
>   prostrations every day.
> To make use of your feet, circumambulate holy objects.
> To make use of your tongue, exert yourself in chanting
>   and in recitation of the six syllables.
> To make use of your possessions, be diligent in gathering
>   the accumulations.
> To make use of your mind, train in emptiness and
>   compassion.

In the line, *keep the vows and the samayas,* 'vows' refers to the *refuge precepts* and *bodhisattva vows,* such as refraining from harming others and trying to help as much as possible. The 'one day precepts' are observed on special days of the month when one does *pujas* and special practices in order to gather the accumulations and purify the obscurations.

It is said to be good to perform a minimum of a hundred prostrations without interruption each day, circumambulate holy shrine objects and so forth. 'Recitation' means to recite the supplications and aspirations, different sutras, and the *six syllables,* OM MANI PADME HUNG, the mantra of Avalokiteshvara.

Making use of one's possessions means the practice of making offerings and cultivating generosity. One should use what wealth and resources one has to further Dharma practice. Finally, *to make use of your mind, train in the unity of emptiness and compassion.*

> You should make use of this illusory body which you have
> temporarily borrowed from the four elements,
> And if necessary, be able to sacrifice it.
> Like a traveler who is well-equipped with pack-animals
> and provisions,
> When traveling on, you will have no misery.

This body you have, while sitting here today, is just like a guest house that we have temporarily borrowed from the five elements of earth, water, fire, wind and space; a physical body composed of these elements which we will use for just a short time. We should not cling to it too much. Even if we have a hard time when practicing, if we must undergo some minor hardships of heat and cold etc., we should be able to bear that discomfort.

When we plan to travel a long distance, we make sure to be well-equipped with plenty of provisions so that trip will not be very difficult. Similarly, we are now traveling to a destination called the *Unified Level of Vajradhara,* complete enlightenment. Gathering the accumulations of merit and wisdom are like provisions that will enable us to complete our spiritual journey.

QUESTIONS AND ANSWERS

STUDENT: What is the relationship between the development stage, completion stage, and yidam practice?

RINPOCHE: Erik, you can explain that.

ERIK: The development stage is something fabricated and the completion stage is unfabricated. Yidam practice includes both development and completion stages.

RINPOCHE: In the beginning of yidam practice, it seems as though the development aspect is emphasized more. One spends more time on visualizing the deity and then, at the end of that, one dissolves it and remains for a short time in the completion stage. But, eventually, as one becomes more proficient in the practice, then the development stage becomes very short. It appears in a flash, as I mentioned before, completed by mere recollection, while the major part of the practice is simply remaining in the composure of the completion stage.

A story is told about one of Nagarjuna's students who was a buffalo herdsman. He came to ask for teachings and Nagarjuna told him to first practice *shamatha,* just focusing on a single point in front of him, without trying to think of anything whatsoever, and to continue with this for a while. Later, the student came back and complained, "Every time I try to focus my attention on this point, I see only the face of a buffalo." This was because his whole life was spent taking care of these buffaloes. Nagarjuna replied, "Don't worry about it, just keep focusing." Again, he returned and complained, "Now it's not just one buffalo. I see more and more of them all the time. It's impossible to concentrate." Nagarjuna said, "Well then, try to imagine that you yourself have a head like a buffalo with horns sticking out."

The herdsman did this for a long time. Sometime later, Nagarjuna received a message from him apologizing for not coming to visit and explaining that he couldn't leave his cave because his horns were too big to fit through the opening. Nagarjuna sent back a message saying "This is very good. You've attained some stability in shamatha, but now you should visualize that the horns have disappeared." After doing this visualization for a while, he could leave his cave. The story is not a mere joke. At that point, because of his stability of mind, later, it was very easy for him to receive the pointing out instruction. This was Nagarjuna's skillful means since this man could concentrate on nothing other than a buffalo's head.

STUDENT: What are the three kayas?

RINPOCHE: In short, dharmakaya is free from mental constructs; sambhogakaya is adorned with the marks and signs; and nirmanakaya tames whoever needs to be tamed in whatever way is necessary.

'Space' is used as an example for dharmakaya because space is free from constructs in the sense of mental formulations. We cannot say that the sky is divided or limited in any way. There's no bottom or top. It is completely devoid of these reference points. That is the meaning of 'free from mental constructs.'

Within the sky, the sun and moon shine. This is an example for sambhogakaya. Without ever leaving dharmakaya, the sambhogakaya manifests as wisdom and knowledge, the enlightened qualities, and also as form, possessing the thirty-two major and eighty minor marks of excellence. This form is perceptible only to bodhisattvas on the spiritual levels and not to ordinary beings. What we ordinary beings perceive is nirmanakaya, which is like the reflection of the sun and the moon. Nirmanakayas are classified into either three or four kinds. The first type is called a *supreme nirmanakaya,* someone like Buddha Shakyamuni. There are also the *incarnated nirmanakayas, created nirmanakayas,* and *variegated nirmanakayas.*

STUDENT: Does recognition of mind essence happen suddenly or gradually? Having recognized it, can one lose it again?

RINPOCHE: The Mahamudra system contains three approaches: sutra Mahamudra, tantra Mahamudra, and essence Mahamudra. According to sutra Mahamudra, one proceeds gradually through the *five paths* and *ten bodhisattva stages,* each practice followed by another. When one has reached a certain point, one continues step by step on to the next practice. One presents one's understanding, and the master will check it. The whole procedure is very gradual and quite safe.

Tantra Mahamudra, like the Six Doctrines of Naropa, includes many yogic practices of controlling the channels, energies, and essences, and many different exercises through which one may experience various sensations, such as heat or cold, bliss or agony. Through this, one can recognize the mind essence. It is faster than sutra Mahamudra. In essence Mahamudra, and also in the various systems of Dzogchen, mind essence is pointed out directly, not necessarily forcefully, but also not gradually. The best recognition is through devotion or compassion. Having recognized mind essence doesn't mean that one is enlightened. One must practice further. The recognition won't disappear, but one definitely has to practice in order to attain stability.

Essence Mahamudra uses various techniques in order to introduce mind essence such as strong faith, strong compassion and even shock or panic. This technique can only be used by a qualified master. Otherwise there might be dangers.

STUDENT: Why is it rare to find a qualified teacher?

RINPOCHE: Various types of Buddhist masters exist for each of the three yanas. There is, for example a *triple-vow vajra-holder,* someone who can keep the vows of each of the three vehicles simultaneously without conflict; such a master is quite rare. Compared to true masters, it is said that in this dark age, false gurus are more popular. This is because a true master doesn't make a big display of his qualities. He simply possesses them without showing off. But someone with just minor powers may pretend to be very important so that ignorant people will think, "Wow, he is the real thing!" and follow him.

A story is told about a great master who passed away, and it was later heard that two of his disciples were fighting about who would take his seat as successor. Another man thought, "What a shame. Such a good master. These disciples are acting shamefully. I better go and see what's going on." He went and discovered that they were fighting not to be his successor. The first disciple was saying, "You must take his seat," and the second was protesting, "No, you must be the successor." They were quite serious about it.

Someone who possesses true selflessness and compassion will have no egotism whatsoever and can really benefit others. If we count such people, compared to the number of human beings in this world, aren't they rare? That's what's meant in this text.

STUDENT: Regarding Naropa and the empowerment through being hit with a shoe, we no longer receive the empowerments like that. How did it develop that we receive them as we do today?

RINPOCHE: These days, empowerments are given, and you cannot claim that no one is receiving empowerments because many people do receive them. There must be some who truly receive them, practice, and attain liberation. Basic wakefulness is individually experienced and cannot be known by another person. But we would be wrong to claim that everyone who receives an empowerment will also be liberated thereby.

STUDENT: I meant in terms of the methods.

RINPOCHE: Some masters still give empowerments like Naropa, but secretly, not in public. In public, they give empowerments very nicely.

STUDENT: I think the importance of faith in the direct path is somewhat tricky for us as Westerners, who did not grow up with many of the Buddhist symbols or ideas you are talking about. I was wondering if you could talk about the development of faith?

RINPOCHE: What you say is true. Milarepa had a student who asked him the same question and he replied, "It's okay. Right now, the main thing is to practice, and although the faith and compassion may not be totally genuine, keep it as an adornment to the practice of meditation. Without separating the two aspects of devotion and insight, develop them as much as you can. Then, once you truly recognize the view of Mahamudra, the ultimate truth free from any mental constructs, then even without having to, you will spontaneously have the feeling towards me, the old father, as though I were a fully enlightened buddha in person."

Right now, we cannot have more than mere artificial faith and artificial compassion, because we cannot really perceive the qualities of our teacher. We can only see that sometimes he smiles, sometimes he's nice to us, sometimes he talks pleasantly. He's being kind and so on and we think, "He's a very nice teacher." That's as much as we can understand. Because of this, our feeling towards him may change a little, sometimes it might be devotion, sometimes compassion, sometimes it might be love. It can change. But as one practices more, then one's understanding increases, and one will know more of his qualities. At that point, faith becomes unshakable confidence.

3
The Song of Thinking of Impermanence, Cause, and Effect

> Kyema kyihu atsamana ang!
> When this vessel-like world disintegrates, it will be
>   destroyed by fire and water.
> Years are also impermanent, as the year-cycle gradually
>   turns.
> The months and seasons, the heat and cold,
> And the half-yearly cycles alternate, while the hours
>   dwindle away,
> With the rising and setting of the sun and the moon.

The first line begins with *kyema* etc., an expression indicating weariness or deep sadness.

The Buddha taught that all of the 84,000 teachings can be explained in terms of the *four summaries of the Dharma:* all compounded things are impermanent; all that is defiled is suffering; all phenomena are empty and without self-entity; and nirvana is great peace.

I will now explain the first summary that all composite things are impermanent. The external world, the beings who live there, and the different experiences of joy and sorrow are all impermanent.

We might think that even though human beings do not last forever, at least the external world is permanent and stable, but this is not true. The whole universe has four great cycles: creation, remaining, destruction, and finally voidness. These four periods are together called a *mahakalpa,* a great aeon. In the end, the universe will be totally destroyed seven times by the element of fire, and once by the element of water. These fires are traditionally said to be suns. The first sun will burn away the plants and trees in the forests throughout the entire world. The second will dry up all the moisture. The third will dry up the major rivers, and the fourth will dry up all the great oceans. This continues until the seventh sun brings about complete destruction by burning away all the mountains, the earth, and everything. It is said that after the fourth sun, no water will be left, not even as much as contained in the hoof print of a horse.

At this time, the whole universe, which traditionally consists of Mount Sumeru, the *four continents,* the *eight subcontinents,* and the surrounding iron ring of mountains, will be consumed and totally destroyed. The fire will consume the lower realms, such as the hells, and will move up through the higher realms until it reaches the *Brahma Realm,* the world of long-living gods. Above the Brahma Realm are other god realms where the gods live for ten million years or more. The young gods will ask their elders, "What is this great fire consuming everything?" and the old gods will say, "Don't worry. This has happened many times before. It won't harm us but will disappear again." In short, whatever we now conceive of as the universe will be completely destroyed and finally disappear. At the conclusion of this mahakalpa, the entire world system will vanish.

Not only is the world impermanent, so also is time. One season follows another. One micro-second is constantly changing into seconds, hours, days, months, and years while the time of death approaches steadily. Whether we are sleeping, walking, or enjoying ourselves, our time is running out and our moment of death is drawing near. We cannot stop time. We can play with our watch and it will stop, but time still moves forward. Throughout the year we see constant change. The days become shorter or longer, hotter or colder, and the scenery changes with foliage turning green or brown.

The movement of the sun is another indication of impermanence. Every single second the sun is moving either up or down in the sky. When the sun is rising, dharma practitioners will notice and think, "Now there is a nice, new opportunity for practicing the Dharma." When the sun is setting, they will think, "Now another day is finished and time is running out. Everything is impermanent."

The hours dwindle without our noticing. We often think, "Where did the time go?" We suddenly find that the day is gone. Without noticing the passing of time, we grow old, get sick, and die.

Everything, from the largest object like Mount Sumeru, down to the tiniest micro-organism, is impermanent. Everything changes and is transformed into something else. Everything has the nature of impermanence.

> The contents, sentient beings who inhabit the world, are born, grow old, fall sick, and die.
> The changes of impermanence are like the ripples on water.
> It is impossible, among all compounded things, to find even one that will remain forever.
> The end result of birth is death and the end result of rising is falling.
> The end result of youth is deterioration and the end result of gathering is depletion.
> The end result of meeting is parting — these one cannot avoid.

All sentient beings who are born into this world grow old, fall sick, and die. Some die as children, some when they have grown old, and some without having had a chance to grow old. Some die when sick, some when healthy; some die from insanity, and some would like to die, but cannot and must live until they grow very old. There are many ways to die.

The changes, from moment to moment, are like ripples on the surface of water, one following the other, without interruption. If we look around and examine the external world, we cannot find any compounded object which will last forever. This is what the Buddha taught. We can examine it for ourselves and see that it is true.

The end result of birth is death. Each and every being born into this world will someday die. No one in the past has ever escaped death. There will never be anyone in the future who lives forever. This is something we can think about and understand to be true. Never have we heard of, nor seen, nor even had the suspicion, that a living being has been born who will not die. It is a fact of impermanence that whoever is born must also die.

The end result of rising is falling. Whatever has been constructed or fabricated — huge skyscrapers, fortresses, castles, and so forth, whether made of stone, concrete, granite, marble, precious materials, or steel — will eventually fall apart and return to dust. Nothing that has been composed in this way can last forever. That is also a fact of impermanence.

Whatever has been gathered will be exhausted or spent, no matter how plentiful or perfect. Whatever one amasses, will, in the end, be depleted.

The end result of youth is deterioration. We may be extremely handsome or beautiful, in good shape, fit and healthy so that everyone who sees us says, "What a beautiful person!" We may be called Miss England or Miss America, but later on in our lives the time will come when we will grow old and even the doctors will say, "Forget the facelift!" It won't matter what kind of color or paint we put on our face nothing will benefit. These are further aspects of impermanence.

The end result of meeting is parting. Right now, we have gathered here to listen to the talk. Later on, at lunch time, fewer people will be here, and, in late afternoon, even fewer. After the seminar, people will go their separate ways. A few may remain in the area, it is quite possible that many of us who have met here will never see each other again. This is another aspect of the fact of impermanence.

To say that what has been amassed will be dispersed is often a painful truth. First, we have the difficulty of trying to accomplish what we want, which we may not be able to achieve. Accumulating desirable objects, we then worry about holding on to them. We may fear that our possessions will be stolen, so we need a guard; or maybe they will be broken or lost. Much worry is involved.

Parting, the end result of meeting, is another painful fact. Within a family, the husband and wife, sister and brother, or parent and child, may love each other so very dearly that they cannot bear separation for even one hour. Yet, a time will come when death carries off one family member after another. Some couples prefer to die together rather than to face separation, though this will prove impossible. Even if they commit suicide together in order to be with each other after death, they are not likely to be reborn under similar circumstances in the next life. They will still be separated. Even a person who is extremely disliked, with few friends, will still have someone from whom he or she cannot bear to be parted.

Thinking of these things may seem quite depressing, but they are the facts of life about which we can do nothing. We are all subject to this law of impermanence. Were we beyond it and beyond death, there would be no point in mentioning impermanence, but we are not.

> The perfectly Awakened One, the pratyekabuddhas, and the arhats,
> And all the ones who attained the supreme and common siddhis,
> Must all, in the end, leave their bodies behind.
> Where is there someone who is superior to them?
> Since even Brahma, Indra, and the universal monarch,
> The king of half the world, as well as
> All the great kings of India, Tibet, Mongolia, and so forth had to die.
> How can there be any certainty as to the time of death for ungifted commoners?

If even the fully enlightened Buddha Shakyamuni and all his accomplished disciples eventually had to die, then why not someone like us? We are not superior to them. All of the gods who possess miraculous powers, like *Brahma* and *Indra,* all of the universal rulers, all of the great kings of India and Tibet, all of the presidents and prime ministers of the western countries, and even those who travel surrounded by body-guards carrying weapons to protect their lives, must one day die. If all these people with great merit and high position had to die, then what about us who have just ordinary positions?

> There are four-hundred kinds of sickness, one-hundred thousand types of obstacles,
> And innumerable dangers to life and limb.
> Like a flame in a hurricane, there is no certainty as to when you will pass away.
> Like a criminal led to the scaffold,
> You approach death with each passing year, month, and day.
> One day, you will meet with Yama, the Lord of Death.

Tibetan culture traditionally identifies four hundred kinds of sickness, many types of obstacles and harmful influences and numerous dangers to life and limb. We might take a nice skiing holiday in Switzerland, have a good time, show off a little bit, fall off a cliff and die. People die in many different ways: some die from having a good time, some die from having a bad time; some from eating poisonous food, some from eating very delicious food; some die from depression, some from laughing themselves into a heart attack.

Right now, though we feel strong and healthy, our life force is like a candle's flame in a hurricane — certain to be extinguished without notice. It depends on when the wind blows forcefully in our direction. Likewise, while alive, different sicknesses and many kinds of obstacles surround us. We can only try to do our best to go on living. We take long-life medicine or vitamins; we wear warm clothes or say special long-life mantras. Yet, we are still like that flame in the hurricane.

> When medicine, protection, and the power of healing ceremonies have failed,
> There will come a day when you will become a corpse.
> Just like the setting sun approaching the mountain tops,
> There will come a day when your death cannot be postponed.
> Without power to take along your relatives and attendants,

> There will come a day when you must depart alone.
> You may have great wealth, but no freedom to take along even one day's provisions.
> Likewise, there will come a day when you must leave empty-handed.
> Roaming aimlessly alone through unknown lands,
> There will come a time when there is no certainty as to your destination.
> Your pains and agony may be great, but there will be no way to share it with others.
> There will come a time when you will undergo such difficulties.

Like a criminal led to the scaffold or an animal to the slaughterhouse, each step brings the victim closer to death. Each passing moment, day, month, and year brings us closer and closer to our own death when we will meet the one traditionally called Yama, the Lord of Death. Nothing can be done to avoid this, though we might try all kinds of medicines or healing ceremonies, different charms and protections. Nothing will avail. One is still destined to become a corpse. As the setting sun approaches the mountain-tops and sinks into the west, no one can put it back up in the sky. Likewise, at the moment of death, when one has to die, nothing can delay this event.

We may have many loved ones, attendants and followers, but at the time of death, we must go on alone. No one can accompany us. Our wealth, possessions, and enjoyments must all be left behind. One may be the wealthiest person in the world, but when death comes, one goes alone without taking along even as much as a small handbag or a needle and thread. We will have to leave completely empty-handed. Even this treasured body, seemingly the most important thing in the world, will have to be discarded. Death, which may arrive while we're eating, dressing, or when we're in the middle of a new job or worldly pursuit, will carry us off involuntarily. Afterwards, there is no certainty as to where one will end up in the next life, perhaps as a snake or as someone with horns. We can never be completely sure, so it's better to be careful right now.

A saying goes; "We spend all our lives making preparations. We die while in the midst of preparing; there is no end to these preparations." Worldly activities have no end. The only end is when one gives them up.

One story tells about a person who took the thought of impermanence to heart. A meditator was living alone in a cave with a thorn bush at the entrance. Every time he went out to the toilet, his clothing got stuck in this bush and he thought, "What a bother, I should trim this bush back!" But upon returning he would always think, "Who knows? I might die tonight, and then I would have wasted all this time cutting a bush. I'd rather practice!" This happened again and again, but each time he came to the same conclusion. Finally, he stayed in the cave for seven years without ever cutting the bush.

Two other analogies express the feeling of impermanence. One concerns a faint-hearted person who suddenly finds a snake in his lap. If that happened, he would drop everything and jump up. The second is about a beautiful girl who was completely enchanted by her own physical beauty. If she suddenly discovered that her hair was on fire, she would drop everything and leap for water. Keep these two good analogies in mind: the nervous person who has the snake dropped into his lap and the beauty whose hair catches fire.

We rarely think we have time to do practice, but even if we find the time, we usually put our practice off until the next day or the day after that. As long as we're alive, we will always hope for a tomorrow so we can delay our practice. We can easily go through our whole lives like this, thinking, tomorrow, tomorrow, tomorrow.

At the time of death, one may experience a lot of suffering. This pain cannot be handed over to someone else but is a personal experience that one must go through all alone.

> Without recognizing the dissolution stages or the
> luminosities of 'appearance' and 'increase,'

> There will come a time when you are at a loss about what
> to do.
> When the sounds, colors, and lights, and the peaceful and
> wrathful deities dawn,
> An evil person will feel alone and as if surrounded by a
> whole army.
> There will come a time of tremendous panic, fear, and
> terror.

This verse is about the intermediate state, the *bardo*. We won't go into this now, but generally there are experiences in these states, such as sounds, colored lights and rays, and the appearance of the peaceful and wrathful deities. All are expressions of one's own personal phenomena or self-display. Recognizing them as such, there is no danger. Otherwise, one will fall into confusion due to one's karmic accumulations and will experience everything, feeling great panic and terror as though one is alone, surrounded by a great army.

> Carried off by the terrifying and fearsome messengers of
> Yama,
> Your 'inherent god and demon' will reveal your virtues
> and evil deeds.
> Lying will not help, as they will be evident in the 'mirror'
> and the 'register.'
> There will come a time when you will regret your past
> misdeeds.
> You may desire some merit, but at this time there is
> nowhere to buy or borrow it.
> The Lord of Death will be separating the white deeds
> from the black.
> If you want to be without regrets at that time and still
> don't practice right now,
> You are fooling yourself, being silly and senseless.

When meeting the metaphorical Yama and his messengers, whatever one has done in the past life will be clearly revealed. One can't pretend that one did not do certain things. Everything will be totally evident. One's 'inherent god and demon' will act like a mirror which clearly reflects everything that appears in it. Metaphorically speaking, a register or logbook holds a record of every being's past actions. So, at this time, one will probably regret having wasted one's life on pointless things or negative actions. One may wish that one had done meritorious deeds, received empowerments, and practiced, but it will, at this time, be too late. One cannot buy, borrow, or find this merit anywhere.

> At present, you cannot bear even the touch of a fire's spark,
> But the flames of hell are seven times hotter than the fires of this world.
> How will your mind be able to bear having to be boiled and burned for aeons,
> Without even being able to die?

The hot hells, which are only karmic phenomena, are still said to be seven times hotter than the fire of this world. How could one bear being fried, boiled, burned, chopped to pieces, just to die and be revived again and again for aeons and aeons? At the present, we cannot perceive these hell realms. We can believe in them or not, but Lord Buddha taught that such realms exist. Try instead to consider what it would feel like to be an animal, such as a cow or a street dog, and reflect upon what kind of life that must be.

> When you cannot bear just wearing thin clothing for even a single winter's day,
> What will you do when, without being able to die,
> You are enclosed within ice, without clothes, freezing for aeons?

This refers to the cold hells, which I'll mention very briefly. For example, in the dead of winter, one cannot bear to stay outdoors for a single day wearing only a thin covering. How then can one hope to bear existence in the cold hells where one feels completely enclosed within a block of ice, one's body blistering from the freezing conditions?

Traditionally, there are eight cold hells. At the first level, one cries out in pain from the agony of freezing, but as one progresses to the lower levels of hell, one's body will begin to blister, ooze, and finally crack into many pieces. Each of these hells has a particular name describing the tortures experienced therein.

> When you keep fasting-silence right now, you feel completely dizzy.
> Later on, for thousands of years, without hearing even the words 'food and drink,'
> What will you do when, at that time, you are not even able to die?
> At present, if some one calls you 'old dog,' you pull out your knife,
> But what will you do if you are actually reborn as a dog?
> Right now, it is enough just to flee from an army or an enemy,
> But what will you do if you are born in the realm of the demigods?
> At present, you feel despair at the slightest degradation,
> But the misery of a fallen god is unbearable.

Fasting-silence is a practice of abstaining from food for one day. The second line of the verse refers to the experience of the suffering of the hungry ghost realm. The suffering of the animal realm is referenced by a special Tibetan insult — being called an 'old dog.' This insult is considered so horrible that it causes Tibetan people to pull out their knives in anger. But what would actually being reborn as a dog be like?

Right now, one can attempt to escape an invading army, but

what would it be like to be born in the realm of the demigods and have to engage in continual warfare?

> The sufferings in the three lower realms are intolerable.
> The pleasures of gods and humans are impermanent and totally transient.
> Birth, old age, sickness, and death are like ripples on water.
> The ocean of samsaric misery is deep.

If one truly contemplates the endless cycle of existence, one will fear the unceasing terrors of samsara from which escape is so difficult. Yet, one's own negative actions and misdeeds are the very cause of these countless sufferings. Therefore, just as one is careful not to consume poison, resolve to avoid negative actions.

Good actions are said to bear good results and negative actions, negative results. Actions, or karma, are of four types: the result of ripening, experience resembling its cause, dominant result, and action resembling its cause.

The result of specific actions causing rebirth in a particular realm is called the result of ripening. This is the first type of result stemming from actions. For example, if one kills, then the ripening result of that is that one will be reborn in a hell realm. Just as an action committed with strong anger will result in a rebirth in hell, an action done with great attachment will result in rebirth as a hungry ghost, and an action stemming from stupidity will result in rebirth as an animal.

The second kind of effect is called the 'result resembling its cause.' There are two kinds, action resembling its cause and experience resembling its cause. For example, if in this life one has killed many animals or human beings, then in a future life, due to the habitual pattern formed from that action, one retains the desire to repeat that same action. This is an example of action resembling its cause. If one has killed many insects, for instance, in a future lifetime, one will experience a shortened life-span, have much illness, or die at birth.

Some people will experience illness throughout their entire life. This is an example of experience resembling its cause, and it results from one's own past actions.

There is an additional effect called dominant result. For example, if one steals from others many times, one can be reborn in a poverty-stricken place and suffer the pains of famine. Or, if one engages in slander and persistent gossip, one can be reborn in a place where the hills are very steep with many dangerous precipices which make walking extremely perilous.

Likewise, positive actions will reap positive results. From actions of generosity, great wealth results. If one decides not to take the lives of other beings, but to save lives, the result of this will be that, in future lives, one will experience little sickness and have a long life. Other positive actions will result in rebirth under pleasant circumstances, such as rebirth in a prosperous country, or the enjoyment of good health and so forth. Each positive action yields its own positive results.

> Since one fears this endless terror, without any chance for escape,
> One should shun misdeeds as if they were poison
> And follow these sacred teachings which bring benefit, as if they were the antidote.
> Venerate the Three Jewels, the supreme protection.

The disturbing emotions are the three poisons and practicing the teachings are their antidote. In other words, negative actions are like poison and virtuous actions are like their antidote.

What causes rebirth within the lower realms? What causes suffering? What is it that gives beings a hard time? The disturbing emotions of attachment, anger, and delusion are the three poisons, but they can be expanded into the five or *six kleshas* when pride, envy, and avarice are added. Therefore, one should apply the remedy of the sacred Dharma.

The text then says, *Venerate the Three Jewels, the supreme protec-*

tion against the fears of samsara. When one wants protection against one's country's enemies, one appeals to the Head of State to secure that protection. Likewise, the supreme protection against the fears of samsara are the Three Jewels.

In general, following the conventional meaning, the Three Jewels are the Buddha, Dharma, and Sangha. The Buddha is the ultimate refuge, the Dharma the path, and the Sangha, our companions on the path. According to the inner teaching, one maintains that recognition and puts it into practice. This last kind of refuge will be the supreme protection.

> If you don't understand the meaning of what I have explained here,
> Look, then, to these examples which are obvious.
> Even when the present kings assemble their armies,
> It is hard for them to gather more than thirty-thousand.
> Also, it is rare to find more than three-hundred thousand human beings in one vassal kingdom.

Obviously, the mention of kings and armies describes the old days, not the present. Years ago, when a king would assemble his army it was hard to get more than 30,000 men. It was difficult to find more than 300,000 human beings in a single vassal kingdom.

> The number of insects in summertime on just a single mountain slope,
> Far surpasses the number of humans in the domain of a great king.
> Likewise, the quantity of ants in a single ant hill is higher than all the troops of a great ruler.
> To see whether or not a human form is hard to find, think of the previous example.

If one compares the number of human beings with the number of insects in the summertime on a single mountain slope, the insects will far surpass the number of human beings under a king's ruling. Even the number of ants in a single anthill exceeds the troops under the rule of a great king. So, are there more insects or human beings in this world? Sentient beings in the hell realms are generally said to be as numerous as dust motes in a vast desert; hungry ghosts to be as numerous as the grains of sand in a great river; and animals like the pieces of husk from a harvest. To become a human being in our world, the Jambu continent, is quite rare. Compared to the multitude of beings in the lower realms, the number of human beings is like the dust motes under one's fingernail.

> Consider equally strong brothers from the same parents
> — some are rich, some poor, and some destitute.
> Some have short lives, sickness, and a lot of misery.
> Some are rarely sick, have long lives, and are mostly happy.
> Although they are alike in having obtained a precious human form,
> Some are powerful and others are destitute,
> Some are rich and others starving, and desolate.
> This is not because some are strong and others weak, some clever, and some dumb,
> Examine this to see that it results from the karma of past lives.

Consider children with the same father and mother. They should be very alike but are not. One child may become wealthy while his brothers and sisters are destitute. One may have a short life, another live for a very long time. One may have excellent health, while another suffers from one illness after the other. One may be miserable, the other perpetually happy. Born of the same parents, children often lead quite different lives. Due to karma from past lives, human beings vary quite a bit, not because some are strong and others weak, some clever and some unintelligent. This is how it happens. There is nothing to be done. One should examine to see if this is true or not.

> All human beings, since the beginning of the aeon until this day,
> Feared death but still found no way to avoid it.
> As not even one single person is left behind alive,
> Try and estimate how many of your acquaintances have died.
> They died last year, and this year more will die.
> You are also not beyond this in the slightest.

The human beings who lived in the beginning of this aeon had very long life spans, few disturbing emotions, little attachment, and bodies composed of light. This is because they had little concept of 'self' and 'other.' They had many enjoyments and did not need to eat ordinary food as they were sustained by samadhi. At that time, they were quite like divine beings — like gods; but slowly they developed attachment and the idea of a self — clinging to things and making everything more and more solid and gross. There is some similarity in this to the Bible's story of Genesis. Yet, these beings died, whether they wanted to or not. Further details can be found in a text called the *Abhidharma Kosha*.

All of us have had a father and a grandfather and, if we wanted to discover the exact number of our forefathers, we could not. Searching out the names of our forefathers, even finding someone who knows more than ten or fifteen by name is extremely rare. We certainly had many more ancestors than this, but we'll never know their names, nor their occupations. They were born, they lived for a time, and then they passed away, whether they wanted to or not. They all feared death, but none could avoid it.

> Everyone knows that there is death, one needs the Dharma when it happens,
> Yet we fool ourselves by thinking there is plenty of time.
> Nowadays it is said that a life-span is about forty years.
> Try and think and reflect upon how many people have died
> Who were the same age or younger than you.

Even now, with every passing hour, numerous sentient beings are born and pass away, just in this world alone. To make a complete count of them is impossible. If we just think of how many people we, ourselves, have known who have died: family members, friends, acquaintances, and so on, it must be quite a lot. Try to remember how many neighbors and friends died just this year and last. We should take notice of this and know that we, too, will someday die. We are not special or different from others. There is no guarantee that we will not die this year or maybe this very day.

The verse says that everyone knows that death will come. A Dharma practitioner who has recognized the ultimate nature of his mind, may, by the power of his practice, be able to attain liberation at the time of death. Having studied the Dharma and having gained understanding of the law of cause and effect, one becomes certain of future lives and firm in the conviction that, at the time of death, the practice of Dharma will be an invaluable aid. Imagining that, one can always practice next year when there is more time, that one can study at one's leisure sometime in the future, or that the retreat that one has been planning can be put off for another year, is really foolish.

These days, the human life span in the West is said to be about 65 years. This doesn't mean that one cannot live longer or shorter, but it means that most people will die around this age. Consider how many people have died who were the same age or younger than yourself and you will know this to be true. The main point to understand from this is that we will certainly die, but the time of death is not certain. The reason to think about this is that taking to heart the thought of death becomes an encouragement to practice. By doing so one will not waste time, but quickly engage oneself in practice, study, and reflection.

> Still, we think we won't die right away.
> We spend our time on defeating enemies, taking care of relatives,
> Making preparations and taking pleasure in misdeeds.

> Without fulfilling our plans, we are all taken away by the
>   Lord of Death.
> Realize that you also are not exempt from this and
>   practice the perfect Dharma.

If we really believe that we are not going to die for many years, then we can spend all of our time, directly or indirectly, trying to defeat others, trying to acquire wealth, making preparations for this and that, and taking care of family matters. Through these activities, we happily accumulate all kinds of negative karma.

We have made all of these plans and preparations, but without having had the chance to complete them, the Lord of Death carries us off. We pass away. In the past, many died while making plans to practice or study. So, if we keep our practice only on the planning board, we may also die without having had the opportunity to accomplish much.

> The method for intending to practice, for entering the
>   Dharma,
> And for reaching perfection in Dharma practice is the
>   pure teaching on sincerely thinking of death.
> If you don't take the thought of death to heart,
> Your Dharma practice will only stray into self-
>   aggrandizement and the performance of rituals for pay.
> The profound advice is to take to heart the thought of
>   death three times every single day.

People have such anxiety about running out of money or not having enough food to eat. They always feel that whatever they have accumulated is not really sufficient. They cling to an illusive world that they think is solid and lasting. When one really understands, takes to heart the thought of death and impermanence, knowing that all sentient beings and all things are perishable and that all experiences of pleasure and pain are transitory, one will naturally have less attachment to the things of this life. Eventually, one's mind will become peaceful and gentle. How much wealth one accumulates makes no difference, for that too will be exhausted. Realizing this, one will strive for liberation, the only true happiness.

The thought of impending death is the reason for entering Dharma practice, for feeling that one should do what is really worthwhile. If one has truly taken the thought of death to heart, one will not take great pleasure in distractions; one will only want to practice. It's like the snake dropping into the lap of a nervous person or the beautiful woman's hair catching fire. One will feel like laying everything else aside, and without further delay, want nothing more than to practice the Dharma.

After entering the Dharma, some practice only occasionally and then forget it for a while. This happens because they have not fully understood the reality of death. Not understanding the imminence of death, practicing Dharma can be distorted into self-aggrandizement, seeking a high position or pleasure-seeking, performing rituals for pay and so forth. This will become an erroneous path.

A few times a day we should think, "I really do have to die. It will happen someday and then it will be important to have practiced the Dharma." Just as we now plan what we will eat tonight, what we will wear tomorrow, and what we will do in a few days or next year, we must also prepare for what will happen in the long run. The thought of death will encourage us, first to enter Dharma, and then to practice continuously with diligence.

If one is not practicing, it's important to think of death, but if one is already practicing then one need not think about it continuously. If the light is off, then turn on the switch; but if it is already on, then don't make yourself depressed thinking about death.

The themes of these last two songs are contained in the following four thoughts which turn the mind away from samsara: the difficulty of attaining the precious human body, impermanence and death, the cause and effect of karma, and defects of samsara.

Although we have already touched upon these topics, I'll elaborate even further. Obtaining a precious human body endowed with the *eight freedoms* and the *ten favorable conditions* is not enough.

One needs to be free from the eight temporarily unfree conditions or obstacles to practice.

The first is called the eruption of the five poisons and refers to the fact that though we may think about practicing the Dharma, we sometimes become completely carried away by disturbing emotions such as attachment to relatives, aversion toward enemies, or by passion, aggression, or ignorance. We spend our time caring for friends and relatives, or trying to subdue others, and in this way, all our time dissipates. We might have a glimpse of inspiration to practice once in a while, but it is not very strong and is usually overpowered by the five poisons. Being governed by these, we are not free to practice the Dharma. This is the main obstacle of these eight.

Although we have engaged in Dharma practice, in studying, reflecting, and meditating, if someone utters just a slight harsh word out of anger towards us, our whole practice collapses and we immediately give up everything and are carried away by our reaction. This is another example of the first point.

The second unfree condition or obstacle is dullness, a state of mind in which one doesn't really hear what is being said. Not able to think clearly, one doesn't really notice what is going on in any precise way. It is worse if the dullness is a recurrent state, as it prevents one from being able to practice correctly. When we practice or study, sometimes we become completely dull, obscured, or stupid so that we can't think clearly. Sometimes we may also become agitated or restless so that our mind jumps from thought to thought, especially when doing sitting practice. We always seem to want to do something else; to get up and drink tea, to go somewhere else, or to experience, see, feel, or hear something rather than just sitting quietly.

The third obstacle is to be taken by a demon, meaning to follow the teacher of a perverted teaching or system. Whoever follows him will be led down an erroneous path.

Laziness is the fourth obstacle. Laziness has different forms. Feeling sluggish and wanting to relax a little too much, lying down and stretching out, and not wanting to bother to practice are, of course, laziness. The worst kind of laziness, however, is called discouraging oneself, putting oneself down, thinking, "How can I find time to practice? I have my children to look after. I'm just a housewife." Or "I have a job to do and there's no time to practice." Or thinking, "I'm not diligent. I can't attain enlightenment. I'm not very clever, so I can't understand these deep teachings." We tell ourselves that it's impossible and thus avoid practicing.

Laziness is also thinking, "Of course I should practice, but right now I don't have the time. I'll start tomorrow for sure." When the next day arrives, there is no time in the morning, so practice is postponed until after lunch. But after lunch there's no time either, so it's postponed again until the evening. But then we are too tired, and we feel we should sleep because we would be too tired to practice correctly. We decide, "For sure, tomorrow morning I'll get up bright and early." But then the morning is a little cold and we want to sleep an extra hour. On and on it goes, just postponing practice until the future. We do want to practice, of course, but small things become very important. We must immediately go to the toilet, or make coffee, wash our face, or tidy the room.

The mind works in quite a funny way. First, one thinks, "Without a good meal and tea or coffee, I won't be able to do proper practice." Then, after the meal, one thinks, "I think I ate a little too much. I can't practice on a full stomach!" and again delays. Excuses are endless: "I'm too tired. I need to lie down for a while" and then, waking up, "If I don't take a walk right now, my mind will not be clear enough," one then walks outside. All of these are examples of laziness, a serious hindrance. Give it up.

The fifth obstacle is called the flood of activity. We have developed a definite wish and sincere desire to practice and we have the impetus to engage ourselves intensively, but we seem to have important things to take care of first. For instance, we need some wealth in order to practice. Once we have money, we feel we should keep increasing this by investing so that it won't dwindle too quickly. After making more, we have to maintain this capital and continue to gather more. There are many activities connected with this, taking care of the family, and accomplishing various things. It becomes endless. People usually think, "First I'll work and get money together and when I feel I have enough, later on, I'll be able to practice." Usually the time never arrives, practice is again postponed.

In short, 'the flood of activity' obstacle means getting carried away by accumulating, hoarding and maintaining possessions. In the end, the desire to practice becomes like a mere flash of lightning in the sky, very fleeting.

The sixth obstacle, called dependency, means that one is under the power of another person and has no free will. Being governed by someone else, one always feels that one must fulfill that person's aims, listen to orders, and follow directions rather than doing what one really wants. Such circumstances allow little opportunity to engage in Dharma practice.

The seventh obstacle can be called seeking security, trying to escape the insecurity of this life. One practices surviving, for example, as a monk or nun in a secure monastery. Practicing so as to simply feel safe for this life is not a correct motive.

The eighth obstacle is called the pretense of Dharmic hypocrisy. One behaves like a first-class practitioner, either dressing up like a yogi or siddha of great accomplishment, or like a very neat and impressive monk or nun, with everything apparently under control. This applies as well to any kind of practitioner who pretends to have some understanding and some realization of the teachings, while internally retaining only an interest in honor, personal gain, wealth, position, and so forth. This can happen for everyone and is dangerous. It easily pops up and is something we should guard against.

If we examine how long we have been alive, how long we have been interested in Dharma, how much time we have spent engaged in Dharma practice, how much time we have actually spent studying, contemplating, and meditating, how much time we've spent working, how much time we've spent having a good time, how much time we've spent doing nothing whatsoever in indifferent neutral actions, the times spent on genuine practice seem as infrequent as stars seen in daytime or as short as the flicker of lightning in the sky.

In this respect, the time we spend on Dharma, or in sitting practice, is something very precious, and is, in fact, invaluable. Later on, whether we easily find the time to practice or not is totally up to us. If we think something is important, we usually find time to do it. We find the time to party, relax, and so on. If we think that practice is worthwhile, we can easily find time for that too. It depends upon the value we attach to it. Please keep this in mind.

QUESTIONS AND ANSWERS

STUDENT: Is there any conflict between being rich and aspiring towards liberation?

RINPOCHE: This is a very good question. There are two kinds of accumulation. Whenever concepts are involved in one's practice, the accumulation is called merit with concepts. The other accumulation, free of concepts, is called the accumulation of wisdom without concepts. If one is generous to others and performs virtuous actions only to be happy, have a long life, and be rich oneself in future lives, this is a very narrow and poor attitude. For example, being generous by giving material things, by offering protection against fear, or by making a gift of the teachings, are acts of generosity — the accumulation of merit. However, if the acts of generosity are embraced by a nonconceptual state of mind, they become the accumulation of wisdom. If one embraces whatever virtuous activity one does with the attitude of bodhichitta, it will have an inexhaustible effect, beyond simply resulting in becoming rich or influential in a future life. But if one fails in this, the results of all of one's virtuous actions will only ripen within the samsaric world. One will reap nothing beyond that.

A story is told about Buddha Shakyamuni's disciple, Nanda. He had a very pretty wife to whom he was extremely attached and whom he loved deeply. Nanda had a small portrait of his wife made to carry around with him. He would often look at it and think, "My wife is the most beautiful woman in the world!" His attachment prevented Nanda from taking vows and becoming an ordained follower of the Buddha, although the Buddha tried to persuade him. Finally, seeing no other way, the Buddha took Nanda to the god realms and showed him women much more beautiful than his own wife. Nanda then thought, "This place is quite nice." In the god realm, he was told that to be reborn in this realm, one needs only to take ordination and practice shamatha and vipashyana. On returning to our world, Nanda immediately took vows and practiced very hard with great diligence. Since expecting a reward in samsara from spiritual practice was not really the proper motivation for practice, the Buddha later changed Nanda's mind again so that he became a pure practitioner. For this, he took Nanda to the hell realms where Nanda saw incredible pain and suffering. Beings were tortured in many ways. When the Buddha and Nanda arrived at one place, they saw a huge pot of boiling oil. Nanda asked the worker what it was for and the worker replied, "In the human world lives a disciple of the Buddha named Nanda who will be reborn in heaven through his merit of keeping the precepts. After exhausting this conditioned merit, his negative karma from past lives will send him right here. This is why we are heating up the oil in this pot." Nanda became frightened and asked the Buddha "Are you playing a joke on me?" The Buddha said "No, it is real. The law of karma is unfailing." Returning to the human world, Nanda completely changed his motivation for Dharma practice. He no longer aimed at a rebirth in a higher realm within samsara but strove for complete liberation in order to benefit all beings.

STUDENT: Yesterday, you spoke of simplicity as being the recognition of ordinary mind as baseless and groundless. What is 'ordinary mind?'

RINPOCHE: 'Ordinary mind' is a Dharma term, a meditation expression with profound meaning. We could also say 'special mind.' Usually, we think that the buddha mind, the state of enlightenment, is something very fantastic, something completely different. That is incorrect. The buddha mind is said to be the nature of things as they are. The word 'ordinary' means something that is not modified, altered or changed in any way. That is buddha mind and it is special.

If you have to call anything special, this is what should be called special.

Student: Earlier, we talked about the different kinds of refuge; outer refuge of the Three Jewels — the Buddha, Dharma, and Sangha; the inner refuge of the Three Roots — the Guru, Yidam, and Dakini; the innermost refuge of the three kayas; and finally, the nadi, prana, and bindu. Can you explain nadi, prana, and bindu?

Rinpoche: Usually, when we talk about refuge, we speak of an external refuge, that of the Buddha, Dharma, and Sangha. There is also an inner refuge, which involves taking refuge through the practice of controlling the key points of the nadi, prana, and bindu and thereby discovering the three kayas to be inherent within ourselves. The nadis are channels we have in our body, the pranas are the energies or forces within the body, and the bindus are essences. When purified through practice, that pure aspect is what is recognized as either essence, nature, and capacity, or the three kayas. In short, this helps for recognizing and training in mind essence. Such a type of refuge is not outside oneself, but within; if one never departs from the state of essence, nature, and capacity, then one is taking the ultimate refuge.

4
The Song of the Meditation Session

> Ema!
> Now for the meditation teaching on the main practice.
> There are first something to understand and then
>   something to train in.
> First, gain an understanding of what is to be understood.
> Then, as much as you can, practice the meditation
>   sessions of the topics to train in.

Ema! expresses amazement: "How wondrous!"

So far we have covered the preliminaries, beginning with the precious human birth including the eight freedoms and the ten endowments, the law of impermanence and the four end results: the end of birth is death, the end of accumulation is dispersion, the end of rising is falling, and the end of meeting is parting.

We have also discussed the three kinds of suffering: the suffering of suffering, the suffering of change, and the all-pervasive suffering. All this information belongs to the preliminaries.

In order to be truly free from suffering, we must practice the teachings of the fully enlightened Buddha. The Buddha taught many levels of teachings according to the needs of beings, beginning with the preliminaries, through the *main practice,* the stages of development and completion, and the highest views of Mahamudra and Dzogchen. Following the preliminaries, we now arrive at the main practice. When studying, we begin with something to understand and move on to something in which to train.

> Since no one else is going to save you from the miseries of
>   samsara,
> Entrust yourself to the unfailing Three Jewels.
> The Buddha, Dharma, and Sangha, according to the
>   sutras,

> And the Gurus, Yidams, and Dakinis, according to the tantras,
> Are all ultimately contained within the Body, Speech, and Mind of your master.
> To entrust yourself to him with complete confidence is the 'taking of refuge.'

Regarding refuge, no ordinary being can save one from the miseries of samsara, so one should rely completely on the unfailing Three Jewels as one's refuge. One is usually taught to take refuge in the Buddha, Dharma, and Sangha, to place one's trust in them. This does not mean that the Buddha can wash away all of one's obscurations and negative karma, or that he, like throwing a stone, can send one to a pure buddhafield in a state of complete enlightenment. This is not possible. What is possible? Through the teaching of the Dharma and through one's own efforts in practicing, one can attain enlightenment. The Buddha said, "I'm showing you the path to liberation; whether you actually reach it or not depends upon you."

Complete enlightenment is not a heaven or paradise somewhere else. It is fully realizing the ultimate nature inherent in oneself.

One first develops trust in the Three Jewels and compassion towards all sentient beings. This will enable one to engage in the main practice of emptiness, the natural state free from mental constructs. For the realization of this natural state, devotion and compassion are invaluable aids. In the beginning, this realization is like planting a flower seed. By adding the fertilizer of faith and the water of compassion, the flower will quickly grow.

All Dharma teachings are contained within two categories: *Sutra* and *Tantra*. According to the Sutra tradition, when one takes refuge, one takes refuge in the Buddha, Dharma, and Sangha. The Sanskrit word is buddha, the Tibetan, *sangye*. *Sang* means cleared or purified; all disturbing emotions and obscurations have been completely cleared away. *Gye* means developed or unfolded; all the enlightened qualities of abandonment and realization have been fully developed. Thus, buddha means purified and developed. Literally, dharma, in Sanskrit, means to hold or to gather, but the Tibetan word *chö* means cure or change. In short, the Dharma is instruction which is helpful and without any harm whatsoever. The Sanskrit word sangha literally means group or community, a gathering. In Tibetan, the word was translated as *gendün* meaning 'those who pursue virtue.'

According to tantra, one takes refuge in the Guru, Yidam, and Dakini. The Sanskrit word *guru* means heavy, heavy with the qualities of abandonment and realization. In Tibetan, it is *lama,* meaning supreme or unexcelled. Why unexcelled? Again, because the Guru has perfected all the qualities of abandonment and realization.

Why is a guru or master important? In order to realize what Mahamudra calls 'ordinary mind,' what Dzogchen calls 'self-existing wakefulness,' and what Madhyamaka calls the 'ultimate, inexpressible and indescribable truth,' we must depend upon a qualified master. We need to supplicate a master, blend our mind with his, and, in short, receive his blessings. The guru is considered the root of blessings.

Vajrayana is characterized by having many methods, few hardships, and easy accessibility for people of higher faculties. For these reasons, Vajrayana is especially exalted. Yidam practice is a skillful means which involves the stages of development, recitation, and completion. As we mentioned before, there are supreme and common accomplishments. In Vajrayana, the yidam is the root of accomplishments.

There are various kinds of obstacles that manifest as outer, inner, and innermost. Whenever one engages in something important, something valuable, difficulties and hindrances arise. If something is very simple to do, it is not surprising to find no obstacles. If I walk to Kathmandu on foot, there is nothing special about that; but, if I ride to Kathmandu on a motorcycle with only one wheel, that is quite unusual and also a little dangerous. Likewise, in practice, many dangers or hindrances prevent one from attaining complete enlightenment. To clear these away, we depend upon the dakinis as well as the protectors of the teachings called *Dharma protectors*. The dakini is said to be the root of activity, a means of clearing away obstacles.

According to the sutras, the Buddha, Dharma, and Sangha are contained within the body, speech, and mind of one's own master. This means that the physical form of the teacher is the Sangha, his speech is the Dharma, and his mind is the Buddha. Essentially, each and every master down to the present has developed the enlightened qualities within himself, in an unbroken transmission which is handed down to us. Therefore, our personal teacher, whom we have been able to meet and from whom we receive teachings, is even more precious, in a sense, than the Buddha himself, not in the ultimate sense, but in a personal sense.

The text also tells us that the Guru, Yidam, and Dakini are contained within one's master in the sense that he is the guru himself; he is the yidam, the source of accomplishments; and he is the dakini that can clear away obstacles. Of the two kinds of accomplishments, supreme and ordinary, the ordinary siddhi is in itself neither outstanding nor ultimate, but if one attains the supreme siddhi, that of full realization, the ordinary accomplishments will accompany that automatically. Moreover, the master's mind is inseparable from the naked state of Dharmakaya. If one receives yidam teachings from one's guru and practices the yidam as inseparable from him, one will develop or attain these siddhis.

Finally, the activity of the dakinis is to clear away obstacles to one's practice. The various kinds of obstacles include the outer obstacles of distractions; the inner obstacles of imbalances in one's physical energies, channels, and essences, which cause sickness and mental disturbance; and the innermost obstacles, which are discursive thoughts. For instance, physically, we may sit on our meditation seat or stay in a retreat hut, but mentally have no control at all, our mind is rampant with many different thoughts. This is the innermost obstacle. But, due to the coincidence of cause and effect, if one supplicates the guru as seated above the crown of one's head and mingles one's mind with his, these obstacles can be pacified. In this sense, the dakini is also contained within the master.

The line, *To entrust yourself to him with complete confidence is the taking of refuge,* is meant, not for beginners, but for people who have already studied and practiced and have understood the Dharma for some time; otherwise, this trust becomes just blind faith and is not very useful.

Before entrusting oneself, one must first examine and assess one's teacher. The student should skillfully examine the teacher to find out if he is really qualified. Then, after having examined the teacher and having heard about the Dharma, one can entrust oneself with complete confidence. Literally, the Tibetan says, "Supplicate the master with the thought, 'You know everything!'" One acknowledges oneself to be merely a deluded sentient being, without the wisdom which the master has already attained. Therefore, one places oneself in the master's hands. In other words, one commits oneself fully to practice the methods that the master gives in order to tame one's mind.

Three different kinds of faith have been described: beginner's faith, which we call enthusiasm or admiration, then longing or strong yearning faith, and finally full trust, which later on becomes unshakable confidence.

As an example of the first type of faith: if we come to a garden with beautiful flowers and think, "How nice! This is so pleasant," or, if we go to a museum or temple, wherever we find something which is impressive or delights us and we become happy, this is 'enthusiasm.'

In 'longing faith,' we have decided that we would like to attain for ourselves that which makes us happy, a material thing or some quality we'd like to develop. In the spiritual sense, when we first meet a teacher, we initially feel very impressed or inspired by him, enthusiastic. In the second stage, we have decided that we would like to become like him ourselves. That is the longing or yearning faith.

The third kind of faith is to feel complete trust in the teacher, to feel that his or her spiritual qualities lie beyond one's reach of thought. One can neither understand nor judge his or her realization. As a dog cannot emulate the mighty leap of a lion, an ordinary being cannot judge a great master. A dog might try to behave like a lion, but he won't be very successful.

You may have read the *Life of Milarepa*. When Milarepa first met his teacher, Marpa was plowing a field, a very ordinary activity. Nevertheless, Milarepa did not give rise to any discriminatory thoughts about it being something 'bad.' At that moment, and for some time after, due to their karmic connection, his ordinary experience totally ceased. Milarepa didn't even know that it was Marpa that he was meeting; but nonetheless, upon seeing him, all his grasping and fixation collapsed for a while.

Regarding faith, a story is told about a man named Ben from Kongpo. Kongpo is a district in southeast Tibet. Ben once made a pilgrimage to Lhasa and there developed great faith in the famous *Jowo* statue, an image of the Buddha. When he arrived at the Jowo Temple no one was around, but in front of the statue itself, Ben saw different offerings of food and butter lamps. Ben was not a very bright fellow and so he thought, "This must be food for that nice lama." The statue has a very beautiful smiling countenance and Ben said, "You must be a very good lama. You sit there so nice and quiet. You must be a really nice person and you have such a nice meal here to eat and butter lamps to keep warm by. You can dip the cakes and bread into the butter lamps and eat them."

The statue didn't answer and made no move to eat. Ben thought, "Okay, if you're not going to eat it, I will." He dipped a torma into a butter lamp and munched away. The statue, of course, didn't protest, so Ben said, "What a good lama! I'm taking your dinner and you're not getting angry at me. Now I want to do a circumambulation and one should do that without shoes on so would you mind keeping an eye on my shoes?" The statue replied, "All right."

He put his shoes up on the altar and started to walk around. When he reached the back of the altar, the caretaker came in and saw the shoes on the altar. He thought, "What kind of disgusting person would put his filthy old shoes on the shrine? How terrible!" He took them and was about to toss them out the door when the statue said, "Hey, don't throw those out! I'm keeping them for the devoted Ben from Kongpo."

The caretaker became very frightened and put the shoes back

on the altar. A moment later, Ben came around from the other side and said, "What people say is really true. You are truly a good lama. Thanks a lot for taking care of my shoes. Now, I'm going home, but please come and visit someday. I'll brew some barley and make some good wine and we'll eat meat together. Please come anytime." And the statue replied, "All right."

Upon his return, completely convinced that this nice lama would come and visit him back in Kongpo, Ben told his friends and relatives that, for sure, Jowo from Lhasa would come and visit him in Kongpo. The others said, "You're really crazy. It's not a person, it's a statue. How can it visit anyone?" Ben made preparations anyway. Then, one day his wife went to the river and saw the image of Jowo in the water. She ran back and told Ben, "The man you invited from Lhasa, he's fallen into the river!" In great distress, Ben ran down to the riverbank and saw that the lama had indeed fallen into the water, so he dove in immediately.

Somehow, he pulled the apparition up on dry land and said, "Thank you very much for coming. What a shame that you took that fall into the river. Now, please come to my home." The buddha-image replied, "No, I'm not going to your house. I have already blessed this place," and dissolved into a rock leaving an image that can still be seen. People have a great deal of faith in this image that spontaneously appeared and regard it as no different from the statue of Jowo in Lhasa itself.

Ben wasn't very intelligent, but he had great faith and that's how these things can happen. Later on, due to this faith, Ben progressed a great deal in his understanding and became a very good practitioner.

What is the reason for developing devotion and compassion? In the moment of feeling deep devotion, it is possible for the mind to be totally uncovered, utterly naked. In that instant, the ultimate, original wakefulness dwelling within oneself is laid bare and can be easily realized. Similarly, at the moment of feeling natural and unfabricated compassion, it is easy to recognize, and a very great opportunity exists for realizing the original wakefulness inherent within oneself. For this reason, the generation of faith and compassion is very important.

When one washes a white cloth that is soiled with dirt, as the dirt disappears, the cloth spontaneously becomes white again. Likewise, when negative karmas and obscurations are purified, realization occurs spontaneously. The best method for clearing away one's obscurations and negative karma is faith and compassion.

> Because all sentient beings have been your kind parents,
> It is not sufficient to attain buddhahood for just oneself alone.
> The seed of enlightenment is the vast aspiration
> To establish them all in the state of buddhahood.

Attaining enlightenment for oneself alone is not sufficient because, in all of our past lives, we have had parents who have taken great care of us. Not a single sentient being has avoided being our own mother and father many times in past life situations. We know right now how a mother takes care of her child, and likewise, all sentient beings have, at one time or another, shown us the same kindness and are therefore called 'kind parents.'

When a mother has a small baby, she doesn't mind when it is dirty. She doesn't find this disgusting. She'll just clean it and care for it, giving it food and clothing, keeping it safe and so forth. She will always put the baby and her other children before herself, believing them to be more precious and more important. Everyone who has a child now knows this to be true.

Consider that all sentient beings have been your own mother and father and have shown you great love and tenderness. Yet these beings are still wandering through the six realms of samsara, experiencing different kinds of misery and suffering. Without really wanting to, they experience pain and perpetuate the cause of suffering — negative actions. They wish to be happy, yet they do not know how to practice the cause of happiness — virtuous actions. One should think with great feeling, "How sad that my former mothers, all sentient beings, are ignorant and suffering," and should develop the wish to attain complete enlightenment and establish them all in that same state of buddhahood. This is called bodhichitta.

This verse is about developing bodhichitta. Traditionally three kinds of bodhichitta are discussed. The first being like a shepherd, the second like a ferryman, and the third like a king.

When a shepherd leads a flock of sheep to a pasture, he first checks to see that the sheep are in a place with enough food and water, and a place where there is no danger. Then, he will sit down, relax, and eat his food. He won't think too much about himself though. He's more concerned about looking after the sheep because that is his job. That kind of attitude is the highest kind of bodhichitta. One takes care that other sentient beings attain enlightenment first, placing all others before oneself. After others have been secured, then one attains enlightenment oneself. With this attitude, engaging in the trainings of a bodhisattva is called 'developing bodhichitta in the style of a shepherd.'

The second type of bodhichitta is like the ferryman who travels together with his passengers to a destination. He doesn't send his passengers ahead, nor does he travel before the others. They go together in one boat and reach the other shore. Developing bodhichitta in the style of a ferryman is that while practicing oneself, one wishes to attain complete enlightenment for the benefit of all others and one helps others equally to attain enlightenment.

The third and lowest type of bodhichitta is developing bodhichitta in the style of a king. A king first attains the throne as his seat of power and then helps his subjects by doing what is beneficial. Likewise, one aspires oneself to attain enlightenment and afterwards to benefit all sentient beings. The highest is 'shepherd,' the middling is 'ferryman,' and the lowest is 'king.'

Traditionally, the generation of bodhichitta occurs in three stages. To develop bodhichitta, the awakened heart, one must first equalize oneself with others, then exchange oneself for others, and finally regard others as more important than oneself. For this, an easy way is to think first about one's present mother and then extend that feeling to include all other sentient beings. Since one's own mother is precious to oneself, without starting with her, one might not care so much about other sentient beings.

We can observe parents with a new-born infant. They fuss over it, making sure to keep it clean and well fed, warm, and happy. They try to entertain it in all different ways, using their fingers and face, showing their teeth and making baby noises. We all know about this. Regardless, if the mother is eating a meal or dressing, if the baby cries, she will drop everything and rush to see what's wrong. When sleeping at night, people usually sleep very heavily, like logs, but after having a baby, a mother doesn't sleep deeply. She's ready to jump up at the slightest sound. If the baby makes a small cry, immediately the mother will go and look, and say, "Okay, the baby is fine," before going back to sleep. If she hears any unusual noise in the night, she'll jump up to see if anything has happened to her child.

Both father and mother show equal kindness to the baby, but the mother is closer to the child. The mother is the one with the milk. If there are small things to do, the father is extremely kind, but if it is something more difficult or something that takes longer, the mother is usually kinder. Both, however, are kind toward the child.

We can see this for ourselves, whether we have children or know others who do. Parents show great kindness to their children. Understanding that all sentient beings have been our own parents in past lives, we have a good reason for developing the three kinds of bodhichitta.

Without bodhichitta, there cannot be complete enlightenment. Bodhichitta, the mind of enlightenment, is like the seed from which enlightenment will grow. After developing bodhichitta, one will engage in the actions of a bodhisattva.

> Buddhas and sentient beings are of equal kindness in benefiting
> One's own attainment of complete enlightenment,
> Because without practicing the six transcending actions,
> There is no way to attain perfect buddhahood.

The first line of this verse refers to the kindness of the buddhas in appearing, giving teachings, and enabling the masters in the lineage to attain enlightenment. The kindness of one's own root teacher in giving teachings enables one to practice and to be able to realize the ultimate truth, the natural state free from mental constructs, fully and completely, exactly as it is.

Sentient beings are also of great importance in our attainment of enlightenment, without them there are no objects upon which to practice the six paramitas of generosity, discipline, patience, diligence, meditation and knowledge; nor are there objects for the development of love and compassion. In the case of generosity, for example, one needs a recipient for the act of giving. Thus, sentient beings are of great importance for one's attainment of complete enlightenment.

> Poor and destitute beings are the objects for practicing generosity.
> The objects for cultivating compassion are sentient beings who suffer.
> Even all your enemies and those who make obstacles, returning harm for help,
> Are aids to enlightenment since they support the cultivation of patience.
> By realizing this, generate the courage of the noble aspiration
> To establish by yourself all beings, without bias or partiality,
> In the state of buddhahood.
> That is the profound teaching called 'generating bodhichitta.'

Poor and destitute beings are the objects for the practice of generosity. All beings who suffer are the objects for developing compassion.

When you are treated badly and others create obstacles, try to develop patience. Enemies also aid you in reaching enlightenment. Realizing this, have no preferences or partiality. Generate the great aspiration to establish all sentient beings in the supreme state of buddhahood. That is the profound teaching of generating bodhichitta.

All sentient beings possess basic wakefulness, the enlightened essence. We have been endowed with this original wakefulness since beginningless time. But, just as the weather is sometimes cloudy, we, being under the clouds with the rain and the mist don't feel the warmth of the sunshine. Likewise, all sentient beings are covered by temporary obscurations that prevent clarity and the ability to manifest enlightened essence.

Obscurations are momentary as well as temporary. They can be purified and cleared away, just as a dirty cloth is never too dirty to be cleaned. The cloth may be difficult to clean, but if the right methods are applied, using a strong soap or a special technique, then the dirt can be removed. Our various obscurations are the same.

Usually, three kinds of obscurations are mentioned: the obscuration of disturbing emotions, the cognitive obscuration, and the obscuration of habitual tendencies. A single technique can't clear all of these away. Some need a very strong method, while some need a more subtle application. One single antidote is not effective with all three obscurations, but with various techniques they can all be cleared away.

> Without confessing it, even the tiniest misdeed can become severe;
> As each day passes, it grows and increases.
> Just as dirty clothes can be cleansed with water,
> If you sincerely confess it, there is no misdeed which cannot be purified.
> The misdeeds done in the past are like having swallowed a strong poison.
> If you feel remorse, they are easily purified.
> But the arrogance of thinking you can handle it is more difficult to purify.

> Therefore, resolve firmly to never commit them again.
>
> You may think to do misdeeds doesn't matter because you can just confess afterwards.
> But the Buddha has taught that then they will not be purified.

The first line of this verse means that if we do not immediately change the pattern of our negative actions, it perpetuates itself, growing and becoming stronger and stronger each day. Negative actions are said to have only one good quality: that they can be purified and cleared away.

Just as a soiled cloth can be washed clean with water, negative actions can be purified once they have been committed. But one must feel as though they are a poison one has swallowed. Like poison, negative actions kill the life-force for liberation and eliminate the opportunity for attaining enlightenment. They should be purified. By feeling strong regret, they can be cleared away. If one thinks one can continue to do them, purification is difficult. Therefore, resolve firmly never to commit negative actions again. One may think that it doesn't matter if one does wrong, because one can confess as one goes along, but the Buddha has said that with this attitude the actions will not be purified.

Negative actions must be purified immediately. If someone has treated us badly, we may hold a grudge thinking, "I'll give him a hard time. If I have a chance to help him, I won't." Kept inside, this kind of attitude constitutes a misdeed. The Kadampa practitioners of the past, as soon as they had a bad thought, immediately took out their mandala plates and made a confession to clear away the negativity. In the same way, we should be on guard and purify negative thoughts immediately.

When having negative thoughts or after performing a negative action, it is easier to purify if one immediately feels remorse. Thinking, "I was wrong, I've been confused, I made a mistake," one should generate strong regret about negative actions. Without feeling remorse, to think, "I can just purify it later, say some mantras and confess," and to continue both practicing Dharma and performing negative actions, for instance reciting OM MANI PADME HUNG, and then slaughtering an animal, will not ever result in purification. But, after feeling regret, if one firmly resolves never to do the negative action again, purification will be very effective.

In a marriage, after a husband and wife quarrel, they will generally make up, perhaps exchange some flowers or something, and clear the air so that everything is fine again. If, instead, one keeps a smiling face and a black heart, holds a grudge and thinks, "I'm going to get you," some negativity will remain inside. So, one must purify one's misdeeds as they occur.

Having done a good deed, one should not just lean back and think, "I did well," but should immediately dedicate it for the welfare of all sentient beings. When doing prostrations, it's especially important to dedicate the merit immediately. Otherwise, one may think, "Today I gave myself a really hard time. My joints ache. It wasn't that necessary to put myself through this."

For example, the Buddha had a disciple named Anguli Mala who killed nine hundred and ninety nine human beings, but, afterwards, through the power of strong resolution and regret, he purified it all and attained realization. Milarepa, in his youth, learned and practiced black magic through which he killed many people and animals. Nonetheless, he subsequently purified it all through his meditation practice and became a great accomplished master, attaining the unified level of Vajradhara in his lifetime. His fame continues to this day.

> Visualize your master, who embodies the Three Jewels, above your head.
> To confess before him is called 'the power of the object.'
> There are many means of confession but reciting the six syllables is the most profound.
> Exert yourself as much as you can in accumulating merit.
> Make mandala offerings, since they are easy to do and give the greatest merit.

As the embodiment of the Three Jewels, one's personal teacher is considered even more precious than the Buddha himself. When we are beginners, perceiving our teacher as just an ordinary being with a physical body of flesh and blood, our faith may wane. For this reason, we should visualize him as a pure being, a deity, such as Vajradhara or Vajrasattva or as the four-armed Avalokiteshvara, the Great Compassionate One. Making our confession in front of him is called the power of the object.

Confession can be made in many ways. Vajrayana includes practices such as the meditation and recitation of *Vajrasattva*. This text, however, teaches that to simply practice the essence by condensing all these practices into the Six Syllable mantra of Avalokiteshvara is more profound. This mantra purifies the six poisons and closes the gate for rebirth in the six realms. If one conjoins this recitation with a strong resolution never to engage in any negative actions again, it is said that, just as the sun shines freely when the clouds have disappeared, realization occurs spontaneously when the negative karmas are purified.

Now, concerning how to accumulate merit and wisdom, there are two kinds of accumulations: the accumulation of merit with concept and the accumulation of wisdom without concept. As mentioned earlier, to use one's body, one makes prostrations and circumambulations; to use one's speech, one recites the mantras like the Six Syllables and so forth; and to use one's mind, one meditates on emptiness, compassion, giving and taking, and so forth.

Tibetans particularly enjoy accumulating 'merit with reference point,' such as going to visit shrines, temples and masters, and making offerings of flowers, incense, food, and so on. Although this is good and does accumulate merit, it's not the supreme way; one should try to do whatever one can.

One easy and effective way to accumulate great merit is through making *mandala offerings*. There are outer, inner, and innermost mandala offerings and we can further classify them into two types: what is mentally created and what is actually offered. The offering depends not upon the actual substance in one's hands, but upon the purity of one's heart and mind.

For example, in the beginning of the teaching we throw rice. This mandala offering has different aspects: what we offer in a material way, the grains of rice, and what we mentally create or visualize at the same time. If we make a vast offering to all the buddhas and bodhisattvas of the ten directions before receiving the teaching, it will further our understanding and accumulation of merit through our studies, reflection, and practice.

Purifying obscurations and gathering the accumulations are very important, as is taught: "In order to realize the ultimate wisdom, one must depend upon the methods of purifying one's obscurations, gathering the accumulations, and receiving the blessings of a realized master. Other ways will only be a cause for exhausting oneself."

To realize the ultimate wisdom, the inseparability of emptiness and compassion, one must combine this wisdom with the accumulation of merit and the purification of one's obscurations as well as with faith and compassion. Just as a bird needs two wings to fly and a car four wheels to travel, one aspect depends upon the other.

Many people these days offer water on their shrines. No one feels stingy about water and no one clings to it afterwards. Hence, it is given with a pure mind. One could easily offer milk or tea or wine, but being more expensive, one might feel unhappy because the milk will sour, and one will think it's been wasted — and that the deities are not making much use of it. One can feel both stingy when offering and feel regret afterwards. For this reason, water can be a pure offering.

The external or outer way of mandala offering means that one offers something real, something concrete in one's hands, like grains of rice on a plate. Traditionally, seven or thirty-seven heaps of rice are placed on the plate while one visualizes the entire universe, with Mount Sumeru, the four continents, all the precious possessions etc., and multiplies this in one's imagination many times. Then, one offers it to all the buddhas in the ten directions, to all the bodhisattvas, and so forth, with the wish that all sentient beings, without exception, may purify their obscurations and negative karmas, and may attain the state of supreme wisdom. By making this offering, an auspicious coincidence is created through which one will purify negative karma, accumulate merit, and further one's ability to attain realization.

The inner mandala offering is offered in an inner way, through what is called nadi, prana, and bindu, or offering one's body, speech, and mind. The innermost mandala offering means to remain in the composure of the ultimate nature, the thatness of ordinary mind, the self-existing wakefulness.

This practice includes various steps. For beginners, although just resting in simplicity seems to be the easiest, it is actually the most difficult to maintain. Therefore, one starts with something concrete and elaborate and, as one succeeds further in purifying, one reaches the practice of resting in simplicity, in the ultimate state. This will also purify a tremendous amount of negative karma spontaneously, and one will gather an immense accumulation of wisdom.

> We haven't the karmic fortune to meet the limitless
>   buddhas of the ten directions,
> The bodhisattvas or the many accomplished masters.
> Therefore, the master who confers empowerment, explains
>   the tantras, and gives you oral instructions,
> Is more kind than all the enlightened ones.

In the past, many buddhas appeared as well as many bodhisattvas and accomplished masters from India and Tibet. They appeared and attained enlightenment. Turning the wheel of Dharma, they ripened and freed an immeasurable number of disciples. Yet, somehow, we were not fortunate enough to be present during those times. We didn't meet these buddhas and masters and weren't benefited by them. Hence, one's personal master is considered to be most important and most kind.

In Vajrayana, 'master' means someone who gives one empowerment, explains the tantras, gives oral instructions, or gives personal advice. When we say, 'root master' or 'root guru,' this refers to the one who points out the essence of one's mind so that one recognizes it. It needn't be a famous or important person sitting on a throne or a wild yogi in the mountains. It can even be one's own grandfather or mother. Whoever points out the essence of mind is the root guru, and is, therefore, more kind than all the enlightened ones.

The *vajra master* is someone who brings us to maturity and liberation. How he does this doesn't matter. It can be accomplished through empowerment, by giving explanations, or by giving direct advice. If he helps us and furthers our understanding and realization, then he is our master.

> Even though your teacher may be an ordinary person,
> If you supplicate him with devotion, seeing him as Vajradhara,
> The good qualities of experience and realization will grow forth and increase.
> This is said to be the compassionate influence of all the buddhas.
> Therefore, visualize the master and supplicate him.

I am just an ordinary person with no special qualities of realization. But if one regards me as a teacher, then because of the coincidence of the compassion of all the buddhas and bodhisattvas and our own faith and devotion, one will, through this power, have some experience and realization.

Even a dog's tooth can issue relics. There is a story in Tibet about an old woman whose son, a trader, used to travel down to India. After he returned from his first trip, his mother said, "You're so fortunate. You've been to the country where Lord Buddha lived, the noblest country in this world. You visited important places. Did you bring me something special?" When he answered that he hadn't, his mother insisted that he bring back a relic of Buddha Shakyamuni for her to place on her shrine and use as an object of veneration. As this was very important to her, he promised to bring her something, but on his next trip to India, he completely forgot.

His mother was very distressed, and as he set out on his next trip to India, she reminded him, "If you forget to bring back a relic of Buddha Shakyamuni, I will, for certain, kill myself right in front of your eyes." Hearing this, of course the son promised repeatedly to find her a relic. Yet, reaching India and becoming absorbed in business, he again forgot all about his promise. Later, approaching his mother's house on his return to Tibet, he suddenly remembered and thought to himself, "Oh, no! What to do? I know my mother and she might do something terrible, as she threatened. I'll have to fool her in some way."

Looking around quickly, he noticed a dog's skeleton lying by the road. He went over and yanked out a tooth, rubbed away the dirt, wrapped it carefully in cloth, and proceeded to his mother's cottage. As a clever businessman, he thought he could just tell his mother it was a holy relic and, not knowing any better she would believe him.

When they met, and he presented his mother with the relic. She was so exhilarated that she shed tears of joy and her hair stood on end. She immediately gave the tooth a special place on her altar and day after day she prayed before it very fervently. After a while it began to issue small relics, certainly not due to the dog's tooth being special, but solely because of her strong faith and devotion.

Due to the power of truth and the coincidence between the compassion of the buddhas and one's own faith, such things are possible. The compassion of the buddhas and their blessings entered the dog's tooth. Later, when this old woman passed away, she attained the *rainbow body* and went to the pure realms. This is quite a famous story in Tibet.

> After having entered the gate of Dharma and received
>   empowerment, reading transmission, and instruction,
> If you don't observe your vows and samayas
> It will ruin you, just like medicine that has turned into
>   poison.

Right now, we have obtained what is difficult to obtain, a human form. We have met one who is difficult to meet, a qualified master, and we have received what is difficult to get, the precious teachings. At this time, having entered the gate of Dharma and having received empowerment, *reading transmission,* and instructions, observing one's vows and samayas is said to be quite important. Vows refer to the precepts of *Individual Liberation,* the Hinayana vows; the *bodhisattva trainings,* the Mahayana vows; and the *samayas* of the knowledge holders, the Vajrayana vows. These must be observed correctly. Otherwise, it is taught that these vows will destroy one just like a medication which has turned into poison.

> If you don't know the details of how to observe them and have difficulty keeping them,
> It will suffice to keep them condensed to their essence, in the following way:
> To place your total confidence in the Three Jewels,
> Will suffice for keeping all the refuge precepts.
> To refrain from ever causing harm to others,
> Will suffice for keeping the disciplines and precepts of Individual Liberation.

Much can be said about taking refuge, but briefly, taking refuge is placing one's total trust in the Three Jewels thinking, "You know everything," or "Everything is up to your wisdom." The enlightened ones possess the eye of wisdom, while sentient beings, being deluded, are blind. Therefore, one thinks, "You know," and places one's trust in the Three Jewels — not to gain fame, greatness, high position, or wealth, but to attain liberation from samsara. One recognizes that all of samsara is suffering and that liberation is to be free from suffering. To attain liberation, one takes refuge.

Simply refraining from causing harm to others is sufficient for keeping the disciplines and precepts of Individual Liberation, which usually refer to the Hinayana vows. Monks and lay persons have different vows. Monks must keep two hundred fifty-three vows. These vows are to help develop mindfulness, presence of mind and alertness. For example, monks must wear the shawl, which is quite an uncomfortable piece of clothing. It very easily falls down and must be put back up, thus forcing one to walk in a certain way so that it won't fall down immediately. This situation supports mindfulness. The begging bowl is round on the bottom and can't be put just anywhere because it will roll over, making it — another support for keeping mindfulness.

> Dedicate all your virtuous deeds to the universal benefit of all beings.
> To try to benefit others as much as you are able,
> Will suffice for keeping the bodhisattva precepts.

Whatever virtuous action one does, never think that it is for your own benefit alone, but dedicate it for the benefit of everyone, all sentient beings as endless as space. Try to benefit others as much as possible; this keeps the bodhisattva precepts.

We can benefit others in many ways. As long as one is an ordinary person, of course one can't benefit beings as the buddhas can through their immense activities. But, one can still do a lot by using one's body, one's speech, and one's mind. If someone trips and is about to fall, one can stretch out one's hand to help them. If two people are fighting, one can go and try to reconcile their differences. These are ways of benefiting others. Keeping a good heart and a pure frame of mind towards others is also beneficial and will suffice for the many bodhisattva precepts and trainings to be kept.

> Regard your root guru as being inseparable from the yidam.
> To refrain from entertaining any wrong views about him,
> Will suffice for keeping all the samayas of Secret Mantra.

In Vajrayana, one's root master is most important since one receives from him the empowerments, instructions, and transmissions. One must keep the right kind of attitude towards him, regarding him as being inseparable from the yidam. To do this, one must have found a qualified master. One should not regard just any teacher as inseparable from one's yidam, but after having examined and discovered a master who one can fully trust, one must never hold any wrong views about him. Though Vajrayana has thousands of samayas or tantric precepts, condensing them all into one is enough.

> The masters will bestow blessings and the yidams will grant their siddhis
> To the one who keeps the precepts and samayas in this way.
> It is certain that the dakinis and Dharma protectors will clear away the obstacles.

Keeping all one's precepts, samayas, and vows in this way, the masters will bestow their blessings, the yidams will grant their siddhis, and the dakinis and Dharma protectors will clear away all obstacles.

> Having understood this, now follows the meditation session that one should train in.
> Visualize above the crown of your head, a lotus and moon disc,
> Buddha Amitabha, who is the single embodiment of the Three Jewels,
> As well as the root and lineage masters with whom you have a connection.

At the beginning of the teaching, the two parts to this song were identified: something to understand and something to practice. We finished the first part, and now we come to the second.

Visualizing yourself either in ordinary form or as Avalokiteshvara, the Great Compassionate One, imagine a lotus flower which symbolizes being untainted by defilements, above the crown of your head. Although the lotus grows in a muddy swamp, it remains totally pure. Likewise, the great masters, living in a samsaric world, nonetheless remain untainted by samsara's defects. To symbolize this, they are usually visualized seated upon a lotus flower.

Above the lotus is a moon disc, symbolizing skillful means and knowledge. Here sits Buddha Amitabha, the embodiment of the Three Jewels and the root and lineage masters; not only all the teachers with whom one has had a connection, but also their teachers, and the teachers before them, extending back in time. It includes all the masters back to the buddhas, as well as the external Three Jewels of the Buddha, Dharma, and Sangha, and all the internal Gurus, Yidams, and Dakinis. The single form condensing all of these and embodying them all is Buddha Amitabha, Boundless Light.

Buddha Amitabha is actually a dharmakaya buddha but dressed in monk's robes. Without the ornaments and jewelry of a sambhogakaya buddha, he wears the triple Dharma robes of a monk and is adorned with the thirty-two major and the eighty minor marks of excellence. His body is red and his two hands, in the gesture of equanimity, hold the begging bowl.

Simply imagine Amitabha as a single figure. For those preferring more details, imagine Avalokiteshvara standing at his right side and Vajrapani at his left. He can also be visualized as surrounded by the Eight Close Sons, the eight main bodhisattvas.

> Then, perform whichever brief or lengthy refuge and
>   bodhichitta liturgy that you know.
> Recite the lines of the mandala offering,
> Imagining that you offer the four continents, Mount
>   Sumeru, and various precious things,
> As well as your body, possessions, and the roots of virtue.

Whatever refuge and bodhichitta prayers one knows are suitable, regardless of their length. If one doesn't know any, one can simply think, "I take refuge in the Buddha, Dharma, and Sangha; may all sentient beings be happy and attain enlightenment."

After this, recite the liturgy of the mandala offering, imagining that one offers the whole universe, the four continents, and Mount

Sumeru, with all the possessions of gods and humans, as well as one's own wealth and fortune, one's body, one's roots of virtue, and so on. If one knows the lines for the mandala offering, then one can offer in this way, multiplying the offering greatly in one's mind. This quickly accumulates merit; it's easy, convenient, and effective.

Also, for temporary benefit, many things can easily be accomplished through making mandala offerings. For example, visualizing that one offers vast numbers of life-vases to all the buddhas and bodhisattvas increases one's life span. By mentally offering books and swords, one increases knowledge and intelligence. By offering medicines and herbs, one increases health. By offering jewels and wealth and so on, one's prosperity will increase. Various purposes can be served.

Many stories from the past tell how various masters, like the great *Drukpa Kagyü* master, *Götsangpa,* attained realization solely through offering everything mentally to their masters and lineage gurus. Götsangpa recognized the nature of mind and attained realization, requiring no other practice to attain liberation.

Mandala offerings are outer, inner, and innermost. The 'innermost' or 'ultimate mandala offering' is to remain in the dharmakaya state of equality. If one is practicing a yidam, one remains in the state of mind in which one's own mind and the mind of the yidam are inseparable.

> With remorse for your past misdeeds, recite the lines of confession and the six syllables.
> Milk-like nectar will then flow down from the bodily form of Amitabha,
> Enter through the crown of your head and fill up your entire body.
> All your misdeeds and obscurations in the form of liquid soot
> Will stream out through your lower openings as well as the soles of your feet,
> And penetrate down into the earth where it is consumed by Yama, the Lord of Death.

> By his satisfaction and contentment, your 'life-debt' has been repaid and the 'life-ransom' given.
> Your body then becomes as immaculate as a crystal sphere.

If we think about it, in all past lives, ignorance and confusion have caused us to perform many misdeeds and negative actions. Though stemming from confusion, these misdeeds were nonetheless wrong. Feeling remorse, one can purify them either through reciting the hundred-syllable mantra of Vajrasattva or through reciting the six syllables of Avalokiteshvara, a completely condensed form which will suffice for purification. At the same time, while visualizing Amitabha, the Buddha of Boundless Light, seated above the crown of one's head, one can also visualize oneself as surrounded by all other sentient beings, particularly one's own father and mother, on one's right and left, respectively. Then one's friends, family, enemies, and all other sentient beings of the six realms, each with a buddha on top of his head, are to be visualized all around. By chanting the mantra of the six syllables, milk-like nectar flows down from the heart of the Buddha of Boundless Light and enters slowly into the crown of one's head, after which it completely fills one's body.

Through this, all the obscurations and evil deeds begin to leave one's body from below. Just as the contents of a container will leak out from a hole in the bottom, likewise all one's misdeeds and obscurations leak out as liquid soot through one's lower openings and the soles of one's feet. The earth beneath oneself opens and the soot flows deep below, to be consumed by Yama, the Lord of Death. One should imagine that he is satisfied and content, and that one's karmic debt, whatever is owed to others, has been repaid through this practice. Then imagine that all one's negative actions, and all one's obscurations — like the obscurations of disturbing emotions, of dualistic knowledge, and of habitual tendencies, are completely purified. One's body becomes immaculate, like a crystal sphere, dazzling and brilliant.

> Generate devotion towards the Buddha, your master,
>   sitting above the crown of your head,
> And repeat whichever supplication you know,
> Or recite the essence of supplications, the Vajra Guru
>   Mantra.

Here, reciting the essence of supplications, the *Vajra Guru Mantra,* is recommended. Since the dharmakaya is Amitabha, sambhogakaya is Avalokiteshvara, and nirmanakaya is *Padmasambhava,* nothing is wrong with saying the Vajra Guru Mantra at this point. At best, say a thousand mantras or at least one rosary — one complete mala.

> Amitabha, the embodiment of all masters and the Three
>   Jewels,
> Melts into light and mingles inseparably with you.
> His enlightened Body, Speech, and Mind, and your body,
>   speech, and mind
> Mingle together, indivisibly, like milk poured into water.
> Imagine that you have thus received all the
>   empowerments and blessings.

Having supplicated again and again and having recited the mantras, Buddha Amitabha then dissolves into light. He is already in the form of light, like a rainbow; but this time he dissolves and mingles into you so that Amitabha and you become inseparable. His enlightened body mixes with one's own body, his speech with one's own speech, and his mind with one's own mind, totally and indivisibly, like water into water. At this point, one should rest in the primordially pure Great Perfection, the self-existing wakefulness, or, in Mahamudra terms, in ordinary mind.

One then imagines that one has received all the four empowerments. Briefly, this means that one has attained whatever enlightened quality which Buddha Amitabha possesses, so that his loving compassion and activities become one's own. With great delight and joy, one remains in composure.

Completing the session, one finishes by *dedicating the merit* of this practice gathered through taking refuge, developing bodhichitta, purifying misdeeds, making mandala offerings, and mingling one's mind with the awakened state. The virtue is dedicated to the welfare of all sentient beings.

This simple practice contains the development, recitation, and completion stages. Visualizing oneself in the form of the enlightened being Avalokiteshvara and having Buddha Amitabha above the crown of one's head is the development stage. Making the supplications and reciting the mantras is the recitation stage. And finally, mingling the mind with the Guru's mind and resting in that state at the end, is the completion stage. Through this, one accomplishes the body, speech, and mind of the Buddha.

QUESTIONS AND ANSWERS

STUDENT: I am curious to know why these are called songs? They don't seem like songs.

RINPOCHE: Tibetan language has various kinds of songs; folk songs, spiritual songs, etc. These are called 'songs' because they can be sung. Written in meter, they are very easy to understand and fall into the same pattern without many complications. The English may be not as poetic, but they sound quite nice in Tibetan.

STUDENT: Who would sing them?

RINPOCHE: In the beginning, the master himself sang the songs. Many masters in the past could sing spontaneously in meter without having to think first and without trying to make the song fit with the meter of the verse. All of Milarepa's songs occurred spontaneously in his mind as he was singing them. He didn't have to construct anything. His disciples wrote them down so they would benefit not just a few, but many. Teachings in the form of songs are very good because if they rhyme or follow verse, they are easy to memorize and remember, and are thus beneficial for one's mind. Many practitioners, nuns, and lay practitioners, for instance, know this whole teaching by heart.

STUDENT: Can Rinpoche say something about the three ways to generate bodhichitta?

TRANSLATOR: Rinpoche says he will drink tea now, so he asked me to say a little bit. First, to equalize oneself with others means to acknowledge the basic equality of all sentient beings. They all suffer, and, in the same way they all want to be happy. Just as we want to be happy and avoid suffering, so does everyone else. There is basically no difference between us and others, and no reason to think that we are special and unlike others in wanting to be free of suffering and so forth.

Secondly, to exchange oneself for others means we put ourselves in another's place and mentally try to experience how the other beings might feel. We try to exchange the happiness we have for the suffering of others.

Finally, to put others above oneself means regarding others as more important. When we consider that all sentient beings have been our own mothers in past lives and have been extremely kind; we feel, out of gratitude, that our mothers are more important than ourselves. Thus, we will put all beings before ourselves.

STUDENT: I have a problem reconciling the statement about the basic equality of all sentient beings on the one hand, and the enormous emphasis which Buddhism lays on differences. Especially differences between what we call the 'ordinary person' and the 'enlightened person' or the 'person on the way to enlightenment' and also the different degrees of capacity and capability.

RINPOCHE: First of all, one should understand the *two truths*. First, the *relative* or *conventional truth* is what is true on an experiential level, concerning the conditioned appearance of things. *Ultimate truth* is what is true in essence, concerning the nature of things. When beings are confused or deluded, they only perceive relative truth, not the ultimate truth. But those who are free from delusion, who have no obscurations, perceive both relative and ultimate truth. According to the degree of confusion one has, the degree to which one's obscurations have been purified, and the degree to which one is realized, one will perceive things in different ways. That's why there are different kinds of beings. In short, regarding the two truths, relative truth is what is true in one's experience and ultimate truth is what is true in essence.

The conditioned things that we experience are 'relative' or 'conventional' truth. The ultimate truth is the nature of things, which is empty. Again, we can say that conventional truth is the truth of how things are experienced — their seeming mode, and ultimate truth is what is true in how things actually are — their real mode.

We do experience things, such as seeing through our eyes, and hearing through our ears. We smell, taste, and touch. Our mind experiences all kinds of thoughts; good, bad, and neutral about past, present, and future. We feel different emotions and so forth. To say all these experiences are unreal or not true would be improper. Yet, because of considering only what appears or what is experienced as reality, we have wandered endlessly in samsara.

Words and names are only something with which we conveniently label things. They do not exist in themselves. Neither the name nor the object to which it is attached truly exists. But, without examining closely, the name and the thing itself seem to be inseparable.

Right now, we can call these things 'table,' 'flower,' and 'vase,' yet, if we truly examine them, then the word 'vase' and the thing itself are different. Even merely saying it is chinaware doesn't help because 'chinaware' is also just a word attached to the object.

In short, if we scrutinize things very carefully, we find nothing which can withstand close examination, nothing that can bear scrutiny. We find that we cannot establish an independent existence of anything whatsoever.

Most of the time, we don't examine things but simply have a very broad conception of what is what. For example, when we say the word 'man,' we immediately think of only one thing. From head to toe, this object is labeled 'man.' For example: our translator, Erik. People believe that his body, from the top of his head to the soles of his feet, is something called 'Erik,' but this involves no real examination. We all agree upon whom we call 'Erik' and can easily identify him, but when we start to analyze, something is funny. Pointing to his hand, if we ask, "Is the hand 'Erik?'" we must agree, "No, it's not." Is the leg 'Erik?' Is the head 'Erik?' No, in themselves they are not 'Erik.' We call this 'Erik's hand' and we call this 'Erik's head,' but that which is 'Erik' himself we cannot find anywhere. Our translator has no basis. Everything is 'Erik's this' and 'Erik's that,' but if there is 'Erik's anything,' shouldn't there also be an 'Erik' to whom these things belong? If we examine everything in this way, we will find that all things are like this — they appear, they are experienced, without really existing.

The Buddha's father asked for teachings and the Buddha replied, "Father, everything is contained within the two truths. There is no third truth. Whatever is experienced, the appearance of conditioned things, is called conventional truth. But the nature of things, the way they really are, which is empty, is also true and is the ultimate truth. You need not merely listen to this but examine it for yourself and you will know."

The truth is divided into just two, the conventional and the ultimate. Each has its own definition. If we ask, "By whom are these two truths understood? To whom do they appear?" then, people differ. There are ordinary people, like someone from the street, and there are people who have adopted a certain philosophy, like those, for example, who are studying the Buddha's teachings. Some people are engaged in different practices and have attained certain meditation states, such as the samadhis. We can divide the two truths for each level of individual. There are many details about this.

Ordinary people believe that degrees of good and bad, pure and impure, quality and benefit, and so forth, are concepts applicable to something inherent to an object. These attributes however do not merely exist within the object. Some objects may be harmful, and others may not but such qualities are not inherent to the object itself.

For example, we have concepts like 'delicious' or 'disgusting,' 'clean' and 'unclean,' 'beautiful' and 'ugly.' We might say that French food is delicious, but everyone may not perceive it that way. Usually, it is particularly delicious to the French. But this also depends as well upon who has prepared the dish and whether it was properly done or not. Otherwise, even a French person may not like it. But if a salad is served to a Tibetan, he might say, "This is rabbit food. It's not for human beings," and he won't be interested at all. Tibetans will extol the virtues of their own food, such as *tsampa,* roasted barely flour, or *khapsey,* deep-fried bread, and speak of how tasty they are, how nutritious, how good the stomach feels after eating them, and so forth. Westerners, however will sometimes feel that tsampa is totally repulsive and they may get diarrhea afterwards.

Compared to the animals, human beings are more intelligent, especially when it comes to food. They will procure the finest vegetables available and wash them carefully with various chemicals, etc. They peel them in just the right way, cut them in the right sizes, prepare them using different herbs and spices so that they will not offend the taste buds. They consider this a very clean and nice thing that they have eaten.

An animal, on the other hand, has no power to do any of this preparation. Forget about cutting food and cleaning it, they can't light a fire and cook; they have no ability to prepare their food at all. They must either steal it, pick it up off the street somewhere, or wait on someone's doorstep hoping something edible might fall their way. In most cases, a dog or pig will eat whatever is put under its nose.

Compared to animals, we human beings are very clever. What we eat seems very clean and is probably clean when it enters the mouth. But it becomes more and more impure and when it finally comes out the other end, it is something which is probably considered the most unclean in all the world. Why is that?

A dog has few concepts about what is pure, impure, clean, or unclean. It sees things differently. What a dog eats and what comes out it's other end should be twice as disgusting as what a human being produces. Somehow though, most people consider their own dirt as the worst. That's illogical, right?

If for example, we discover human excrement in our room, we become completely flustered. Many people refuse even to look at it. We try not to smell it or touch it and we become very nervous about it. That's pretty common. But if it's from a dog, then it's bad, but not that bad; and if it's from a bird or an insect we don't mind so much. We just take it with our fingers and flick it away, wipe our fingers on our pants and don't pay much thought to it. Why is that?

Human beings consider themselves the cleverest and the most intelligent, but if we really look at how they sometimes behave, then it seems that they are the most silly or strange.

Take fashion for example. If we wear the clothing styles of five or ten years ago, people will laugh. Why is that? Had we worn the same clothes when they were in style, people would have said, "Wow. You look really fantastic." But now they laugh. Why?

Let's go back thousands of years when people wore no clothes. If someone suddenly appeared in a three-piece suit or dressed as a king, then, even though the people might not have the word 'hippie,' that person would probably be called that. Why? It was then very comfortable to go without clothes. No one thought about it. Today, if we walk around publicly without clothing, everyone will get very funny about it and probably talk a lot. Why is that?

In short, the mind is quite strange. We believe that our own way of looking at things, our own way of thinking, and our own value systems, are very accurate, very reasonable, and correct. This tendency is especially strong regarding our culture's way of viewing things, but actually, if we look into it, it is something we have to laugh about. As with the questions we asked before, if we must produce logical answers for these questions, it becomes difficult. That's how it is.

Regarding conventional and ultimate truth, there are different categories. We can say there are different kinds of individuals, those with higher capacity, those with mediocre capacity, and those with lower capacity. These people have, correspondingly, various ways of perceiving the two truths.

For example, if we ask a question of an ordinary person such as, "What is this?" He will reply, "a table." He probably hasn't thought much about it and most likely, later on, won't even remember having been asked the question. A table is simply a table.

Yet, if we ask the same question of another person who has studied some philosophy, or who has studied, reflected, and practiced meditation, he may think about it and wonder, "Actually, what is this thing called 'table'?" He can see that it consists of different parts: the legs, the top, the corners, and so forth, but each of these parts separately is not the 'table.' He might consider that all the parts combined make up the table, but this too, becomes unreasonable, because it remains still just a pile of parts that are thought of as a whole and then labeled 'table.' The word 'table' is just a word. One might be tempted to call the whole thing 'wood,' but wood is just another word. Finally, one finds that if the object is dissected further and further, there is no ultimate thing or support onto which the label 'table' can be attached. There's no label-basis. So, first the label does not exist as a thing in itself and next, there is no basis for its application.

The true Dharma is something that should be reasonable, logical, and sensible, something that can be proved both through one's own understanding and through one's own experience. Through study and reflection, one's understanding of 'how things are' becomes increasingly clear. In addition, if one combines this intellectual understanding with the direct knowledge resulting from meditation practice, one can gain full realization of how things are.

This can also be illustrated with a simple cup of water. The different beings in the six realms experience the same cup of water in six completely different ways. Which of these perceptions is true? Which is the real one? In fact, they are all real, individually, for those particular beings.

Hell-beings perceive water as liquid burning metal, hungry ghosts perceive it as rotten blood and pus, animals, like fish, perceive it as a dwelling place, human beings perceive water as something to quench thirst, and gods perceive it as nectar. Each of their experiences is real because that is how water appears for that particular being. Yet, comparing them with one another, compared with a hell-being's perception of water as liquid metal, the human perception is more real, relatively closer to reality, because humans have fewer obscurations than hell-beings. We are less disturbed. Compared to ours, however, a practitioner will have an even more real perception of water.

Usually we hear, see, and feel different things, one after the other, without thinking much about what's happening. We simply experience sensations. However, if we suddenly start to analyze what is going on, and ask ourselves, "What is sight? What is sound? What is it to hear, to taste, to see?" Then, we must find some kind of answer to this. We must try to describe or define our perception in some way, and once we start to have some understanding of what is going on, our perceptions will differ from those of someone who has never analyzed anything. That's why there are differences between people.

STUDENT: Can you explain more about a safe and correct relationship between a master and disciple?

RINPOCHE: Traditionally it is said, that the student should examine the teacher, and the teacher should examine the student. If a disciple fails to examine his teacher well and follows a wrong teacher, it will kill the life-force for liberation. Like blindly jumping off a precipice while holding someone else's hand, it is detrimental. If the teacher fails to examine the student well, and if the student is someone who will turn against him later on, this is the same as eating poison. Therefore, before entering a close relationship, it is extremely important that the teacher and the student both examine each other carefully.

After finding that they can trust each other, the student should be very constant, and practice the teachings that he has been given with trust and confidence. The teacher should be very kind. There are many ways of being kind, but the most important way is through teachings; to give the correct instructions is the greatest kindness. The teacher should regard the student as a parent cares for a child.

If, after a disciple has received many teachings, all the general instructions, as well as the Vajrayana empowerment, explanation of the tantras, and the practices of Mahamudra and Dzogchen, the key instructions on Trekchö and Tögal, he practices these for a while, and then gives rise to wrong views, thinking, "This is all pointless, the master is no good, he is completely fake," he may turn against the master. This attitude will completely destroy the effect that the disciple may have from doing the practice and the blessings will dissipate completely. Everything will have been in vain. It would be harmful not only for the disciple, but also for the master. If a student turns against him, even an enlightened teacher can be harmed.

A spiritual master's mind is said to be like a clear mirror, but the karmic result of broken samaya vows is like the condensation of water on a mirror, making it unclear and obscured, as if we closed the windows here today and watched the water collect on the glass. Thus, wrong views harm both student and teacher.

STUDENT: We sometimes think that though lamas have very great realization, they still don't understand the Western mind. Is this in itself a wrong view?

RINPOCHE: It's alright to think that because it's probably true, but it's not alright to think that he doesn't know the teachings of the Dharma. That can get one into trouble. What the Tibetan masters learn, traditionally, are the outer and inner sciences according to their own tradition. They don't study the Western sciences or Western culture as part of their scholastic training, so it's not incorrect to say that they don't know these things. That's just how it is. Yet still, from their root guru they have received the unbroken transmission which comes from the Buddha, in an uninterrupted lineage of direct transmission from master to disciple. So, if one thinks the lamas don't know the teachings, this is incorrect.

Because Westerners grow up in a different culture with different sciences, when they hear teachings that fit their own understanding, they become very elated and think, "This is really true." Because they are intelligent, they can discriminate. When they find something logical or reasonable, they feel there is some sense to it. Then, they feel some faith, a little trust in the teachings. But sometimes some things don't fit their usual understanding and it seems as though it doesn't belong. They then feel very skeptical, critical, and doubtful. But slowly their understanding will increase.

5
The Song for the Beginner to Train Directly in Development and Completion

> The essential point, the unified path of development and completion,
> Has something to be understood and something to practice.

This song concerns a topic which is more difficult, but also more important. In general, 'ordinary vehicles' and the 'extraordinary vehicles' are spoken of. The ordinary vehicle of Hinayana has little risk but takes a long time. The tantric practices of Mahamudra or Dzogchen, involve more danger, but bring greater profit. This is because, among all the disturbing emotions, delusion or ignorance, is the most difficult to identify and the most difficult to relinquish. In short, if there is knowledge, that is buddhahood. Lacking knowledge is the state of a sentient being. In other words, if ignorance is purified, that is the state of a buddha, but when there is ignorance, that is the state of a sentient being.

The tantric vehicles include the three outer tantras called Kriya, Upa, and Yoga and the three inner tantras called Maha, Anu, and Ati. The Nyingma system has six tantras with development and completion stages indispensable in each. This text teaches development and completion as a unity in a method very easy and convenient to practice. The essential point of the unified path of development and completion is that one should first examine, contemplate, understand, and then put that understanding into practice.

> The essence of the mind of all sentient beings
> Is, since the very beginning, the essence of the enlightened ones.
> That is to say, the empty essence is the nonarising dharmakaya.

> The pure and distinct luminosity is sambhogakaya.
> The manifold and unobstructed capacity is nirmanakaya.
> The undivided unity of these three is svabhavikakaya.
> And their total changelessness is mahasukhakaya.

We are taught that all sentient beings have possessed the enlightened essence since the very beginning. Because of possessing this essence, there is not a single being who cannot attain enlightenment. One might assume that an extremely evil person could never attain enlightenment, but that is untrue. He won't attain enlightenment for a long time, but this doesn't mean never. There is no one for whom enlightenment is completely impossible.

The enlightened essence of a small worm or insect, our own enlightened essence, and the enlightened essence of a completely enlightened buddha are exactly the same, without the slightest difference in size or quality.

A flower seed can grow into a flower, but it must be put into soil and it needs to meet the right conditions of moisture, sunlight, time, and so forth. If these needs are met, a fully developed plant will certainly result. Likewise, given the right conditions, such as practice and so forth, we will be able to realize the nonarising dharmakaya.

We call something 'enlightened essence,' but what does it mean? What is it like? If there is a name, there must be something onto which that name attaches. New students will wonder what we are referring to; even advanced practitioners sometimes get suspicious and have doubts, wondering, "What is actually being discussed?" One must study and think about it and slowly find out through one's practice.

Concerning buddha nature, we talk about three aspects: *essence, nature,* and *capacity*. Being empty in essence means that it has no color, shape, or form. It doesn't exist in any concrete way. It lacks anything tangible or identifiable. It is empty and this empty essence is what we call the *nonarising* dharmakaya.

Nonarising means that the dharmakaya is devoid of arising, dwelling, and ceasing. When we first talk and think about space and nonarising dharmakaya, these two concepts seem to have the same characteristics and attributes, that nothing whatsoever exists. It is just a name given to something that is vacant. In fact, however, space is just blank voidness, mere openness; whereas the nonarising dharmakaya is empty in essence, yet at the same time capable of knowing, of cognizing. We can understand, we can perceive, we can cognize. This capacity of *cognizance*, this awareness, is usually translated as '*luminosity*.' Luminosity does not mean something shining like electric light; it refers to 'knowing,' precisely and clearly.

The three terms dharmakaya, sambhogakaya, and nirmanakaya are well known and are always being talked about in Vajrayana. These three, mentioned again and again in many places, are actually complete within one's enlightened essence.

The essence, which is empty, is the dharmakaya. Its luminous or cognizant nature is sambhogakaya, and its unobstructed expression, its capacity aspect, is nirmanakaya. These three are an indivisible unity. Giving an exact example is difficult, but we can say it's like water and its wetness or, like a flame and its heat which cannot be separated and are an undivided unity. Furthermore, the undivided unity of these three is *svabhavikakaya*, the 'essence body;' and their total changelessness is *mahasukhakaya*, the 'body of great bliss.'

> They are, since primordial time, your natural possession.
> They do not come about through the compassion of the buddhas, the blessing of your teacher,
> Or through a profound key point of your Dharma practice,
> But because you possess them since the primordial beginning.
>
> If all the sutras and tantras agree on this point,
> Why is it that one wanders through samsara?
> The answer is that one wanders because of the confusion of not knowing one's own nature.
> For example, if a person possesses a stone containing gold in his fireplace,

> He might, when not recognizing it to be gold, undergo the misery of starvation.
> Likewise, when your master points out your essence, it is an expression of great kindness.

Since primordial time, these have been one's natural possession, intrinsic and inherent to one's being. We learn here that these kayas are not something that one achieves, or which occurs through the compassion of the buddhas or the blessings of one's root gurus. It cannot be produced through applying the key points of Dharma practice. One has possessed them since the very beginning. The kayas are absolutely inherent to oneself, to one's own nature. The kayas exist spontaneously within oneself. Their presence is not a product of blessings or something slowly produced through practice. One cannot create or manufacture one's enlightened essence through one's own intelligence or through study of the teachings. One possesses them primordially. The sutras and tantras all agree on this point.

But, if no difference exists between our own enlightened essence, that of a sentient being, and that of all of the buddhas, then why do we still wander in confusion through the realms of samsara? We wander because of not knowing our own nature, our enlightened essence. This samsaric wandering stems from ignorance.

The tantric texts teach three kinds of ignorance: *ignorance of single identity, coemergent ignorance,* and *conceptual ignorance.* These three kinds of ignorance cause us to wander in samsara.

In Tibet, households traditionally have fireplaces made of three hearth-stones or of dried mud. Suppose that, unknown to the householder, the fireplace conceals a large chunk of gold. Not realizing what he has, the occupant may feel very poor, may beg from others, and perhaps may even starve. Yet, if someone came and revealed the treasure buried beneath the hearth-stone, his whole situation would change. In the same way, because of not recognizing one's ordinary mind, it must first be pointed out.

Merely being shown that one possesses gold is not enough. One must use the gold in order to dispel one's suffering. In the same way, being shown one's ordinary mind or being taught that the nature of mind is the enlightened essence is not sufficient. When receiving the transmission of mind essence, what is important is first to recognize, second to train, and finally to attain stability. Simply recognizing the nature of mind doesn't make one a fully enlightened buddha any more than simply seeing the gold dispels one's hunger. One must put the recognition to use.

Therefore, when one's master points out the essence, he does so through an enormous kindness. Having one's essence pointed out so that one recognizes it, is not being given something that one didn't already possess. One merely acknowledges what one already has.

> It does not help a starving person's hunger merely to be shown that he has gold,
> Unless he sells it, acquires grain, then roasts and grinds it.
> Then, having cooked and prepared a meal, he can satisfy his hunger.
> Likewise, you should clear away confusion and be liberated
> Through practicing that which has been pointed out by your teacher.

To use a Tibetan example, one first acquires grain, then roasts it, grinds it, and cooks it in order to prepare a meal and satisfy one's hunger. Similarly, having been shown the nature of mind, one should clear away confusion and be liberated through practicing what one's teacher has pointed out.

I mentioned before the term *ground wisdom, path wisdom,* and *fruition wisdom*. Ground wisdom is this enlightened essence, self-existing wakefulness, which one's teacher points out and which one recognizes and takes as path. But that alone is not enough; as in the case of taking birth and being an infant, one must grow up.

A small child can do nothing on his own. He must be fed and cared for, nurtured and sustained so that he will slowly grow up and be able to walk by himself. Later, when fully grown, this person can carry out different tasks and accomplish various purposes. Likewise, after the mind essence has been pointed out and one has recognized it, one must practice and train. Finally, through perfecting the training, one attains stability, and that stability corresponds to attaining complete enlightenment. The sutras teach that this occurs at the end of the *ten bhumis*. Vajrayana recognizes thirteen bhumis.

> All the sutras of the greater vehicle and the tantras of the Secret Mantra
> Agree that your mind is the 'enlightened one.'
> But the sutras do not point out that one's body is a buddha.
> Therefore, it is a longer path
> Since it is taught that buddhahood is achieved after three incalculable aeons.
>
> The profundity of the fact that enlightenment is attained within one lifetime through Anuttara,
> Is due to pointing out one's body to be divine.
> It is therefore extensively taught in all the Anuttara tantras
> Such as Chakrasamvara, Guhyasamaja, the eight heruka sadhanas, and others,
> That one's body is the mandala of deities.
>
> In brief, the old and new schools all agree that the five aggregates are the five buddhas,
> The five elements are the five female buddhas,
> The eight collections are the eight bodhisattvas,
> And the eight objects are the eight female bodhisattvas.

The sutras teach that buddhahood is achieved after three incalculable aeons, a very long time. But enlightenment is attained in one lifetime through *Anuttara Yoga*, the highest Vajrayana teaching, because of the profundity of the practices used, such as visualizing one's form as the enlightened body, one's speech as the enlightened speech or mantra, and one's mind as the profound samadhi.

Through the various development and completion stage practices, and through the practices of yogas involving nadi, prana, and bindu, one can attain complete enlightenment, the unified level of Vajradhara, within one lifetime. Therefore, the Vajrayana is more profound.

All the Anuttara tantras such as the tantras of Chakrasamvara, Guhyasamaja, and others, extensively teach that one's body is a mandala of deities. Many tantric practices involve this viewpoint. All the old and new schools, the Nyingma and Sarma, agree that one's five aggregates of form, sensation, conception, formation, and consciousness are the five male buddhas; the five elements of earth, water, fire, wind, and space are the five female buddhas; the eight collections of consciousness are the eight main bodhisattvas, and the eight objects are the eight female bodhisattvas.

Maintaining this viewpoint, one trains in all-encompassing purity, developing what has been introduced as the ground wisdom. Practicing this is called path wisdom. It's like flying in a supersonic jet, an extremely skillful means.

> In particular, in the center of your heart are the forty-two peaceful ones.
> At the place of your throat are the pure vidyadharas.
> Within your brain are the fifty-eight herukas.
> They are all truly present in the forms of nadi, prana, and bindu.

In the center of one's heart are the forty-two peaceful deities. Deities here is the term used for the expression or manifestation of one's enlightened essence. Its various functions are called 'deities.' These so-called deities within oneself, the forty-two peaceful deities in one's heart, the pure *vidyadharas* in one's throat center, and the *fifty-eight wrathful herukas* in the head center, all truly exist as the pure aspects of the nadis, pranas, and bindus.

> As a sign of that, through the nadi linking the heart to the eyes,

> Rainbow lights and circles will manifest in the sky of Dzogchen.
> At the time of death, your inherent deities emerge from your body
> And manifest in person filling the expanse of space.

These lines concern the Dzogchen meditation practice called Tögal, Direct crossing, which one practices after having been introduced to and recognized the correct view of Dzogchen, Trekchö, Cutting Through. Without having recognized the view, one cannot practice Tögal. Recognition, therefore, is imperative before beginning.

We might mention here that after reaching the correct viewpoint in Mahamudra, the view of ordinary mind, various meditation practices should be used to enhance or improve that view. In Mahamudra, one uses the Six Yogas of Naropa to further one's realization of the view.

> Not recognizing them to be deities, you perceive them to be the Lord of Death.
> Panicking, afraid, and terrified, you faint and fall into the lower realms.
> For example, on a road where there is great danger
> You will flee from your welcoming party thinking that they are enemies.
> When pursued, it seems that you are being chased, and you become terrified.
> But, when you recognize them, you feel fearlessness and delight.
> You can go to the pure realms when you recognize them to be yidam deities.
> In order to grow familiar with them right now,
> You should practice seeing the major and minor circles of Tögal.

The deities that emerge from one's body and manifest at the time of death are not concrete but are more like energies or expressions of the enlightened essence. Failing to recognize them as being such a 'self-display,' one might think that they are the Lord of Death and his henchmen. One will panic, be afraid, be terrified, and will faint from fear.

If one has had mind essence pointed out, but hasn't practiced much, one might not attain enlightenment in this very lifetime. Nonetheless, a great opportunity can still occur at the time of death. If one makes fervent supplication and has great faith in or devotion to one's teacher as well as genuine compassion towards all sentient beings, and simply rests in, or sustains the mind essence, there will be a great opportunity for perfecting the practice. But, if this does not happen and one wanders through the bardo, the intermediate state after death, since one is without a physical body at that time, another great opportunity arises.

The physical body weighs one down like a trap, but after death one only has a mental body. If one can remember whatever practice one trained in during this lifetime and can recognize the mind essence during the bardo, there is a great opportunity to attain realization very quickly. If one doesn't do this, one will become terrified and think that whatever appears in the bardo is something else. Feeling "I'm afraid of that!" one creates the causes for new rebirth.

An example for this is, when one travels in a territory full of many dangers and bandits, the welcoming party that comes to greet one may appear from afar to be enemies. One may try to escape. When the welcoming party runs after one bringing refreshments, one becomes completely paranoid and terrified, thinking they are giving chase. One will run away. The bardo is like this example. If however, the welcoming party is recognized, then instead of being totally terrified, one will be delighted, fearing nothing. Likewise, recognizing what arises at the moment after death, one can go to the pure realms. 'Pure realm' is a metaphor and doesn't mean that one actually goes somewhere. It simply means that the liberated state is attained.

> For example, although a lode stone may contain silver,
> It cannot be used without being melted down and purified.
> Similarly, it is not enough just to know that your body is the mandala of the yidam deity,
> You should actually accomplish it through practice.

Just learning about 'ground wisdom' isn't enough. It is like only looking at a delicious meal when hungry. Just as one needs to eat food in order to dispel one's hunger, one must put the teachings into practice. Learning and thinking alone will never bring realization. Realization occurs only through practice.

If one is deaf and cannot hear, yet still talented at music, one can play for others so they can listen and enjoy, without hearing anything oneself. This is like talking about the Dharma without having realized it oneself through practice.

We know, for instance, that milk contains butter but unless we churn it, butter will never form. Similarly, we might hear or even understand that our mind is basically the 'Enlightened One.' Simply knowing this and doing nothing about it changes nothing. Therefore, without practice, this 'buddha' will not manifest and one will not fully realize one's enlightened nature. Understand the meaning and practice.

> Although there are many yidams,
> Noble Avalokiteshvara who embodies all yidams is the destined deity for Tibet.
> Although there are many brief and extensive ways of visualizing,
> This way of completion by mere recollection
> Is convenient to practice and easy to understand.

There are many kinds of yidam deities or forms of buddhas. Avalokiteshvara, the Great Compassionate One, is said to embody the Buddha's compassion. The embodiment of knowledge is Manjushri and the embodiment of ability and power is Vajrapani, but these can all be condensed into one. The deity for Tibet, for example, is Avalokiteshvara, who embodies all of these yidams. This one deity can be practiced in various ways, abbreviated or extensive. A technique called 'completion by mere recollection' is the easiest and most convenient to practice. One simply thinks or recollects that everything is there, and the form of the deity becomes vividly and clearly present. This doesn't happen immediately, but one can train in this technique.

> For this reason, visualize your body in the form of the
>   Great Compassionate One
> Who is white, has one face and four arms, in accordance
>   with the liturgy.
> In his heart center is a white lotus with six petals.
> In the center of this is a HRIH, and on the six petals are
>   the six syllables.
> Visualize all of them standing upright, effulgent,
>   sparkling, and vividly present.

One should visualize oneself in the form of Avalokiteshvara, the Great Compassionate One, who is completely white, like clear crystal, with one face and four arms. Find a picture to see exactly how he looks. Two of his arms are joined at the heart center holding a jewel; the two upper arms are poised in the air, one hand holding a lotus flower, the other a crystal rosary. Do not think of yourself being alone, but visualize all other sentient beings surrounding you on all sides, especially your father and mother. All these beings, as many as the sky is vast, are also in the form of the Great Compassionate One.

In the heart center of each sentient being, visualize the seed syllable HRIH. The bodies are transparent, not made of any concrete substance like flesh and blood, but totally transparent like rainbow light. In your heart center is a white lotus with six petals; in the center of this, standing upright, is the syllable HRIH. Upon each petal, one syllable of the mantra OM MA NI PAD ME HUNG, also stands upright. They are all shining, sparkling and vividly present.

> The syllable HRIH is unmoving and the six syllables revolve clockwise.
> From them, rays of light stream out into the ten directions and make offerings to all the buddhas and bodhisattvas.
> They all turn into the form of the Great Compassionate One
> And dissolve into oneself like gently falling rain.
>
> Once more, rays of light stream out from the six syllables
> And purify the misdeeds and obscurations of all the six classes of sentient beings.
> All these beings turn into the form of the Great Compassionate One
> And each one hums with the tones of the six syllables.
> The vessel-like universe has become the realm of Great Bliss.

The HRIH in the center is stationary, but the six other syllables revolve around the HRIH, resembling a chain. While you recite the mantra, the syllables send out light in all directions. Visualize the buddhas and bodhisattvas of the ten directions just in front of you and send rays of light from your heart center towards them. The light becomes the various offering goddesses who carry the most pleasant objects of sight, sound, taste, smell, and textures and who offer these to all the buddhas and bodhisattvas.

Having made these offerings, the offering goddesses dissolve into light. The blessings and powers, wisdom-knowledge, loving compassion, enlightened deeds and so forth, of all the buddhas and bodhisattvas stream towards you and all the other beings in the form of rays of light, like a gently falling rain, and dissolve into all of you. The light streams downwards to all sentient beings as generosity, purifying all their misdeeds and obscurations. The six syllables purify the six poisons and the gates for rebirth in the six realms are thereby blocked.

Form the aspiration that the disturbing emotions of all human and nonhuman beings are totally pacified by absorbing this light.

Pray that all warfare and strife may calm down and that profound peace will reign within yourself, your family, and throughout the whole world. Imagine that all sentient beings engender the profound thought of bodhichitta, and that for those who have already developed bodhichitta, it increases and develops even further. Keep this aspiration while reciting the six syllables. The rays of light streaming from oneself take the shape of whatever any being might desire, food for the hungry, clothes for the needy, etc. All the beings take the form of Avalokiteshvara and each *hums/Hung with the tones of the six syllables, like the droning of many bees. This happens through the coincidence of one's practice, the blessings of all the buddhas, their aspirations, and the power of the truth of reality.

At this point, the whole universe has become the realm of great bliss, the pure land of the Great Compassionate One. All forms become the deity and one's speech and mind are indivisible from the yidam itself. Thus, one meditates in all-encompassing purity. That is one meditation practice. Now comes another.

> Sometimes keep your attention one-pointedly focused on the HRIH,
> And when your mind remains still for a long time without wandering elsewhere,
> Then practice shamatha with an object, the union of development and completion.
> When you then look directly into the mind that has visualized this,
> Whatever is visualized vanishes into emptiness.

Now we come to the practice of the union of development and completion. 'Development,' here, is the visualization of oneself as the deity Avalokiteshvara. What does one focus on in this shamatha practice? On the syllable HRIH in one's heart center, you visualize yourself as Avalokiteshvara with a small HRIH standing erect in your heart center. Keep your mind focused on that, without allowing it to wander or be distracted in any way whatsoever.

Visualize the HRIH as sometimes very tiny and sometimes quite colossal in size. The main point is to refrain from being distracted. The HRIH should be brilliant and clear. This part is the shamatha practice.

Now comes the *vipashyana* aspect. It is the mind itself that has visualized the HRIH and Avalokiteshvara's form. The text says, *when you look directly into the mind,* meaning that the mind should look directly into itself. Everything visualized up to this point, the HRIH, Avalokiteshvara, and the environment as the Blissful Realm, totally vanishes into emptiness.

> Mind has no form, color, or concrete substance.
> It is not to be found anywhere outside or within your body, nor in between.
> It is not found to be a concrete thing,
> Even if you were to search throughout the ten directions.
> It does not arise from anywhere, nor does it abide and disappear at any place.
>
> Yet, it is not nonexistent, since your mind is vividly awake.
> It is not a singularity, because it manifests in manifold ways.
> Nor is it a plurality, because all these are of one essence.
> There is no one who can describe its nature.
> But, when expressing its resemblance, there is no end to what can be said.
> It may be given many kinds of names such as 'mind essence,' 'I,' or the 'all-ground.'
> It is the very basis of all of samsara and nirvana.

The word mind is used for 'that which experiences' or 'that which knows' joy, sorrow, happiness, sadness and so on. This so-called mind has no form, no color, nor any concrete substance whatsoever. We can't find it in any specific location, within, without, or in-between. It is neither inside nor outside the body. Mind can't be found as a concrete 'thing'. Even if one searched throughout the ten directions, one could never find any tangible characteristics of mind. Not arising from anywhere, and not abiding or disappearing at any specific place, yet it is not a complete blank because mind is vividly awake and cognizant.

The mind is not just 'oneness' or a singular entity because it manifests in manifold ways. It is not a plurality or many things, either, because these numerous manifestations all have one essence. No one can describe its nature saying, "It is exactly like this!" It is indescribable, unutterable, inconceivable, nonarising, unceasing, and nondwelling, like the essence of space. Mind nature is discovered within the experience of awareness and is cognized individually.

One cannot describe mind exactly, but by using analogies or discussing what it resembles, there is no end to what can be said. Scholars may find a lot of debate about what the mind is. Simple meditators resolve that although mind can be called many different things: such as mind essence or mind nature, 'me,' or 'I,' or the *all-ground, alaya;* actually, mind is the 'thinker' of all that can be thought of, the very basis of samsara and nirvana.

> The attainment of buddhahood and falling into the lower realms,
> Wandering through the bardo and taking a good or bad rebirth,
> Feeling dislike and anger, desire and attachment,
> Having faith, pure perception, love and compassion,
> And attaining the virtues of experience and realization, on the path and stages and so forth,
> Are all performed precisely by this mind.

Whatever happens takes place because of mind. The attainment of Buddhahood results from purifying the mind and realizing it. Falling into lower realms results from the mind's engagement in negative actions as a result of ignorance. It is the mind that wanders through the bardo. Taking rebirth, good or bad, is also experienced by the mind. The mind experiences all feelings such as dislike, anger, desire, and attachment. Faith, pure perception, love, and compassion occur in the mind as well. When performing virtue, or experiencing realization, the mind is the actor. The path, the stages of the bodhisattva, and so forth, are all attained by the mind.

> Mind is the root of all entanglement and ruin.
> For whomever realizes the meaning of this and puts it into practice,
> There is not a single teaching not contained within this,
> Just as all the senses cease when the life vein is cut.

Good and bad both happen through the mind. The mind is said to be the root of all entanglements. If we have many tangled strings, we try to find one loose end to unravel. Mind is like that one end.

Mind can also be the root of all ruin. For example, a fire which burns one hundred houses must have started somewhere. One small spark set it off or one person torched the first house. Somewhere it began. Likewise, everything boils down to mind. Even a very complicated illness has its beginnings, its' root, somewhere in a very minute point. The mind is like that root.

Just as the branches on a tree wither when the root is cut, the senses cease simultaneously when the life-vein is severed. To kill a tree, cutting just one branch at a time is not enough. One must go directly to the root. Whoever realizes what this means finds that there is no single practice not contained within finding the root of mind.

> Mind does not have even a hair-tip of something to meditate upon,
> So, it is sufficient to just look, undistractedly, into its essence.
> Give up hoping for something good and fearing the unpleasant.
> Without giving any consideration as to whether or not it is the right thing,

> No matter whether it remains or thinks, is clear or unclear,
> Look wakefully into the essence of whatever occurs.

The perfectly enlightened Buddha taught according to sentient beings' different mental faculties and dispositions. He taught by means of three vehicles as well as the four philosophical views of the Vaibhashika, Sautrantika, Mind Only, and the Middle Way schools. Through these views, he explained 'how things appear' and 'how they really are,' the conventional and ultimate truth.

The *four philosophical schools* are the various approaches by which one discerns and examines the mind through such questions as: "What is experience? What is it that experiences? What are objects?" These approaches attempt to establish exactly what is real.

The first two philosophical schools, Vaibhashika and Sautrantika, agree that the solid things that we experience do not truly exist. They assert, however, that some indivisible or partless atom, a basic component from which objects are made, does ultimately exist. Likewise, as to the mind, these schools assert that there is no gross 'thing' that we can call the 'mind,' but that ultimately there exists an indivisible or partless instant of consciousness. Regarding time, they assert that the past, present, and future do not truly exist, but that there does exist an indivisible instant of time out of which all time is made.

We mention this because the text says there is not *even a hair-tip of something to meditate upon*. Therefore, at this point, we should talk about these four philosophical schools.

People have varying intellectual capabilities: higher, middling and lower. If we were to tell someone with lower intelligence that a table does not exist, he would not readily believe it. If we add, "But it is made out of a lot of atoms," it becomes easy for him to understand. These atoms are said to possess the properties of earth, water, fire, and wind and to have form, smell, taste, and texture. Each particle has these eight properties. The reason that 'things' such as large objects, can change, disintegrate, and be destroyed, is because of an imbalance between these eight properties.

Concerning consciousness, there does not exist one thing called 'consciousness.' These two schools believe in a chain of indivisible instants of consciousness which forms a continuity.

When the two higher viewpoints, the Mind Only and Madhyamika schools, examine this they contend, "What you believe, that coarse things do not truly exist, is true. We claim the same. However, you maintain that individual particles of form and moments of consciousness ultimately exist. We assert that this is untrue." Through logic and reasoning, they refute the position posited by the Vaibhashika and Sautrantika schools saying that belief in the ultimate existence of a subtle, indivisible, and partless particle that is indestructible and unchangeable, is unreasonable when thoroughly examined. Western scientists are also studying this subject.

What could they reply when debating the possibility of an indivisible particle that cannot be cut or divided in any way? The higher schools ask, "Does this particle, which you hold to be ultimately real and unchangeable, indivisible, and so forth, have different sides and directions or not?" Responding to this, one cannot say that the particle does not have different sides. If we think about it ourselves, can we conceive of a particle without sides or directions? Can we imagine a particle with no dimensions at all?

If there is such a particle made of material substance, real and concrete, then it must have not just two sides, but at least six. If we consider even a very tiny and subtle particle which has some material substance, it can be connected to other similar particles so that they touch each other at some place. They won't touch each other at the same spot. Since six particles could touch a particle located in their center in six different places, it must have at least six different parts to it. Hence, we can't conceive of an indivisible or partless atom.

When we examine consciousness as a string of moments, we first examine to see whether each moment is indivisible or not. We must see if each of these moments touch one another, the one before and the one after. If they do in fact touch, then there are two parts and, therefore, that time span is not indivisible. One can conclude that no truly indivisible instant of consciousness exists.

If we think about past, present, and future, then finding the present moment as one indivisible instant becomes impossible. We talk about the past because something existed before the present, and the future is something which comes after, but we have trouble finding a moment that is exactly 'the present.' So, we cannot say that the three times of past, present, and future, truly exist. Therefore, we finally arrive at the Madhyamika point of view and find it true, not just because of its cleverness that triumphs over the other viewpoints, but because it is in accordance with the way things actually are. Western scientists are examining these same theories as well.

What belief does the Madhyamika school hold? They neither hold that things exist nor that they don't. In this way, Madhyamika points to that which is free from any mental fabrication and is therefore beyond conceptual mind. That is ultimate truth, the way things are.

When we talk about mind, we say that it does not exist because even the Buddha has not seen it; nor has he found it anywhere. Thus, no concrete substance exists anywhere that can be called 'mind.' If we examine and try to find a 'thing' somewhere, we cannot. This is fact, the nature of things. At the same time, however, mind is not nonexistent because it is the very basis for both samsara and nirvana. Mind is the basis for everything. It is not totally void or blank, mere empty space. This is not a contradiction. It is the middle path of unity. The fact that it is beyond any mental fabrication or assumption is the ultimate truth.

Ultimate truth is said to be beyond the *four extremes* and *eight constructs*. The four extremes are: existence and nonexistence, both and neither. The eight constructs are: arising and ceasing, being singular or plural, coming and going, and being the same or being different.

One can, through theoretical understanding, get some kind of feeling or conviction that all phenomena are emptiness, that they do not truly exist. But that is not sufficient. Without practice, one will not have the real experience or full taste that this is true. Still, thinking about this subject will give one some idea about emptiness.

We usually have a very gross perception of things. When we think 'house,' we just imagine the whole thing together as 'house.' Likewise, with 'table' or 'car,' we think of one big thing. If we truly examine to find out what we are labeling 'house,' we find that the walls are not the house, but simply the walls of the house. Similarly, the windows, the floor, the roof, and so forth seem to belong to the house, yet if we try to locate the actual 'house' itself, to which these parts belong, we cannot find or identify such an entity at all. When we say something is 'unidentifiable' or 'intangible,' this is what we mean.

It is the same with us. We always think, "My arm, my head, my this, my that," but when we try to discover what this 'I' is to which these parts belong, we cannot identify it. The 'I' is ungraspable and unidentifiable. In short, this means that everything appears or is experienced without truly existing. If we point at a window and say 'roof,' people will laugh, but, if we wave our finger around in the air and say 'house,' somehow people will not laugh but will understand what we are referring to.

If anyone asks, "Who's cup is this?" and we point to our hand and say, "This is my cup," people will laugh, even though the hand always holds the cup. If we point to our mouth and say, "My cup," people will also laugh, even though the cup is always put to the mouth. Yet, if we point to our chest, our heart, and say, "My cup," then no one will laugh. Examining this, we will see that the whole thing lacks logic.

Because we always take things at face value, without examining, when someone says, "Bring the table," we bring the table, and everybody is happy. If we brought the table leg, they'd get angry and say, "You idiot! You brought only the leg. We asked for the table." We could respond that the leg is also the table, part of the table, but nobody would agree on this.

We all agree on something called 'space.' If we say, "Do you see the sky? Do you see the space?" everybody says, "Yes! I see it." But if you ask, "Where is it?" the response will be, "It's right here." Such a statement is made only because of not really examining the situation. If we look into what it is that we call 'space,' there is nothing to point to anywhere. 'Space' is just a word used for something with no basis whatsoever. If we truly examine everything, we'll find that all phenomena are like space, with no basis for attaching their individual labels.

For example, when we dismantle a car, we think that the car consists of all the parts correctly put together. Only then is it a truly real and existing car. If it were in pieces on the ground in front of us, each part, one by one, would have its own name and is not 'the car.' We might tend to think that these parts exist, but they are also, like the wheel, merely a label. Each component consists of various smaller parts which we can again take apart. The wheel, for instance, includes the tire, the hubcap, the inner tube, the nuts, and the bolts. If these are assembled, we think we have 'the wheel,' yet they are merely parts and no such thing as the wheel itself exists. These parts can be further taken apart endlessly, so that we find nothing which can truly be called anything.

What does this all mean? It means that phenomena do appear, but without truly existing. They are like dreams. In dreams, although we do experience what is happening, we think it is real. If we fall down, the pain feels real. If we are happy or sad, it feels real — as though everything were actually occurring. Were we aware that we were dreaming, we could have quite a lot of fun, because even if we fell from a very high place, we wouldn't die. We could do many things, but this requires some advancement in practice. In the same way, with a sufficiently high view in the waking state, there are many possibilities.

This object on the table before me is called a 'vase,' but 'vase' is just a word. The thing itself is not the word. We can say, "It's ceramic, made of baked clay," but these are also just words. No matter how we try, we can't find out what the object really is. We can only apply our own concepts to it. With this understanding, then all phenomena are empty yet apparent.

The fact that whatever we think of we try to label is quite funny and strange. Whatever names we can conceive of are just our own words for labeling phenomena. All of our concepts, like clean and unclean, pleasant and unpleasant, and so forth are just mental constructs without any existence whatsoever.

In short, mind is empty. It has no concrete substance, but it is also not a blank voidness. There is cognizance or the capacity to know. These two things, being empty and being cognizant, are an indivisible unity and this unity is naturally present in all sentient beings. It is not something we need to construct or manufacture. If we want to call it by a name, we can say enlightened essence or *tathagatagarbha* or dharmakaya.

The dharmakaya, in our present situation, is a dharmakaya or state in which the enlightened qualities have not yet manifested. The dharmakaya state of buddhahood is the state in which all the enlightened qualities are fully developed.

When we say ground wisdom, ground luminosity, or ordinary mind, we mean the ground dharmakaya in which emptiness and cognizance are a unity. Later on, the path wisdom or path luminosity is the same thing, not something new. Even at the time of fruition, it is still ordinary mind, the unity of emptiness and luminosity. The only difference is that the clarity aspect, the manifestation of enlightened qualities, is further developed. One attains nothing new. Nothing is given as a blessing and nothing is manufactured anew.

The phrase 'ordinary mind' is a very good term to use because it means that our basic nature is the unobstructed unity of being empty and cognizant, without being tampered with or altered, accepted, rejected, or modified. That is the meaning of 'ordinary mind.' We usually think that something that is ordinary is not very special, that there is nothing much to it. But ordinary mind is very special in the sense that it is not tampered with or spoiled by disturbing emotions. As soon as something is changed or altered by a disturbing emotion, it is no longer ordinary mind. It is something contrived and not the buddha mind.

There is not even a hair-tip of something to meditate upon. Just looking undistractedly into the essence of mind is sufficient. One doesn't need to meditate upon something. At the time of the development stage, we talk about 'doing meditation,' meaning that we keep something in mind; but here, there is nothing upon which to meditate. Just remain one-pointedly, undistracted in ordinary mind, without trying to cultivate or manufacture anything. Give up hoping for something good or fearing something bad.

Don't hope that something fantastic will happen, nor fear that the whole thing is going wrong. Don't think, "Now I've got it!" or "Oh, this is completely wrong!" or "Is this the real thing or is it something else?" One should not get involved in any of these considerations whatsoever.

> At the time of practicing the main part in this way,
> 'Stillness' is to abide totally free from thinking,
> And 'occurrence' is when mind roams about through the ten directions without staying still.
> 'Awareness,' here, is to notice whatever takes place, be it stillness or occurrence.
> Although these show themselves in different ways, they are of but a single essence.

The Mahamudra system mentions four yogas, each divided into three. As a prelude to entering these twelve stages of Mahamudra, there is a practice called *stillness, occurrence, and awareness*. One first tries to keep the mind perfectly still without any thinking. 'Stillness' means the period without thought activity. 'Occurrence' is when the mind thinks, when there is thought activity. 'Awareness' is noticing whether there is stillness or thought occurrence, such as "Now there is stillness," or "Now there's occurrence." At this point, simply noticing is called 'awareness.'

In general, the practice of noticing stillness and occurrence comes before the mind essence is pointed out. Mahamudra, however, teaches that even if one has recognized mind essence, practicing stillness, occurrence, and awareness will further the realization of simplicity.

Stillness means abiding totally free from thinking. Occurrence means the mind is roaming through the ten directions. Don't think too literally about the ten directions; this means that many different thoughts occur. Awareness means noticing whatever is there, either stillness or thought occurrence. These are all aspects of the same thing. Stillness is when the mind is still, occurrence is when the mind is moving or thinking, and awareness is the mind noticing what is going on. Their identity, however, is the same.

> Stillness is dharmakaya and occurrence is nirmanakaya.
> Awareness is sambhogakaya and their indivisibility is svabhavikakaya.
> These are the causes or seeds for accomplishing the three kayas.
> In this way, there is no difference in quality between stillness and occurrence,
> So, don't make preferences, just maintain the practice in whatever happens.
>
> In the beginning, look again and again during short sessions repeated many times.
> Next, look gradually for a longer and longer duration.

As a beginner one should practice in short sessions repeated frequently. If the sessions aren't short, one may fall into the trap of drowsiness, agitation, or being fascinated by the experience. Slowly, as one becomes more and more proficient in practice and recognizes the unified state of emptiness and wakefulness, one can then prolong the sessions.

QUESTIONS AND ANSWERS

STUDENT: Could Rinpoche explain shamatha practice in more detail?

RINPOCHE: Concerning shamatha practice, it is the mind that experiences all joys and sorrows, as well as feelings of indifference.

Hence, if our mind remains in stillness, our body will also remain quiet. Through this, our speech will be calm, too. So, practicing shamatha is very important.

Shamatha, or stillness practice, has different aspects, such as *shamatha with support* and *shamatha without support*. For example, in one shamatha practice you focus on a representation of the enlightened body, enlightened speech, or enlightened mind. The different techniques are all alike in that their only purpose is to calm your mind so that it can abide peacefully.

"Water clears when undisturbed," it is said. If water in a pond is disturbed, it becomes murky. But if left alone, it naturally remains clear. Likewise, when your mind remains focused on a single object, whatever it might be, and doesn't follow after gross or even subtle thoughts of the past, the present, or the future, it automatically relaxes and remains still, calm, and peaceful. This properly laid foundation is of great benefit for training in the more advanced practices.

Shamatha literally means abiding calmly or peacefully. Everyone is pursuing peace and happiness. Each and every person in this world, each and every animal, down to the tiniest insect, wants happiness and a sense of well-being. We see that even a tiny insect crawling on the ground, when bothered by the sun's heat, will seek shade, or, if too cold, search for warmth. Everyone is searching for a state free from harm or disturbance.

Happiness cannot necessarily be found externally, however. Peace is not only outside. It is the mind that experiences joy and sorrow, peace or disquiet. The training to tame one's own mind, if one can apply the practices, makes peace and happiness easy to attain.

The unrest in this world basically results from human beings' inability to control the disturbing emotions within their own minds. In particular, motivated by pride, jealousy, or competitiveness, we begin to fight over small things, like children quarreling over a sweet. The children act either from attachment to the piece of candy, thinking, "I should have it!" or from jealousy, pride, or anger at the other child. In short, it is disturbing emotions that cause the fights of even small children. If a chunk of meat is tossed to a pack of dogs, they will snap each other and bite, sometimes fighting to the death for that food, all because of their disturbing emotions.

Within a family, the inability to control disturbing emotions causes husband and wife to quarrel. Unwilling to admit their own shortcomings, each will find reasons for arguing and will always say, "You are the one who is wrong!" never, "I was wrong." A person willing to take blame on him or herself is rare.

More widely, the truly great danger of nuclear weapons these days has brought about great fear and anxiety among nations. People feel very afraid. Some dig big holes in the ground in which to hide, in case something happens; others seek a safe place deep in the mountains where they can feel secure if something goes wrong. People have great worries and try to find all kinds of ways out, but no one knows if hiding will be of any benefit. People feel desperate. If asked, "What do you fear?" people say, "We fear the bomb!"

The nuclear weapon itself, harbors no ill-will. It is not the bomb itself that can harm beings, but it is those humans who made the weapons and those others who make the decisions to use them.

Through the five poisons, people of various countries who are unable to control their different disturbing emotions have been motivated to actually manufacture and use these weapons. What provides the basis for all of this to occur? It is simply the result of mind poisons, which have been allowed to run out of control.

We may shout, "Let there be peace!" but this won't really bring peace. Peace will appear in the world around us only when each individual learns to tame the disturbances arising within his or her own mind. Then, peace will come automatically.

When practicing shamatha, the full vajra-posture is best, but if that position is uncomfortable, simply sit cross-legged. Allow the breathing to be natural and free-flowing. We will have thoughts and they all fall into the three categories of being either good, bad, or neutral. Good thoughts are those that benefit others, having an altruistic attitude, compassion, and so forth. Bad thoughts are thoughts of ill-will and hostility. Neutral thoughts are simple passing thoughts that are never particularly forceful or intense, like "this is white; that is red." They just come and go and are forgotten about in the next moment. Good thoughts and bad thoughts, however, are never really forgotten. We can remember them, especially if they are very intense, like strong anger or strong happiness, even after several days or even years. An extremely intense thought, for instance being shocked by some very bad news or having an intense experience, can cause a similar feeling to reoccur later, even in dreams.

Sit, if you can, in full vajra-posture, otherwise just loosely cross-legged. Either put your hands in the meditation gesture or rest your palms on your knees, whichever is more comfortable.

We have *five sense consciousnesses* that are like different openings or doors, but they must be connected to the mind within, otherwise our consciousness is not employed. If one fails to take hold of the consciousness within, it will distract itself through these different doors. Some people say, "If I don't close my eyes in meditation, I get distracted." Actually, it is through not controlling the mind that we are distracted, either through the eyes, nose, or ears. We must control the mind itself.

In short, remain cross-legged with the hands in meditation gesture and the mouth slightly open with the tip of the tongue lightly touching the palate. The breath should move naturally, unforced. Don't let your attention wander. Achieve this by focusing on one object. Objects are of various kinds, but at this point, simply focusing on the inward and outward movement of one's breath will suffice. Breathing out, notice, "Now, the breath is moving out." Inhaling, notice, "Now, the breath is moving in." You needn't think anything else. Just return to awareness of the breath.

This practice will cause all our various thoughts, our hopes and fears, expectations, anxieties, and so forth, to naturally subside. Our many thoughts about things will calm down and our negative and disturbing emotions will naturally cease. Thus, our body and our mind will automatically remain in a state of stillness and great peace. As our practice develops, this becomes the basis for further qualities to arise.

You've probably heard or read about this frequently, but it must be practiced. A strong inter-relationship exists between the breath and the mind. As they are completely interrelated, controlling the breath will also control the mind. If the breath is out of control, likewise, the mind will be out of control.

The mind is often compared to a horseman and the breath to the horse. A wild and untamed horse is difficult for the rider; a very good and well-trained horse is quite useful. If both rider and horse are extremely well trained and skilled, an excellent combination has been made.

Keep the eyes half-open, looking down in the direction of the tip of the nose. If you experience a lot of thought activity and disturbances, then you can close the eyes.

The best position for this practice, slightly different, is called the sevenfold posture of Vairochana. Hold the hands in the meditation mudra. The channel of disturbing emotions is located at the base of the ring finger. If a person becomes psychotic, tying a cord around his ring finger and applying pressure often helps a lot.

Close the fingers around the thumb and then place your closed fists on your thighs. Right now, as beginners, this practice is a bit difficult, but slowly, slowly… This posture at first glance appears very uncomfortable, but actually if one is trained in it, it is extremely pleasant.

Keep the mouth slightly open. Do not follow thoughts, whether good or bad. Don't entertain memories of what happened yesterday or in the past. Don't plan what will happen tomorrow. Don't become involved with either good, bad, or neutral thoughts. Keep only one thought: while exhaling think, "Exhaling!" and when breathing in think, "Inhaling!" Breathe smoothly and slowly.

When remaining like this, some defects can occur. 'Sluggishness' means we sit without noticing anything; we become completely unaware. 'Excitement' or 'agitation' means that our mind becomes unruly and will not remain in the natural state. But right now, we can experience the taste of shamatha. Concern yourself with just a single thought — acknowledging the movement of the breath — body and mind will automatically become still and peaceful. This is called 'experiencing the taste of shamatha.'

At the onset, as a beginner, one will think without even trying. But try to keep mindful and alert and decide firmly, "I won't follow after that thought." Then, just focus on the practice.

STUDENT: What benefits come from practicing shamatha meditation?

RINPOCHE: Since among body, speech and mind, mind is the most important, it is said that when practicing shamatha or stillness of mind, if one's mind is peaceful and relaxed, one's body will also be peaceful and loose. Due to the stillness that occurs from shamatha practice, one's mind will be free from the disturbing emotions of pride, competitiveness, etc. When a group of people practice together, the group will mutually, among themselves, be free from these disturbing emotions. If the whole country or the whole world were to practice shamatha and be calm and free from the disturbing emotions, such as attachment, aggression, and so-forth, then warfare would no longer exist. This is only a good wish that one can make, since everyone in the world is unlikely to learn to practice shamatha, and it is not realistic to think that everyone would maintain the practice. Therefore, simply practice yourself and if you can attain stillness of mind, that, in itself, is of great benefit.

The shamatha I have taught here is based upon following the movement of breath. Breath, or wind, relates very closely to consciousness. Later on, you can practice retaining the *vase breath,* where a portion of the breath in the lower part of the body is held, enabling you to make one breath last for quite a long time. The Six Yogas of Naropa, particularly *tummo* practice, use this technique. In another technique, the practitioner holds one portion of the breath continuously and breathes with the rest. Throughout the day, the held portion provides a basis for mindfulness and also for controlling the disturbing emotions, so that one will always be peaceful and not agitated or disturbed in any way. Moreover, all the defects of meditation like drowsiness, agitation, and so on, will be easily controlled.

The winds are related to the stability of the mind. When someone becomes furious or intensely angry, his or her face becomes completely red and the hands begin to shake. It is the winds that express this emotion from within. Wind is a medium that functions in either a positive or a negative way.

A lot of talk is not beneficial; the important point is applying the practice to one's state of mind. When beginning shamatha practice, do not fix your mind too tightly upon the object of focus, such as the breath. Use it merely as a support for not becoming distracted, as something to return to when the mind wanders. You will slowly start to feel the taste of shamatha, a state of mind totally undisturbed by any emotion like joy or sorrow, but at the same time not oblivious or dull-minded. Feeling very free, easy, and comfortable, peaceful and blissful, this is the beginning of having a taste of shamatha meditation. What is your experience like? Please tell us.

STUDENT: I experience quite a bit of heat rising from my chest. This just happens sometimes.

RINPOCHE: Different kinds of experiences or sensations occur, but they are specific for the individual. There is no general rule that everyone will have experiences in the same way. Some mainly feel that everything is void or empty; some, that everything is clear or blissful; some, that the body is very light or buoyant; others that the body is heavy or uncomfortable; and some feel hot or cold in various parts of the body. These experiences come and go. If one does not get too fascinated with a good experience, thinking "This is great" and does not get depressed if the experience is unpleasant, then all the experiences will yield some good quality. Tightness or too much heat in the upper part of the body results from holding too tightly to the breath. If that happens just breathe very smoothly and naturally.

In short, does the mind stay peaceful or not? After having done this practice, do you see improvement, or is it getting worse? It probably will not get worse, but it may definitely seem like that. This is because we never before took much notice of our thought activity. In the past, we were always either trying to have a good time, to be entertained, to get drunk, or to take some medicines, both those that are allowed and those that are prohibited. [Laughter]

Our present situation with shamatha practice is devoid of those desires. It is simply the naked mind by itself, as it is. It must stand alone, independently, and we will come to know its basic situation, more and more clearly. Now, while we are practicing shamatha and trying to remain undistracted, we seem to have more thoughts the more we try to quiet our mental disturbances. Yet, the mere fact of noticing a lot of mental activity happening is good since we can then do something about it. Without noticing, there would be nothing to do.

If, for example, we have an external enemy or a physical illness, we can identify it as our problem; we can do something about it, by either befriending it or trying to chase it away. Problems can be solved in different ways. If something is disturbing or harming us, and we cannot identify it, then we are in trouble. It is like having an unidentified thief in the house. We notice that things are beginning to disappear, but if we believe that the thief comes from outside, he will be quite difficult to catch, and eventually all our things will disappear.

At this moment our life is in our own hands. We have the freedom to choose what we want to do. We can give ourselves a good time or a hard time; we can do something positive or something negative. Since it is our own decision, we should try to tame our disturbing emotions and be truly free.

Some people have great difficulty in following the movement of the breath, so they can instead focus on an object in front of themselves. Anything in particular, even a spot in the field of vision can be used as a support for concentration. Do not allow the mind to wander elsewhere, keep mindful of the object of concentration. Since the mind won't stay still by itself, you should control it with mindfulness and sit alert as though keeping constant guard.

STUDENT: Can Rinpoche say when these practices should be done and by whom? How can the shamatha practice be incorporated with the practice taught earlier?

RINPOCHE: This text is actually something that takes a long time to teach and a long time to practice, and is usually given in small portions over a long period of time. We haven't much time and yet I hoped to teach it all in one seminar. Were we to practice each specific practice according to the text, trying to assimilate it into our experience as we went along, we would find it impractical to do in ten days. You will have much more time in the future. Therefore, try to keep in mind what is being taught, and later on, try to practice it in the mornings and evenings. This text is complete, containing all the key points of the three yanas, Hinayana, Mahayana, and Vajrayana, in the refuge, bodhichitta, development and completion stages. The problem may be due to the text covering too much. So much material may be a little too rich to grasp.

Yet, one can combine the entire text into a single session. First, sit down in your meditation seat, and consider the four thoughts that change the mind: the precious human body, impermanence, karma and suffering. Then, in a flash, become Avalokiteshvara, the Great Compassionate One, surrounded by all sentient beings. Take refuge and arouse bodhichitta. In your heart center, focus on the syllable HRIH as a support for shamatha practice. Remain focused on this, without distraction, for some time. Later on, look into "Who is it that meditates?" With nothing to find, the meditator's experience becomes intangible. This is sufficient for right now. Next, emanate rays of light and make offerings to the buddhas to accumulate merit. Then, emanate light that purifies all the obscurations of sentient beings. In the end, complete the session by dedicating the merit. Such a session completes the topics of the whole text. If you combine this practice with receiving the stream of nectar from Amitabha, then the preliminaries are complete.

When you sit down to practice, contemplate the four mind changings. You can do so very briefly by talking to yourself: "Now, take advantage of this good opportunity of having attained a precious human body completely endowed with all the right circumstances. Don't waste it." By doing Dharma practice, one is making use of one's precious human body which is hard to find and easy to lose. When not under the sway of the eight temporary unfree conditions, one can now engage in the practice with delight and happiness.

Regarding impermanence, this human body will not last forever. Remind yourself, "You won't always be here. Dying is easy, so don't waste time. Don't postpone, but practice right now."

As for karmic cause and effect, you should think: "Were it not for the law of karma, everyone who wants happiness would find it. Life would be the same for everyone. In fact, because each individual has individual karma, each person experiences different results. This is because of the law of cause and effect."

About the suffering of samsara, remind yourself: "Right now, I'm in good health, I have food, clothing and a place to live; but, nevertheless, my mind is still not that happy. Therefore, the proof of suffering in samsara exists right within myself."

You needn't spend more time than this on the four thoughts at the beginning of a session but reminding yourself is important. Next, in an instant visualize yourself as Avalokiteshvara with Amitabha above or in front of you. Take refuge and develop bodhichitta, and spend the major part of the session focusing on the letter HRIH in the heart center. Before focusing on the HRIH, imagine for a short time, a stream of nectar flowing down from Amitabha, who is above your head.

The HRIH stands erect atop a beautiful lotus flower with six petals. Very small in size, it is encircled by the other six syllables on the surrounding petals. Focus mainly on the HRIH which is radiant, sending out rays of light. The main part of the session is simply this. The rays of light, as the basis of wisdom, are also important in that they clear away one's ignorance and make one's sleep less dull.

Later in the session, ask yourself, "Who is it that meditates?" Look into "What is it that visualizes or thinks?" Since it is totally intangible, there is nothing to find, nothing to be seen or taken hold of in any way, and nothing we can either think of or discern by means of thoughts or concepts. If we start to fall into the trap of thinking, "There is a 'thing' and it's like this," that is *eternalism* — one extreme. If we fall into the trap of thinking "There is nothing whatsoever," that is *nihilism* — the other extreme. Don't bother with these two extreme concepts.

According to a proverb, thinking that mind is concrete, one is as stupid as a cow; but, thinking that it is nothing, one is even more stupid. So, falling into neither extreme, remain in ordinary mind. This is called vipashyana, whereas focusing on the HRIH is the shamatha. As beginners, we will spend less time on vipashyana, spending most of our time on shamatha.

At the end of the session, rest in natural mind and then dedicate the merit. This is a simple way of combining all the teachings in Karma Chagmey's text into one session.

STUDENT: From time to time Rinpoche uses the phrase 'self-display.' What does this mean?

TRANSLATOR: In this context a better translation than self-display for the Tibetan expression *rangnang* would be 'personal experience.'

RINPOCHE: Whatever we experience, be it as a fish or human, what appears to us as dwelling place, food, environment, and so on, is our personal experience, and is not necessarily the same for other beings. A mouse, for instance, has a certain experience of what its home is like, what 'home' or 'dwelling place' means, so if it enters the home of a human being, it will not feel that the room is a dwelling. When we talk about 'pure' or 'impure' experience, the 'purity' depends upon how much we solidify our experience — how much we fixate on concrete reality. As this fixation lessens and falls away, we say that personal experience becomes pure experience.

Dreams at night are a good example of what 'personal experience' or 'self-display' means. Dreams are completely personal. Another example is of beings from different realms experiencing a single cup of water as completely differing things. This is also personal experience. For us, human excrement is disgusting, but for some animals, it is food, something to eat. That is their personal experience. To some, excrement is something filthy, to others, it is edible. What you find beautiful and attractive may not be attractive or beautiful to someone else. Your favorite dish is not necessarily anyone else's favorite meal. Smell, taste, textures, and so forth are all like this.

STUDENT: Could you say something more about coemergent ignorance and conceptual ignorance?

TRANSLATOR: Rinpoche asked me to explain these two types of ignorance. In terms of sitting practice, coemergent ignorance means forgetting the natural state of mind, becoming carried away. Conceptual ignorance means starting to think of something else in terms of dualistic or conceptual thoughts.

STUDENT: Then, what is the 'single nature ignorance?'

TRANSLATOR: That's the basis for both of them. [Laughter]

STUDENT: What are pure lands or pure realms?

RINPOCHE: The ultimate or real sense of a pure land or pure realm is what is called 'pure experience.' Pure personal experience is the 'buddha realm,' but at the same time, there is also a pure land manifested by buddhas for the sake of beings, where they may wish to be reborn and, in fact, can be reborn for the sake of practice and progress. Ultimately, though, a pure land is pure experience. In our own world, there are said to be some hidden pure lands in various places, but these are generally something which we hear about, but cannot actually see. The stories are probably true. Some old predictions state that when the world is being filled with strange kinds of machinery and evil substances which endanger human beings' existence, some of these lands will open and provide a safe haven.

STUDENT: Earlier when you were talking about the Madhyamika view and the other three philosophical schools, what was the idea of an ultimate particle?

RINPOCHE: According to the Vaibhashika, gross things are empty, but the subtle are not. It's not that they proved that the particle is ultimate because it is indivisible. It's the other way around. Unless there is something that is ultimate, they asserted, ordinary things could not exist. Therefore, there should be an ultimate particle. It's not that they have proven it through logic. They only infer the ultimate existence of a subtle particle by saying, "How can there be big objects, if there isn't a basic particle, something that they are made out of?"

For instance, if we talk about powder, it seems as though there is a thing, but if we try to find that thing then there is nothing to find. Still, according to the Vaibhashika, we cannot say there is nothing, because they believe there really are tiny particles of which it is composed.

There's a lot to be said about this and if you want to study it in finer detail, it's good to consult the *Abhidharma Kosha* and the *Abhidharma Samucchaya*.

We can also consider the question, "Does a sound have a physical form or not?" If one says "no," then why should it be obstructed by a wall? If one says "yes," then what does it look like? It's the same with odor. An odor can't be seen or taken hold of, but still, it's based upon something material, and it's difficult for someone to walk into the room with a good or a bad smell without noticing the odor. At the same time, if I say, "Show me the odor," then there's not much to show. Traditionally, there is a lot of discussion about this topic.

6
The Song of Clearing the Obstacles for Experiences to Occur

> Emaho!
> In these times, when there are many who teach the oral instructions,
> There are many people who have some partial knowledge.
> But the appearances of this life are beguiling and enticing,
> And, because of not taking the thought of impermanence and death to heart,
> There are many whose knowledge remains as mere theory.
> Although they receive many instructions, they are stubborn and insensitive.
> Without shying away from wrong-doing, their actions are like a mere commoner.

Emaho is an expression that means "How wondrous!"

In these times, many teachers are giving oral instructions that are short and unelaborate. They may be instructions on Mahamudra and Dzogchen, or on the Six Yogas, and so forth. There are quite a few teachers in various places. As a result, many people receive bits and pieces of teachings and end up with a fragmented knowledge of the Dharma.

The appearances of this life are beguiling and enticing. The Tibetan phrase is 'skilled in deceiving.' With only a partial knowledge of Dharma teachings, people are easily carried away because of being gullible and fickle-minded and are easily overpowered by the *eight temporary unfree conditions*.

The appearances of this life are beguiling, and not taking to heart the thought of death, we are naive. If we don't take seriously the thought of our own death, we can easily fall under the power of laziness and postpone practice until later. But, taking to heart the thought of death and impermanence, we won't feel like wasting time. Knowing that we possess the enlightened essence, we should also know that if we put into practice the instructions received from a qualified teacher, we will be able to attain complete enlightenment. Still, carried away by the appearances of this life, all the knowledge about practice is left behind as mere theory.

> Those who receive the teachings only criticize the faults of others.
> This is because they lack revulsion, the foot of meditation.
> If you know the path but do not traverse it,
> It is like having no chance to visit the Jowo Temple.

We may have received many instructions, but still remain stubborn and insensitive. For example, if we have a buffalo that we beat repeatedly, after a few beatings it won't care very much anymore. Feeling that the beating doesn't matter, it will refuse to move. Similarly, in the beginning, when we hear a lot of teachings, we are enthusiastic to study, very diligent, and anxious to understand. But after a while, we feel we have heard so often about the precious human body and impermanence that we feel fed-up and tired of it. We've heard so much about emptiness that we think, "Sure, all things are empty and it's probably true but so what?"

In this way, we become jaded and insensitive, stubborn, and we don't really take the teachings to heart. In our understanding, the dharma remains mere dry words. We don't apply the teachings, we don't shy away from wrong-doing, and our actions remain like those of ordinary people. Because we lack revulsion and renunciation, the foot of meditation, no matter how many teachings we get, we still criticize others and examine their faults.

The next two lines talk about going to Lhasa. The text was written in Kham, eastern Tibet, so the example used is about visiting the Jowo Temple, a famous shrine in Lhasa. If one knows how to go there, but fails to travel the prescribed route, how can one visit the Jowo Temple? Similarly, if we have received the teachings and know how to practice to attain enlightenment, but fail to apply what we know, the opportunity for progress is spoiled.

> In this respect, people have higher, medium, and lower capacities.
> The person of the highest capacity does not need to renounce worldly actions,
> But can practice while mixing mundane actions with the practice.
> This partaking of sense pleasures as the path, without abandoning them,
> Is the example of King Indrabodhi.

Different kinds of people have different capacities: higher, medium, and lower. People of highest capacity need not renounce or reject any worldly actions of this life. King Indrabodhi belonged to the highest type, someone whose understanding and liberation was simultaneous.

In Tibet, for example, Marpa the Translator did not take ordination. He had a wife, family, household, and farm, and yet, he never strayed from his practice of the view of Mahamudra. He simultaneously looked after all his mundane responsibilities and remained in uncontrived mind. In this way, he attained, in a single lifetime, what Dzogchen calls the 'exhaustion of concepts and phenomena.' Mahamudra calls this attainment the 'royal throne of dharmakaya.' People of the highest capacity can and should practice like that.

Someone who is able to practice in this way should do so without being influenced by disturbing emotions such as aggression, attachment, and delusion. If one can mingle one's mundane actions with the practice, keeping the view of Mahamudra or Dzogchen while remaining totally untainted and without becoming a mere commoner, then one can practice just like King Indrabodhi and Marpa, that is, without abandoning sense pleasures.

> The person of medium capacity abandons most worldly actions.
> He practices while keeping the behavior of a monk.
> Trying to acquire food, drink, and clothing
> Is the life-style of most learned and accomplished masters of India and Tibet.

The person of mediocre capacity should abandon most worldly actions and perhaps live like a renunciant, content with just a simple life, simple food and clothing, satisfied without an expensive wardrobe, good food, or a beautiful expensively furnished home. Not needing a large variety of delicious food and drink, nor having to eat or drink something vile, such a person is content to have simple meals — just enough to fill the stomach. He or she needs only enough clothing to keep warm. Most of the learned and accomplished masters of India and Tibet lived like this.

> The person of lowest capacity cannot fulfill his aims while keeping two frames of mind.
> He is unable to engage in both Dharmic and mundane pursuits
> And practices, having cast away concerns for the food and clothing of this life.
> This is the life-style of such masters as Milarepa and Götsangpa.

Just as one can't sew with a double-pointed needle, the person of the lowest capacity cannot, at the same time, both strive to fulfill the aims of this life and simultaneously practice Dharma. Thus, it is taught that such a person should give up all consideration for the *eight worldly concerns,* such as attachment to honor and gain, pleasure and praise, and aversion to their opposites; and, should live like Milarepa and Götsangpa who abandoned all concerns of this life and concentrated exclusively on practice.

> Whichever way you follow, do it continuously.
> If you practice without giving up, experience and
>   realization will dawn.

Whichever of these three lifestyles one is able to apply: higher, like King Indrabodhi and Marpa; medium, like the accomplished masters; or lower, like Milarepa the great yogi; one should keep to that. Keep to the chosen lifestyle continuously, not just for a short time to see how things work out, later changing to something else or giving up one's practice entirely.

Diligence is crucial for beginners. If one does not exert oneself or persevere in the practice, nothing will happen. One will simply not have any progress. If one practices without abandoning the style of practice one has adopted, then realization will take place.

> Due to the constitution and faculties of the individual,
>   what occurs to one person will not occur to others.
> Some are pure and will have high experiences and
>   realization.
> While others, after each experience, will feel despair.
> For some, experiences gradually improve, more and more.
> However, I will now explain gradually
> The way in which experiences take place.

As mentioned earlier, all individuals are unique. Dispositions, physical constitutions, and mental faculties vary from person to person. Therefore, when practicing, one person's experience is not necessarily the same as another's experience. Some people will immediately have very deep experiences of bliss, clarity, and nonthought. Others may feel that nothing has happened, though slowly, slowly something will change.

Some people have very pure faculties and they will have very high experiences right away. Others, after each experience, will feel despair. They may have some difficulties. For some, experiences will gradually improve, further and further. So, now we will discuss how experiences take place.

> In the beginning, the mind does not want to remain still for even an instant.
> It chases after everything, jumping from one thought to the next.
> At that time, straighten your body posture and rest loosely.
> Let your mind run wherever it wants, while keeping watchful guard.
> In this way, it will return home and be still for a short while.

In the beginning, when we start to do Dharma practice, our mind won't stay still for even an instant; it skips from one thing to another, thinking about this and that, running after everything. If we see something, we immediately begin to think about it. If we hear a sound, it triggers a train of thought. Some thoughts may cause us to burst out laughing. The mind can think of the most impossible and unexpected things.

We might think, "How nice if I could fly right now!" or "What would immortality be like?" Again, and again, we think about attaining impossible things. Yet, keeping the key points of correct body posture, the energies or pranas will flow freely and we will be able to rest loosely, peacefully, and freely. The mind will think this and that, all kinds of thoughts. Let it express whatever it wants without inhibiting it in any way, however, keep on guard and remain watchful. Be mindful

The paradox is that, leaving the mind to itself to freely think of whatever it wants, it will stop. Yet, if we try to control it, saying, "Now concentrate. Don't think of anything!" it will think of all kinds of things. Just like a monkey or a little child, if you say, "Be quiet!" it will of course jump around and make trouble; but if you say "Just jump around and do whatever you want," it will quickly tire and stay still. Mind is the same. So, the idea here is to just leave the mind to itself and let it rest loosely.

> Both stillness and thought occurrence belong to shamatha.
> The insight that their essence is empty is vipashyana.
> Their unity is to realize, as an indivisible oneness
> The emptiness of both stillness and occurrence.

There are two aspects: stillness, when the mental activities subside and the mind remains still; and thought occurrence, when a great deal of thought activity is taking place. Both belong to shamatha. Stillness or occurrence are again mere concepts, but if one looks into "What is it that is still? What is it that abides calmly? What is it that thinks?" one then discovers the empty essence, totally free from any extremes or mental constructs. This is called the uncompounded unity of being empty and cognizant, called vipashyana or insight. 'Vipashyana' means to see clearly, but 'seeing' doesn't imply 'something to see.' Here, we are completely beyond there being a 'person who sees,' a 'thing which is seen,' and the 'act of seeing.' It is totally beyond all kinds of mental constructs.

> Although you have understood this to be so,
> Sometimes, when resting in practice, you become exuberant and exhilarated.
> Your mind gets fascinated, thinking "This is it!"

At the moment of stillness or thought occurrence, one should recognize the empty essence, without making preferences between these two states. As long as one doesn't become blank or dull at the time of stillness and doesn't fixate on thought at the time of occurrence, one can realize the unity of indivisible cognizance and emptiness. If, during practice, one experiences a strong sensation of bliss and a dominant feeling of stillness; when, like water spreading out, everything becomes very quiet and tranquil, then one may become exuberant and exhilarated thinking, "This is wonderful." One's mind becomes fascinated, deciding, "This is it! Now I've finally got it." But this is only a temporary experience.

> Sometimes it will not remain still but is scattered and moves about like the wind.
> Although you look, it is evanescent and fleeting with nothing to be found or seen.
> Then you become frustrated, thinking "Oh no! This is not right. It is gone!"
> At that time, recognize the thought that occurs.
> By looking where it came from, where it remains, and where it vanishes, you will find nothing but emptiness.

At other times, one's mind may be totally scattered like leaves blown about by the wind or like popcorn popping, so that one feels very nervous and totally restless. At any of these times, if one tries to find the mind that experiences, it completely slips away. It is evanescent and fleeting; nothing can be seen or found anywhere. One becomes frustrated, thinking, "Oh, now I've lost it. This isn't right. My stillness is gone." At this time, try to recognize the essence of whatever thought occurs by examining where it came from, where it remains, and where it vanishes. Through this observation, one will find nothing but emptiness.

> For example, if you cut one piece of bamboo and look within it,
> You will understand that the inside of all bamboos are empty.
> Likewise, when you realize that one thought is hollow, since all thoughts are the same way,
> There is no reason to be elated about stillness and depressed about thought occurrence.
>
> Just as there is no difference between water and its wave,
> Look into the essence of whatever takes place

> Without making distinctions between stillness and
> occurrence.

Calm water is simply water and so are turbulent waves. No difference whatsoever exists between their nature. Likewise, the mind being still is just one's concept. If it makes thoughts and thinks, that also is just one's concept. Therefore, making distinctions between stillness and occurrence serves no purpose. What is important, on the other hand, is to look into the essence of that which creates concepts like stillness. Look into the essence of that which thinks, "Now there are thoughts." Then, one should just remain in thatness, in ordinary mind. This is the most essential.

There is a danger called 'straying into a blank state of cessation of cognizance' that can occur during shamatha practice. A true story is told about three men from Kham on pilgrimage to Lhasa. Along the way, they rested at a certain spot. One fellow fetched firewood, another collected water, and the third set up a campfire. While wandering about, the fellow who went for wood discovered a small cave and thought, "It looks so comfortable, I think I'll go inside and sit for a little while." He went inside, sat down, and, being an experienced practitioner of shamatha, entered a state where all cognition and thought activity ceased. He remained like that without noticing anything until the others began to wonder where he had disappeared. They called his name for hours, with no response.

The next day they searched but couldn't find him anywhere. No one answered their calls; he had completely vanished. They finally concluded that he must have fallen down somewhere or been killed by wild animals. He had completely vanished. They continued their journey without him, reached Lhasa, and visited many holy places. Three years later, returning home to Kham, they happened to stop again in the same spot. One said to the other, "Hey, isn't this where we lost our friend? We should check around. We might still find something."

By chance, they came across the cave entrance. Looking in, they could see by the sunlight streaming in, a figure seated on the floor of the cave. One man said, "Somebody's sitting in there. Maybe it's a statue or something. Let's take a look." They went inside and discovered their friend. One fellow called into their friend's ear and then tried ringing a bell to awaken him. They could feel that his chest was still a little warm. Slowly, he began to wake up. He looked at his friends and said, "Okay, okay. I was just sitting here for a few minutes. Now, I'll get the firewood." He had no idea that three years had elapsed. Such a state of *cessation* should be avoided.

Here's another example of a negative form of temporary experience. When I was living in Rumtek, my meditation master told me this story about himself. When he was young, his teacher told him to stay in retreat. He did one three-year retreat and then a second three-year retreat, alone, in a cave in the mountains. He used to get up very early in the morning, make a *torma* offering and do his practice. One night, he went to sleep and awakened feeling as though he had only slept for a very short time, yet it was broad daylight outside and the sun had already risen high in the sky. He thought, "This is terrible! I never oversleep like this!" and he hurriedly put together his tormas and preparations for the practice he would do.

Soon after, a stranger leading a horse came by and said, "Your sister is very sick and about to die. You must come immediately." The meditator refused, saying, "I'm sorry, but I've taken a solemn vow before my teacher to remain here for three years. I cannot go." The man argued, "Your sister wants only you, because if she dies without you to do the ceremonies, her spirit will be very unhappy and will roam for a long time restlessly. You must come. I've even brought you a horse."

He looked and saw the horse and thought, "How strange! It's difficult enough for a person to climb up here, let alone a horse. How can this be?" He asked the man how he had managed the climb and the fellow replied, "Rinpoche, we tried whatever we could so that you could have a pleasant journey down the mountain." He thought, "If I stay here, it may be selfish. If I go, it's not for my sake, but for the benefit of others and it seems my sister has great faith in me and great love also. Maybe I'd better go."

Yet, while preparing to leave, he suddenly felt suspicious. Just as he was about to climb onto the horse he thought, "My guru has told me I should never go anywhere without taking the thangka he gave me." He went into his cave to fetch it, came back out, and was just about to climb onto the horse when everything vanished into the blackness of night. Only the stars remained, shining in the sky.

The meditation master became terrified. He couldn't see anything in the pitch dark, so he crawled slowly back to his cave and sat shaking with fear on his meditation seat, wondering, "What's going on, has my meditation gone wrong?" He made fervent supplications to his master and meditated on compassion. At daybreak, he left the cave and discovered that where the 'horse' had stood, where he had been about to step, was nothing but a very steep cliff. Afterwards, his meditation improved tremendously.

> When you feel agitated or disturbed, relax both body and mind.
> When feeling dull, unclear, and sluggish, you should concentrate and watch.
> After that, at some point, thought occurrences will diminish
> And you will remain in total peace with infrequent thinking.
> But, although thinking occurs, you quickly return to stillness.
> This is named 'attainment of stillness.'

Based upon shamatha and vipashyana practice, one accumulates a great abundance of merit while, at the same time, purifying obscurations. Visible signs of successful practice occur. During the day, one feels more spacious, relaxed, open, and free and the body feels lighter and comfortable.

Sometimes we become angry and upset with a reasonable cause, but on other occasions we feel moody or depressed with no external justification whatsoever. Practicing vipashyana and shamatha will cause these disturbances to diminish. We can prove this to ourselves. Becoming more and more proficient in shamatha and vipashyana practice, our unwarranted moods, those with no relation to our daily lives, will vanish. Though we may still become angry, irritated, or upset for substantial reasons, the feelings automatically dissipate as quickly as they arise. We will not cling to these emotions as rigidly as before.

Sometimes people lacking stability in practice become so upset as to feel totally overwhelmed, as though their heart were breaking. But, for those with stability in the practice, this won't happen. Earlier, we mentioned the eruption of the five poisons that interrupts Dharma practice and carries people away, but this obstacle will not happen after attaining some stability in the practices of shamatha and vipashyana as explained here.

At present, we might become so upset and disturbed that we feel we can't eat or sleep, but with stability in this practice we will not lose our appetite nor lose any sleep at night. We will, of course, feel disturbed from time to time, but never as deeply as before. A person who has not developed the power of concentration through these two practices may become completely overheated and red in the face when disturbed by negative emotions, or may feel cold and clammy and grow pale. Strong emotions may even cause facial twitching. Different kinds of physical effects can manifest from the disturbing emotions. A person who has attained some stability in these practices will not experience this to any great extent.

We might believe that taking pain-killers or tranquilizers will help, but usually medicine for a headache helps only to cure a headache, and not to vanquish disturbing emotions. You should apply the true medicine, the practice of shamatha and vipashyana.

At night, the signs of practice can manifest in dreams, such as dreaming of putting on new clothes and throwing away the old, dreaming that impurities and filth are leaving our body, or dreaming that we arrive in delightful places. One may feel compassion and great love towards sentient beings, or devotion while dreaming. In dreams it may happen that one's mind will feel very free and easy, and one's body very light and buoyant. Various other signs can occur in dreams. All these indicate that one's negative karmas and obscurations are diminishing and being purified, and that meditation practice is progressing.

In short, the real signs of practice are as follows: the sign of learning is being gentle and disciplined, while the sign of practice is a diminishing of the disturbing emotions. A person who has studied the Dharma becomes gentler and disciplined and more careful in speaking and acting, especially in actions towards others. A practitioner does not offend other people but is very pleasant and kind. These are signs of having understood the teachings. The sign of a good meditator is the decrease of negative emotions. One doesn't become angry or upset at others and doesn't stubbornly hold onto things and emotions.

Yet, being mere ordinary people, though we practice the Dharma, we still experience disturbing emotions during the course of a day. Not just occasionally, but, if we really observe, frequently. One deals with the emotion by not holding onto it or making it into something real; it will then automatically disappear by itself. But, if one tries to control or hold on, the emotion becomes intensified.

Although we have attained the precious human body, free from the eight temporary unfree states, and although we engage ourselves in shamatha and vipashyana practice, in stillness and insight, two enemies can yet appear in meditation. They come, not from the outside, but from within, and are called dullness and excitement. When I was young, I received instructions on mind essence from Dudjom Rinpoche. At that time His Holiness said, "Just stay with what you have already learned. That's it. But watch out for the two thieves who can sneak in and make trouble. Guard against these two thieves and you'll be free from difficulties." Thinking about this later, I realized what a very profound and important teaching it was. Dullness and excitement can indeed be thieves.

Looking at a meditator from the outside, we may see him sitting in an elegant posture, hands held correctly, and it may appear as though he is really meditating. But no one knows what is occurring in his mind. Especially, in the beginning of shamatha practice, attempts to let the mind rest naturally won't be successful. The mind will be very restless, as when two small children are put together and become overactive. When one child tries to sit still and be quiet, the other becomes restless. In the same way, trying to sit quietly with the mind, it will think many different thoughts, hopping from one idea to the next.

When disturbed and agitated, relax body and mind. There's not much to relax really because one is already relaxed while practicing but lower the gaze slightly and loosen the body's tension. 'Dullness' is a state in which we, from the outside, may appear to be meditative, but the mind is not very awake; it is not sleeping, but is not wakeful either. Some thinking is occurring, but not much is noticed; it's a kind of blurry, undercurrent of thoughts. One simply sits obliviously. One might begin to drool without realizing it, like a cow or an old horse, chewing its cud with saliva going everywhere. This is called the state of dullness.

Being unclear is an obscured state with no sharpness or precision in one's mind. One just sits and feels obscured, not really aware of what's going on. One does think of different things, but if asked afterwards, "What did you think about?" One has no recollection whatsoever. Of course, these states of being dull and unclear happen to everyone often, but they are severe defects when one is engaged in them during practice.

When one does feel dull, unclear, and sluggish, the text says one should concentrate and watch. 'Concentrate' here means to pull yourself together, to straighten your posture, to raise your gaze to a higher position, at best, gaze into a clear blue sky, and wear fewer clothes if you are too warm. This will make your awareness sharper. If one is very agitated or disturbed, one should wear warmer clothing, lower one's gaze and relax, or loosen one's body tension.

'Watch' in this case doesn't mean to watch a certain thing, but to rest in the wakefulness in which clarity and emptiness are inseparable.

The context of this teaching is for students who have practiced shamatha, and in addition, have received from a master the pointing-out instructions indicating the true vipashyana, the nonconceptual wakefulness or nondualistic awareness. This recognition is then combined with the shamatha practice.

When practicing, in the beginning, one will experience many strong thoughts, either happy, so that one laughs aloud, or perhaps sad, so that one feels like crying. But thoughts will slowly diminish. Even the unnoticed thoughts, those which come one after the other, one thought occupying the mind and being forgotten when the next appears, will slowly diminish. One will reach a state in which emptiness and wakefulness are inseparable, a free, open, and tranquil state.

At this time, thought occurrence is not regular. Sometimes thoughts erupt strongly and then vanish; sometimes there is a small eruption, but the mind is mostly still. Although thoughts and emotions occasionally occur, the combined practices of shamatha and viphashana, practiced according to one's ability, enables one, despite thoughts, to quickly return to stillness and remain totally serene and still.

In this context, 'stillness' does not exactly refer to the correct shamatha. It is more 'stillness devoid of clarity,' devoid of wakefulness. For a full understanding, however, these teachings must accompany one's own personal practice so that one's own experience corresponds to what is being taught. Right now, we haven't the time.

> Following this, while sustaining the practice,
> There occurs a vividly clear and awake openness.
> This is like the example of a lake being unharmed by waves,
> Because one is not harmed by even the slightest occurrence of thought.
> Sometimes it happens in this way, sometimes not.
> Sometimes it feels difficult to meditate or even to keep your posture.
> At times these experiences happen even without meditating.

A lake unavoidably has waves, but the wave neither harms the lake water nor does it improve the lake. Likewise, with stability in nonconceptual wakefulness, one is not harmed by thoughts and need not try to avoid their occurrence. One cannot avoid them in any event, because thoughts do not simply cease. But, as the Mahamudra tradition teaches, "Within thought, I discovered nonthought." Although a thought is not something good, the essence of thought, its' nature, is the naked dharmakaya, the ordinary mind, Mahamudra, or self-existing wakefulness, whatever we want to call it. In this way, it is said, "The more thoughts, the more wakefulness." Thought occurrence causes no harm to wakefulness.

The occurrence and the freeing of a thought sometimes take place simultaneously, when one recognizes the essence of thought as it is occurring. The thought arises, is freed, arises, is freed, and so forth. Sometimes it happens this way, sometimes not.

Sometimes, we intend to practice and think, "Now I will let my body, speech, and mind rest in naturalness. I'll just rest in the state of Mahamudra," but keeping the meditation posture and the meditation itself feels extremely difficult. No matter what one tries, one doesn't remain in naturalness.

Sometimes, one may resolve to practice intensively in a secluded situation, even try to keep a sense of discipline by setting aside certain times of the day for practice. Then one sits down in a meditation posture and thinks, "Now I'll practice Mahamudra!" But still it doesn't happen at all; rather one becomes disturbed, unable to meditate. On the other hand, the state of wakefulness may spontaneously occur as one is going through the usual activities of everyday life. This won't happen without some previous experience of practice, but it can sometimes occur spontaneously without any preparation.

The *ground wisdom* or basic wakefulness is very tricky. If we try to cultivate it, it doesn't occur. But without trying, it suddenly arises. At this time, one should rely on the oral instructions of a teacher.

If we compare a chronically ill person who has experienced many different illnesses and consumed many different medicines over a long period of time with an inexperienced doctor, we might find that although the doctor has completed his studies and can talk for hours and hours about diseases and medicines, the sickly person will, in fact, have more expertise in administering medications and diagnosing other patients. Likewise, receiving instructions from an experienced meditator, a teacher who has practiced a lot, is much more effective than receiving teachings from one who has merely studied a lot.

> Following this, your body and mind remain in total blissfulness,
> Unharmed by ordinary actions like walking and sitting.
> The inspiration for desiring to practice is then found.

After a long period of practice, it may happen that during the session our body and mind remain totally blissful. The body will feel relaxed and smooth, and the mind very open, free, and tranquil, as though we have had some very good, smooth liquor. We're not totally intoxicated, but have had just exactly the right amount, so we feel a little blissed out, a little exhilarated, and very tranquil. We feel we don't hold onto anything very tightly, but neither are we stupidly drunk. We may also find that whatever ordinary actions we perform, like walking, sitting, talking, or working, our practice is undisturbed. We can carry on the practice continuously.

This state of not clinging so much, not grasping so much, feeling elated and in a delightful frame of mind is good, but not if we fixate on it, holding onto it as something special. It indicates a certain level of realization, of profound experience, but one should not cling to it. Yet, at that point one truly starts to feel some eagerness for practice. Before that, practice had been just hoping for, or expecting to, attain something. One always sits down to meditate with the feeling that it will have some effect or cause some change in oneself. At this point, some chance of attainment truly exists. At the same time, there is also the danger of becoming attached to this sense of delight and freedom. Pride can easily develop as well.

> Sometimes it happens that you recognize dreams.
> Thinking, "My experience and realization are excellent!"
> Feeling fascinated and attached, you fixate tightly on it.
> At that time, don't cling, but look into the essence.

Sometimes, during dreams, we recognize that we are dreaming and sleep in a very free and blissful, smooth state.

After having practiced for some time, we reach a state in which we no longer face many problems or troubles during the day and, whether sitting or walking around, practice occurs spontaneously. Our minds feel free and easy. We no longer experience paranoia or claustrophobia, no matter what the situation. Both day and night, the mind remains in a very open state. We might even begin to congratulate ourselves, thinking, "How nice! I've finally made it!" and to fixate on this state. But in fact, the key point here is not to become attached, not to cling to these feelings.

One may be tempted to think, "My experience and realization is excellent!" Experience and realization are keywords, but, as the teachings say, "Experience is like mist, it fades and disappears. Realization is unchanging like the sky." But for a beginner, experience and realization are mixed together. One cannot be sure which is which.

Three kinds of *temporary experience* are usually described: bliss, clarity, and nonthought. The experience of nonthought is the feeling that everything has disappeared — the earth, its mountains, one's house, body, and so on. One feels that nothing remains. Yet, one holds on with the thought, "I am experiencing this emptiness," and one likes it. The experience of clarity can be so intense that even with closed eyes, one can still see unimpededly.

Such experiences are always temporary and always include some sense of attachment, with the thought, "I am experiencing this." Realization, however, is unchanging. Thus, the teaching here is "Don't be fascinated, don't hold on to it, don't be attached, don't fixate." At the time of the experience, don't cling, but look into the essence. 'Look' doesn't imply something to look at or a person who looks, but means to simply rest in the unity of awareness and emptiness, without a watcher, and without something watched.

Mahamudra has various distinctions known as the Mahamudra of bliss and emptiness, the Mahamudra of clarity and emptiness, and the Mahamudra of awareness and emptiness. These distinctions come from whichever aspect is emphasized in the experience, whether bliss, awareness, or clarity predominates. The teachings say that the Madhyamika experience is like utter emptiness, the Mahamudra experience like pure bliss, the Dzogchen experience like naked awareness. These are the terms mostly emphasized.

Based upon shamatha practice one is able to attain what are traditionally called higher cognitions or *superknowledges*. One of these, called the divine eye, means that, combining the practice of shamatha with the experience of strong clarity, one can see unimpededly, with closed eyes, both one's surrounding environment and that which is far away. Other common siddhis can also be attained. For example, the siddhi called 'swift feet' whereby, controlling the prana, one can cover great distances in a very short time. Another is the siddhi called invisibility.

At the outset, people in Tibet took these common siddhis very seriously. If, for instance, someone could fly or leave footprints in stone, people thought him a great master and felt strong devotion. Someone who didn't display these abilities was assumed to be not very advanced. Tibetans had great interest in common siddhis at first, thinking, "This is really something very special. We must attain these powers!" Later on, qualified masters came to Tibet, gave further teachings, and advised that, "Such accomplishments are just for fooling yourselves and are not the ultimate attainment that results not from shamatha alone, but manifests when combined with vipashyana practice." People then began to emphasize vipashyana more in their practice.

Paltrül Rinpoche said, "What's so amazing about flying in the sky or drilling yourself down into the ground? If you truly generate bodhichitta, that is the most precious accomplishment." Paltrül Rinpoche, an extremely learned and accomplished master, would sometimes just lie around the whole day. In the general Dharma teachings, this is a sign of laziness that brings no experience in practice. In his time, Paltrül was said to be even more learned than Jamgön Kongtrül and Jamyang Khyentse, with whom he had studied when they were all young.

Both Jamgön Kongtrül and Jamyang Khyentse were from rich families and had money and good food, while Paltrül Rinpoche came from a poor family and had little to eat. When they studied together, the others shared their food with him. After their daily teachings, Jamgön Kongtrül and Jamyang Khyentse studied very hard to keep up, but Paltrül would just pull his shawl over his head and lie down. Eventually, the other two said, "What's going on? You're just eating our food and then going to sleep. What does eating and sleeping have to do with studying?"

Paltrül replied, "Isn't it just enough to repeat what the *Khenpo* has taught?" They answered, "Of course, if you can do that, but needn't you study first?" Paltrül said, "No, no. I just do what I feel like doing." One day, Paltrül was examined in class and, because of his extreme intelligence, he was able to repeat, word for word, the Khenpo's exact teachings, like a replica made from a mold. Later in life, all three were extremely famous and great masters, but with quite different lifestyles. However, despite their great respect for one another, they always criticized each other. They had strong faith, but the other two often called Paltrül Rinpoche, 'Crazy Paltrül.'

Paltrül Rinpoche was a very simple yogi without attachment to material things. As a great master, people lined up to meet him and offered all kinds of precious things, but he simply threw the offerings away, never keeping any of them.

After a while, his disciples started to say, "Rinpoche, what a shame! You should use these things for something virtuous." Rinpoche thought, "Okay," and invited all the local beggars to come see him. He fed them and they sat and carved all the stones in the area with mantras and *dharanis* from the sutras. Finally, after they had made a huge heap of mani stones, like a small hill, Paltrül Rinpoche sent a message inviting Jamyang Khyentse to come and consecrate the carved stones. Khyentse Rinpoche could not come because of the distance and his advanced age, so he promised to consecrate them from a distance. He sent a small package of saffron-colored barley, which he said to toss on the pile on a particular date.

When the day came, everyone was ready for the consecration. Khyentse Rinpoche hadn't arrived, but still he would pray from afar. Incense was lit and Paltrül Rinpoche said, "He's not here, but old Khyentse does some unusual things once in a while, so watch out!" They performed the consecration ceremony and when they finished, a big cloud came overhead. Just over the mani stones, grains of barley suddenly rained down. When compared with the small handful of barley Khyentse Rinpoche had sent before, it was exactly the same saffron-colored grain. In eastern Tibet, this story is very wellknown and many people still have keepsakes of this barley. My father, Tulku Urgyen, has a few grains.

Another story about these three great masters concerns the extremely learned Khenpo Tashi Özer, who also became a great accomplished master. The *Rain of Wisdom* includes some of his songs. Nonsectarian, he took teachings from many masters of different schools and so also received teachings from these three.

Tashi Özer was at first a very strict monk, studying with Jamgön Kongtrül, wearing the yellow shawl, carrying the begging bowl and staff, and keeping the discipline very carefully. Kongtrül Rinpoche ordered him to behave this way. Later on, however, he went to study with Paltrül Rinpoche and Paltrül asked him, "What's the use of all of these elaborations?"

At that time, the tradition in Tibet was to approach a master and say, "Please give me food, clothing, and teachings." Tashi Özer went to Paltrül Rinpoche in this prescribed manner but couldn't see him for a few days. Their meeting was postponed several times, but finally he came before Rinpoche, and asked, "Please give me food, clothing, and teachings." Rinpoche said, "Come back later." When he returned, he found food, an article of clothing, and a book. Rinpoche said, "Okay. Here you are. Good-by." But Tashi Özer begged for a long time and was finally allowed to stay. He received quite a few teachings from Paltrül Rinpoche.

Since Paltrül Rinpoche was so simple, with no elaborations, the other two masters criticized him and said, "He's a little too simple. If he could just do something useful instead of being a crazy simpleton!" Anyway, Tashi Özer stayed with him and became a simple yogi as well, just wearing old rags and living on whatever happened along.

Sometime later, Tashi Özer went to study with Jamyang Khyentse. When he first arrived, he wasn't allowed in to see Rinpoche, but was told to rest for a few days after his long journey. He was put off for three days, but eventually he was called into the room with Rinpoche.

When he entered the room, Jamyang Khyentse was seated on a low seat beside a high throne laid out with brocades and a hat. Rinpoche held a big stick in his hand. He told Tashi Özer, "Alright, put on these important robes and get up there on the throne. Why have you been running around like a stupid beggar? You want to be a mad disciple of Crazy Paltrül or what? You're now going to be the head of a big monastery and give teachings to many people. If you don't become an excellent expounder of the teachings immediately, I'm going to beat you up with this stick!" From then on, Tashi Özer was forced to give up his wild yogi behavior.

Returning to the instructions on meditation, having recognized the natural state, the emptiness endowed with the supreme of all aspects, the basic wakefulness or ground wisdom within oneself, then, when practicing, one must be totally free from all clinging, all fixation, and all grasping whatsoever, especially grasping toward the temporary experiences. Be totally free from elation when an experience occurs and depression when it doesn't. Do not try to accept or reject, produce or suppress, these experiences in any way at all. When free from clinging or attachment, this is the correct view.

Attachment or clinging to anything is generally taught to be bad, especially during practice. When remaining in the composure of the wakefulness of inseparable emptiness and clarity, if one clings to the view, thinking it excellent, and fixates on that, then particularly at this point, clinging becomes a defect.

The general system of these teachings includes the 'sixfold taking as the path.' This involves such practices as taking disturbing emotions as path, taking obstacles as path, taking negative forces as path, and so forth. We won't get into the details of all six variations here, but you should know how to deal with whatever takes place in your experience, be it attachment, aggression, or strong dullness. Sometimes the mind is agonized by craving after some external object, so that one becomes completely disturbed, yearning single-pointedly for the object of desire and becoming totally consumed by it. Or one can be totally engulfed in anger towards someone or something, or have an intense feeling of stupidity or dullness, like wearing a heavy iron mask, not feeling or noticing much, being obscured.

Many other experiences, both pleasant and unpleasant, can occur, but instead of seeking a specific antidote for each, there is a method called 'knowing one frees all,' a simple technique to liberate us from all these different states.

I shall now give a summary of some teachings on Mahamudra which the great master Milarepa taught to Gampopa: the natural state of mind, the ultimate truth, cannot be accurately described through words, nor truly indicated by examples, nor even taken as an object of thought. Milarepa said, "When explaining the nature of mind, even the Buddha's tongue is mute."

To rephrase Milarepa's teachings on the natural state, this mind essence has known neither existence nor nonexistence. It has never fallen into any category. It is a totally unbiased state that has never improved or deteriorated, and has never changed or been modified in any way whatsoever. That describes the ground wisdom in its basic state. How are we to put it into practice as the path? This is done without cultivating, and also without forgetting; without hope and without fear; without trying to produce or trying to suppress anything. At the time of fruition, like the sun in a cloudless sky, totally beyond anything to be accepted or rejected, it is the exhaustion of phenomena beyond concepts.

Milarepa further said, "In short, Mahamudra has three points: recognizing the natural state, resolving how it is, and training in 'thatness' as path."

Resolving the natural state refers to becoming clear about our basic wakefulness, ground Mahamudra. One will then naturally know how to put 'how it is' into practice. Speaking first about ground wisdom, or what in general terms we call buddha nature, what is it like in its basic state? It is without causes and conditions, without path, without fruition, without techniques, and without means. That's actually how it is in its basic state.

To recognize your essence, ground Mahamudra, it should be pointed out by a qualified master. It needs be recognized. After recognizing this natural state of mind, train, perfect the training, and finally attain stability. It was previously taught that ground Mahamudra has no cause, no circumstance, no technique, no path, and no fruition. Despite this truth, Milarepa went on to say, that although Mahamudra is without cause, strong devotion to one's root teacher will cause the realization of Mahamudra. Although Mahamudra is without circumstance, a qualified master is the influential circumstance for realizing Mahamudra because it is through devotion combined with the master's oral instructions that you can recognize the natural state of mind, ground Mahamudra. Therefore, one must rely on a teacher. Realization doesn't happen by itself.

Although Mahamudra is beyond a means, *nonfabrication* is the technique of Mahamudra. Nonfabrication means not trying to alter, change, correct, or fabricate anything; simply letting it remain as it is. Although Mahamudra has no path, *nondistraction* is the Mahamudra path; not forgetting and not letting oneself get carried away. Again, undistracted mind is the path of Mahamudra.

The general system of Mahayana involves many paths and stages, such as the path of accumulation, the path of joining, the path of seeing, the path of cultivation, and the path of no-learning. There are also the stages of the ten bodhisattva bhumis and various other categories, but Mahamudra makes no distinction as to different paths or levels.

The external Mahamudra system talks about the twelve Mahamudra levels of the four yogas, dividing the four yogas into three each, but Mahamudra itself remains beyond path. Undistracted mind is taught to be the path of Mahamudra. Although Mahamudra is beyond any fruition, the liberation of concepts into dharmata is the fruition of Mahamudra.

Milarepa's third point is training in thatness as path. In short, it means 'not parting from the view of Mahamudra.' His instruction teaches how to practice Mahamudra correctly with no mistakes or sidetracks. You should take this to heart and be very clear about it. You might otherwise think, "I understand Mahamudra perfectly. My practice is flawless! I understand the state of emptiness and wakefulness as being inseparable." This may be so, but if you also retain some attachment, then the fascination with, and clinging to your experiences become the cause for rebirth in the samsaric realm of the gods of desire.

> The expression of bliss and the essence of emptiness
> Will then dawn as the Mahamudra of indivisible bliss and emptiness.
> If you become attached and cling, it is the cause of rebirth as a god in the Realms of Desire.

> As the text states, being attached to a sense of bliss causes rebirth as a god in the Realms of Desire.

Some people regard thoughts as being enemies,
And believe that meditation is remaining without thought.
This is called the view of the Chinese Hashangs.
Simply remaining totally still, with no thoughts whatsoever,
Is but a resemblance of 'cessation' and the cause for rebirth as an animal.

One can go wrong in other ways too. Although the natural state means simply remaining in the unity of cognizance and emptiness, we might get certain ideas and make some small adjustments, correcting it a little bit. Trying to be free from thoughts, considering thoughts as enemies which disturb our meditation, is called the *Hashang view,* a specific viewpoint of trying to remain totally free from thoughts, believing that to be the ultimate. In fact, it is a mere semblance of cessation and the cause for being reborn as an animal.

> Having gathered consciousness within the heart center,
> To remain without allowing anything to be thought of whatsoever,
> Is called 'cessation' and is the path of the shravakas.
> Therefore, do not deliberately try to block thought activity.
> Also, do not deliberately try to think, but watch the essence.
> By looking, it is seen to have no substance whatsoever.
> That is the time of seeing the real emptiness.
> Watch, without seeing a 'thing,' in the state of non-seeing.

Shravaka training, through the strong practice of shamatha, cultivates a state called cessation. This state is free from samsara, and the practitioner remains stuck there a very long period of time. While not an erroneous path, it delays the complete enlightenment of buddhahood and is therefore a hindrance. In this state, it is figuratively said that the consciousnesses are gathered within the heart center, that is, one's *six sense cognitions* are withdrawn, brought to a total halt, in a state of cessation. One simply rests in this state for a tremendously long period of time.

Practitioners can go astray in many ways. Through attachment, one is reborn in the Desire Realm; clinging to the Hashang view leads one to rebirth as an animal. Following the shravaka path extendedly also delays complete enlightenment for a very long time.

One should not deliberately try to block thought activity, but neither should one deliberately try to think. Just watch the essence. By looking into the essence, its total lack of substance is perceived. That is seeing the real emptiness. "Watch without seeing a thing, in the state of non-seeing." This was the teaching of Lingje Repa, the great Drukpa Kagyü master, when he said, "My guru said 'meditate!' but now meditator and meditation object have vanished. My sessions and breaks have fallen apart. What should I do now?"

The text here contains various indications of possible ways of going astray and also information about the remedies, using the proper modes of application as a means of correcting the errors. One relies on a teacher to avoid such sidetracks.

A traditional teaching says that the master firstly should be a human being. Next, your teacher can be a book. Finally, the master should be one's own mind. In order to have a book as a master, you must first have received personal instructions on how to practice according to the text from a truly qualified living master. Having heard these instructions, since staying continually near to a great teacher may not always be possible, you should take the oral instructions to heart and practice in solitude, using the text as a guideline. As you gradually become more experienced, you can follow along with the text trying to correct your own mistakes. Finally, the master will be your own mind, the naked awareness itself.

> Sometimes, although you watch, it is unclear and hazy.
> Thought activity is jumpy and disturbed and you become frustrated.
> This is not something to be too upset about.
> Sometimes, you will have doubt arising as conceptual thoughts.
> These are only 'unpleasant experiences' and they are nothing bad.
> Relax your body and mind and direct your gaze into space.
> Look while letting your mind mingle with the clear blue sky;

> Your mind will be clarified and a wakeful emptiness will dawn.

Mahamudra recognizes nothing to watch or see, no seer, and no act of seeing. Yet, we have to call it something. Therefore, we speak of 'looking into' or 'sustaining' the essence, meaning remaining in the state without a watcher or anything being watched.

Sometimes, one may feel hazy and unclear, as though shrouded in mist or obscured. Thought activity is sometimes very jumpy and restless; one feels disturbed, frustrated, and so on. Sometimes doubts arise as conceptual thoughts. Don't become too upset by this. These are all merely what are called unpleasant experiences, mere temporary experiences and not something bad. One deals with them by relaxing the body and mind and directing the gaze into space. Straighten the body and gaze openly and freely into a clear blue sky, letting the mind mingle freely with space. Through this, mind will be clarified. Here, 'clarified' indicates the dispelling of the feeling of being obscured. The essence itself is beyond being clear or unclear, yet its nature is clarity. Practicing like this, wakeful emptiness will dawn.

> At times, clarity, awareness, and emptiness are laid utterly naked
> And you feel proud thinking, "This is high realization!"
> You may feel a conviction that no one will be able to change your mind.
> At that time, if you let certainty be governed by pride,
> That is the cause for rebirth among the gods in the Realms of Form.
> When you look into the essence of this clarity, it is emptiness,
> And will dawn as Mahamudra, the unity of clarity and emptiness.

Although certainty is important, it becomes a great obstacle if it falls under the power of pride and that itself can cause rebirth among the gods in the Realms of Form. Ground Mahamudra is beyond errors or sidetracks, but one can make mistakes when putting it into practice, when training on the path. The gross negative emotions are easy to identify, but the more subtle ones, like pride, are very difficult to detect. One can easily go wrong in this way.

> Sometimes, your body, mind, and everything becomes voidness.
> Perceiving everything as being empty, you will start to use high Dharma words.
> You might think that just as the empty sky can not be tainted by anything whatsoever,
> There is no reason for good and evil deeds to bring benefit or harm.
>
> If you keep a wild life-style and do not practice what is virtuous,
> This nihilistic view of emptiness is the cause of falling to the lower realms.
> It is called the 'perverted view regarding emptiness.'
> Although you may perceive everything to be empty in that way,
> Maintain the essence and exert yourself in accepting and rejecting that which concerns cause and effect.

Sometimes, one's mind and body, everything, becomes totally void and it feels as though the dwelling place, the meditator's state of mind, and everything else has become like pure space. Experiencing this, one may start to use high Dharma words, thinking, "How can good or evil deeds exist? How can past or future lives exist? There is no identity, no one who can take rebirth. Good and evil deeds cannot stick anywhere. It is like the sky. If I throw good cake into the air, the sky will not become happy; if I toss shit or urine into the air, it won't feel depressed. Likewise, in my state of realization that is totally beyond concepts, there are no evil or good deeds. I'm totally beyond these things!"

If one begins to talk like this, using high Dharma language, one may believe that one is just like the empty sky that cannot be tainted by anything. Not believing that good or evil deeds can bring benefit or harm, one might adopt a very coarse and wild lifestyle, acting however one likes. This nihilistic view of emptiness is a perverted view and a cause of falling directly into the lower realms.

Instead of considering that everything is empty, and one can do whatever one wants, one should sustain the essence, and at the same time engage in positive actions and reject negative ones in the appropriate way concerning cause and effect. Padmasambhava said, "Although one's view may be as high as the sky, one's conduct should be as fine as barley flour." Despite one's high view, one doesn't disregard cause and effect.

We usually mention three steps: theory, experience, and realization, and say, "Theory is like a patch on cloth which will wear out and fall off; experience, like mist, will vanish; but realization is unchanging like space."

Theoretical understanding is something we acquire through attending seminars and studying texts. We get some idea about the teachings, but not a stable understanding. It can be improved or worsened. If we examine our notes again, for example, our understanding of what was taught will improve steadily.

> All these stages of experience,
> Including those which stay for a long time as well as the
>   short ones that quickly vanish,
> Never remain the same, like the changing of the weather.

Different kinds of experience, like bliss, clarity, and nonthought, may occur and may last for long or short periods of time. But they are nevertheless transitory and never last forever; they fluctuate like the weather.

> After this, conceptual thoughts may still not diminish,
> But even many thoughts will not cause any harm to your meditation.
> Instead, like rain falling on a lake, they will dawn as practice.

Unless you cling to them, experiences can't harm you. With clinging, experiences can become a great defect. After practicing for a while, conceptual thinking, thought activity, may not disappear. Sometimes thoughts rush by, sometimes no thoughts occur, but this doesn't matter; the number of thoughts doesn't matter. The important thing is to recognize the essence within the thought. In this way, you will neither be harmed by many thoughts nor benefited by few thoughts. Thoughts will be like rain falling on a lake. Just as the raindrops never harm the lake, thought will dawn as meditation practice.

> After this, you will not need to alternate between development and completion;
> While practicing, never being apart from the 'seal' of emptiness,
> Visualize your body in the form of the yidam, the Great Compassionate One,
> Like a rainbow manifesting in space.
> Recite the six syllables so that only your shirt collar can hear them.

Vajrayana includes both development and completion stages. Generally, we understand the development stage to mean visualizing a deity, reciting a mantra, resting in composure, applying the different concentrations and finally, practicing the stages of *dissolution and emergence,* during which one applies the view of Mahamudra and Dzogchen. In this text, however, both the development and completion stages are condensed into a single, very simple practice. One simply visualizes oneself in the form of the deity, but without leaving the seal of emptiness, meaning the view of Mahamudra and Dzogchen. In short, one practices the development stage without separating it from the completion stage.

Throughout the practice, one maintains the view of the indivisibility of emptiness and compassion. As the meditation, one visualizes oneself in the form of the yidam, whichever it may be, and one recites the mantra. In this case, the yidam is Avalokiteshvara, the Great Compassionate One, and the mantra is the Six Syllable mantra.

This visualization is not of something substantial or concrete, like visualizing a physical body, but the visualized forms should be as transparent as a rainbow appearing in the sky. The recitation needn't be shouted but should be loud enough for one's shirt collar or the people in the immediate vicinity to hear.

> Not to stray from these three is the 'easy way to practice.'
> When, at the time of meditating, you arrive in the practice
> Without any hardship or difficulty, by the mere recollection of it,
> That is called 'the ease of sustaining one's practice.'

These three: the view, visualization, and recitation should always be combined. This is the simple way to practice. At this point your state of practice is such that despite occasional distraction you will still, by the mere recollection of the practice, immediately arrive again in the natural mind, the indivisibility of wakefulness and emptiness. No hardship or difficulty is involved here. Hence, it is called the 'ease of sustaining one's practice.'

> Following this, when looking at the earth, the greenery, the mountains, rocks, and so forth,
> Although everything is seen distinctly,
> It is just like mist and is perceived to be empty in essence.
> Your mind and space mingle into inseparable oneness,

> And you might think that your mind reaches as far as
>   space itself.
>
> You may think, "Everything is mind! Mind is devoid of
>   substance!
> It is emptiness that is nothing whatsoever!
> It has no existence. It hasn't even an atom of materiality!
> It is not nonexistence, since manifold things are manifest!
> It is something which is neither existent nor nonexistent!"

In this situation, one may think, "Mind has no substance or concreteness. It is complete emptiness, nothing at all. Lacking existence, it hasn't even an atom of materiality. Yet, since many things manifest, it is not nonexistent. This is because, while its essence is empty, its nature is luminosity or cognizance. It is something with neither existence nor nonexistence." The view itself should be free from any fixation. As long as one holds to the thought, "This is such and such!" or "This is not such and such!" the view is impaired by partiality. The great master Mipham Rinpoche said, "Being primordially pure of all constructs, the extreme of existence has been discarded. As the manifestation of awareness is spontaneously present, it is free from the extreme of nonexistence."

> If you become fettered by the tight grip of these thoughts,
> You will stray into the four perception-spheres of the
>   Formless Realms.
> This is called 'the conviction of open-ended fixation.'

These various so-called 'understandings' or 'realizations' are just subtle concepts, subtle mental fabrications. They occur through having practiced shamatha intensely and having become attached to the resulting experiences, as well as clinging to ideas such as "This is how it is!" One who retains this slight attachment or clinging and becomes fettered by the tight grip of these thoughts and concepts, will fall into what are called the *four perception-spheres of the Formless Realms*. Compared to the lower realms, the higher realms are quite pleasant, but still they are not liberation. One is still circling within the samsaric realms and can still fall into the hells. Since these experiences are not liberation, you should not endanger yourself by clinging to them.

As long as you hold on to a thought, such as "Mind is existent!" "Mind is nonexistent!" "Mind is both existent and nonexistent!" or "Mind is neither existent nor nonexistent," you are still just clinging to a concept, to yet another fixation.

> Without fixating, look naturally into the essence of whatever occurs.
> The watcher and the watched will then mingle into one,
> Without any fixation concerning 'looking' and 'meditating.'

This practice of naturally 'looking' means remaining in the natural state. In the beginning, there seems to be a 'meditator' and something 'meditated upon,' but as practice progresses, watcher and watched mingle into oneness, as in the quote by Lingje Repa mentioned earlier.

Mahamudra teachings refer to this as the *fourth time of great equality*. What we call time is a mere mental fabrication. To reach beyond the mental construct of the three times of past, present, and future is what is meant by the fourth time of great equality.

> Like an ordinary person who is free from thoughts of this and that,
> There will come a time when, besides just remaining totally ordinary,
> All aims and deeds whatsoever will have been exhausted.
> You will even be free from the previous experiences of bliss, clarity, and nonthought.
> Someone of little learning will think "My meditation is lost!"

> Trying to get back to your former 'state', it doesn't happen and you despair.
> If you are extremely presumptuous, you might think that you have reached the 'stage of nonmeditation.'
> But, instead, this is simply called 'seeing the essence.'
> It is the realization of naked, ordinary mind.

Ground Mahamudra is completely unspoiled by the confusion of sentient beings and not at all improved upon by attaining realization. It can't be cultivated or manufactured by any means whatsoever, nor can it be an object of thought, such as a reference point. It can never be changed in the least. After sufficient practice, you will naturally reach a point of becoming just like an ordinary person. You will feel like an ordinary person, without any particular thought of this or that. You will not feel like before, when you experienced many special things happening, such as the experience of nonthought, or of strong bliss, and smoothness, or clarity. At that time, you felt, "For sure, now I have some supercognitions." All those experiences will vanish however, and a person of little learning may think, "Oh no! My meditation is lost. Nothing is happening. I'm just like an ordinary person."

At this point, since all the different kinds of former states, the different meditation experiences, have vanished, you might feel a sense of loss and try to reproduce these experiences. If they don't occur, then you will become depressed and despair, thinking, "Everything is lost!" This results from having little learning. Someone who is somewhat learned and conceited may think, "Now I have reached the dharmakaya throne of nonmeditation!" But actually, it's not the state of nonmeditation yet, but only what is called seeing the essence, undistortedly, without modification or change. It is simply 'seeing the essence of mind;' not the full attainment of the state of nonmeditation, but the realization of ordinary mind. This is only the first step of recognizing your essence. You will still have to perfect the training and attain stability. You must continue the state of recognition.

> Resolve all things to be your own mind;
> That mind is emptiness beyond expression, thought, or description.
> Although there is nothing to do besides resting naturally in nonfabrication,
> When you sometimes become distracted,
> You fail to recognize your essence and stray into the state of ordinary confusion.
>
> Recognize, through mindfulness and remorse, the thought, "I was distracted!"
> Because as long as you do not remain mindful, you are just an ordinary person.
> But by merely keeping mindfulness, you arrive again at the practice.
> At this time, remind yourself again and again through mindfulness.

Resolve all your experiences to be your own mind and that mind is emptiness beyond thought and description. Besides resting naturally in meditation, there is nothing else to do. However, you may sometimes become distracted, fail to recognize your essence, and stray into the state of ordinary confusion. Be mindful and recognize that you were distracted. When you fail to maintain mindfulness, you are merely an ordinary person. 'Ordinary person' here means an ordinary confused person, not someone with ordinary mind.

Mindfulness makes the crucial difference. Simply by keeping mindful, the practice will again occur. Remind yourself repeatedly through such presence of mind. This is extremely important! The third Karmapa, Rangjung Dorje, remarked, "Recognizing mind essence is not amazing, not very special. The important thing is to maintain it continuously."

After recognizing the view of Mahamudra, the natural state of indivisible wakefulness and emptiness, you must, through practice, enhance this understanding and gain stability in the view.

According to Mahamudra, one's realization of the view is enhanced through the meditation on the Six Yogas; according to Dzogchen, through the practice of Trekchö. One can also go to various frightening places, like *charnel grounds,* and practice *Chö,* offering one's body to the demons and spirits. Chö is said to greatly improve one's view and meditation practice.

> By keeping the gaze again and again, clarity increases.
> Sometimes practice one-pointedly in seclusion,
> And sometimes mingle practice with daily life.
> At this point, when you read the scriptures
> And all the teachings of the siddhas of India and Tibet,
> They will be in harmony with your mind.

Sometimes, by shifting the gaze and changing the body's position one can improve the practice. If you feel dull, you should raise your gaze and look into the sky. Clarity will then increase. On the other hand, if you feel agitated, lower the gaze. At all times, mingle practice with daily life activities. While eating, talking, or walking, maintain the practice. When lying down, try as much as possible to keep the mindfulness of practice, even while falling asleep. From time to time, to practice in an isolated situation where the body is secluded, the speech silent, and the mind free of worldly distractions is also important. Practice will definitely improve in such situations.

At this point, having reached some stability in practice, you will discover something suited to your mind within all the scriptures that you read, within all the different teachings of the accomplished masters from India and Tibet. They will all be beneficial in some way. The teachings all talk about either the basic nature of mind or how to perfect the training of its realization. They will all seem very appropriate and meaningful.

> If your diligence is great, you will repeatedly recognize dreams.
> If your exertion is slack, the number of recognitions will diminish.

Exertion is very important, but not in a rigid way. Diligence or exertion should be like the steady flow of a river. Practitioners should not occasionally whip themselves and push very hard and, at other times, give up all together. Diligence means being very constant and regular.

Speaking of Mahamudra, His Holiness Karmapa and other great masters have said, "Throughout the whole day, I never stray from the view. Even after falling asleep, during what for ordinary people is called the 'habitual pattern of dreaming,' I never lose the view. I can maintain the practice continually, although, when falling asleep there is a brief instance where it's a little difficult." So, one can keep the practice continuously.

>Following this, all of the external world and its beings,
>Though their appearances are individually distinct and clear,
>In their essence, just as ice melts and becomes water,
>They will all mingle inseparably with emptiness and mind.
>If you meditate, they are mind and if you don't meditate, they are also mind.
>You will then realize that mind is emptiness, without concrete existence since the beginning.
>This is the essential point of original emptiness without distinctions,
>Such as meditating or not meditating, being distracted or not distracted.

At this point, whether or not you meditate, everything is just mind. 'Mind' here refers to what is termed *rigpa*, nondualistic awareness. You will realize that mind is emptiness, primordially without concrete existence, the essential point of original emptiness. It is totally free from distinctions such as meditating or not and being distracted or not. Everything is only awareness.

>The minds of all the buddhas and the minds of the six classes of beings,

> Primordially are emptiness, inseparable in essence.
> This view, the meaning of the indivisibility of samsara and nirvana,
> Without being mere dry understanding
> From the study of books and the sayings of your masters,
> Will then dawn from within your being.
> When this has happened, don't consider yourself to be exalted
> Because of merely receiving the title 'realized person.'

The minds of all the buddhas of the ten directions, of all the bodhisattvas, and of the six classes of beings are primordially emptiness and identical in essence. Again, 'mind' refers here to awareness, the enlightened essence.

Without remaining mere dry understanding derived through the study of books and the sayings of masters, this view, the indivisibility of samsara and nirvana, will then dawn from within your being. You will have attained a true experience and understanding, not merely another theory. 'Theory' is like patchwork; after wearing it for a while it falls off.

In the beginning, however, after having acquired an intellectual understanding, one gets some taste of what is being talked about when putting it into practice. In this context, the full taste of the meaning is what we call experience. One then has not just an idea about what the teachings are, but will have, from within, actually attained some experience.

Mahamudra includes both what is termed the *path of means*, the six doctrines of Naropa, and the *path of liberation*, the view itself. Here we are discussing the view.

Dzogchen also has two aspects: Trekchö or cutting through and Tögal or direct crossing. Here we are teaching the Trekchö view of primordial purity.

One needs, first of all, to be introduced to the view. Having recognized it through the master's direct oral instructions, one needs to maintain the continuity, to sustain the essence. Simply recognizing the view once will not suffice. One must maintain that recognition continuously without falling into any of the errors or resemblances mentioned earlier in the text. The different possible sidetracks cause one to stray into the higher realms of samsara, such as the Realms of Form and the Formless Realms of the four infinite perception-spheres. Hence, one should guard against falling into these errors. Being too focused on shamatha can also cause one to stray into the state termed 'cessation of the shravakas.'

When maintaining the view, it must be without any fixation, grasping, or speculation, and without any distortion or fabricated meditation whatsoever. Becoming adept in this, one may sometimes be called a 'high meditator' or 'realized person.'

> I am telling you this from my own experience, with a pure intention.
> If I have divulged any secrecy, I confess to the yidam and my masters.
> My own experience and learning does not reach further than this,
> So, if you want knowledge of it, look in all the scriptures.

This text contains many teachings that are usually kept secret. Dharma protectors, the guardians of the Dharma, such as the Mahakalas and Mahakalis and so forth, protect these teachings. Before these beings and before his own masters, Karma Chagmey confesses his own fault if any secrets have been wrongly divulged.

Vajrayana teachings are usually concealed within the seals of the *six limits* and the *four modes*. Having unraveled and 'bared to the core' some of these concealed teachings, if they happen to fall upon the ears of an unqualified person, Karma Chagmey says, "I am deeply sorry!"

The quintessence of all the vast teachings of the nine vehicles, the essence which is the union of Mahamudra and Dzogchen, is here explained very concisely and clearly. If one still desires more fine details and extensive teachings, one should study various other scriptures.

> As to the so-called 'sealing' by means of the dedication of 'threefold purity'
> Of all the conditioned and unconditioned virtue,—
> Just as the example of directing a horse with the reins,
> There may be many ways of explaining this threefold purity,
> But it will be sufficient just to dedicate the merit from within the state of this practice.

At the end of a practice, we should 'seal' the practice with the dedication of the *threefold purity*. The threefold purity means dedicating the merit without clinging to the concepts of the three spheres: subject, object, and action. Conditioned virtue means a practice not embraced by the threefold purity, and unconditioned virtue means a practice which is so embraced. This method of dedicating merit is a way of rendering all the merit inexhaustible. As when directing a horse with the reins: turning the reins to the south, the horse will move that way, turning them to the north, the horse will head north. Merit can be directed in the same way, and for this reason, dedication is important. Although this threefold purity can be expressed in many ways, simply dedicating the merit from within the state of the practice itself is sufficient. While remaining within the state of indivisible compassion and emptiness, dedicate the merit by embracing it with the nonconceptual threefold purity. This is enough.

> Make aspirations to be reborn in Sukhavati,
> Since it is easy to take rebirth there and has immense benefit.
> Cast away all doubt about whether or not you can be reborn there,
> Since the certainty of being reborn there is the aspiration of the Buddha.

We hear a lot of talk about pure realms like Sukhavati, the blissful realm of Buddha Amitabha, but in fact, the term pure realm refers to one's experience when it is purified. If your perception is pure, then this in itself is a pure realm. Realizing the ultimate nature as it is, there is no Sukhavati other than just that. In a conventional sense however, due to the aspirations and compassion of the buddhas, certain pure realms exist which are very conducive to practice. The Copper-Colored Mountain, Guru Rinpoche's pure land, and the Blissful Realm of Sukhavati are examples. Practitioners can aspire to take rebirth in one of these realms. If you haven't realized a very high view yet, but still have accumulated a lot of merit, you can then take rebirth in a pure land. After death, through one-pointed devotion and compassion, you can, according to your wish, be born in such a place.

Due to the aspirations of Buddha Amitabha, it's said to be easy to take rebirth in Sukhavati. There, one will abide in the presence of Buddha Amitabha and the bodhisattvas. By receiving the Mahayana teachings, and through practice, one will quickly progress along the five paths and ten bhumis, and will finally become inseparable from the state of enlightenment of Buddha Amitabha himself. It is not only easy to take birth there, but it is also of immense benefit: one cannot again fall back into samsaric realms. With deep-felt devotion and one-pointedness of mind, just like an arrow released from a bow, one can truly go to a pure realm at the time of death. For this very reason, you should again and again form the aspiration to be reborn in a pure realm.

At the moment of death, you must cast away all doubts about whether or not you can be reborn in Sukhavati; being reborn there depends totally upon one's faith, aspirations, and merit.

> When at some point, you realize that you are wandering through the bardo,
> It is certain that you will go to the pure realm.
> So, from this very moment, keep it acutely in mind
> And you will arrive there the very moment you remember it in the bardo.

Having taken birth, one must definitely die. There is no escape from that. After death one's spirit will roam through the bardo. At that time, the most vital point is to simply rest in the state of innate wakefulness as pointed out by one's teacher. Through this, one will surely appear in one of the pure realms of the three kayas. For that to happen, one must be very familiar with this practice during one's life either through resting in wakefulness or through imagining that one is right now in the bardo state thinking, "What should I do now?" One must make sure now that one will be able to remember the practice during the bardo state. This is very important.

QUESTIONS AND ANSWERS

STUDENT: Would you say something more about 'temporary experience?'

RINPOCHE: We call it a *nyam*. At present, our fixation on solid reality is only slightly better than that of an animal — not much more intelligent. As we progress in practice, we cling less and less. As a result of this, our qualities increase. So, also, may our obstacles. We can have many different things happen, both in dreams and in what are called nyam or temporary meditation experiences.

Another story is told about a student whose master said to come at a certain time of day to see him. The student went and found no one in the cave, but only a puddle of water. Thinking, "This is strange," he left. He ran into a Dharma friend and asked, "Where's the master?" His friend said, "He's in his cave," and the student replied, "But I just went there and didn't see anyone." "Well, maybe you were confused or something, but he is right there." The student returned and discovered that the cave now held a small pond. He thought, "This is certainly strange." He tossed a pebble into the water and left.

Again, he met his Dharma friend. They returned together to the cave and found the master sitting in meditation posture with the pebble in his hand. He said to them, "Maybe you didn't see me. I was practicing samadhi."

One can have many different experiences through meditation practice, but they are all just temporary. They come and go but are dangerous if clung to and considered to be real.

It is also said that on attaining realization, one can see all the beings that normal people don't see — invisible beings, spirits, and so forth.

STUDENT: When we're practicing these teachings and doubt arises, there seem to be three things we can do: resolve it intellectually, discuss it with our teacher, or simply consider the doubt to be more waves on the water. Can you talk about what the guidelines are?

RINPOCHE: Each of these three is important, but on different occasions. The best is to clear the doubts away yourself, but if you cannot, you should ask to have it clarified. The very best is to see the essence of the doubt as just another thought, which causes it to vanish. You then remain in the state where wakefulness and emptiness are inseparable, without trying to fabricate and without being at all distracted. After analyzing your doubts, if this happens, it is the very best method of resolution. It may not always work, and then consulting a qualified teacher is important. But, as practice improves gradually, and you become more adept in meditation, you will have many more opportunities to be your own teacher.

STUDENT: Rinpoche, what relationship, if any, is there between the 'preliminary practices' and this practice of Mahamudra?

RINPOCHE: Generally, the preliminaries are considered to be important as a foundation for the main practice, just as when building a house, one needs to begin with a strong foundation so that the house won't later collapse. Likewise, practicing the preliminaries provides a solid foundation for the main part of practice. In short, the preliminaries are said to facilitate one's realization.

One can also practice the preliminaries while embracing them with the main practice. When practicing the meditation and recitation of Vajrasattva, for instance, one visualizes and recites. This is the development stage, but at the conclusion comes a point where, if one has recognized it, one rests in the natural state of mind of Mahamudra. A beginner who hasn't recognized the natural state simply rests in ordinary shamatha.

The specific purposes of the four preliminaries are to purify obscurations, to gather the two accumulations, and especially through the *guru yoga,* to receive the blessings for quickly realizing the view of Mahamudra.

STUDENT: Why do people, from the very time they are born, have such strong desire for everything: "I want this, I want that." What's the reason for this?

RINPOCHE: This is the main cause for samsara. We first think 'I' and then 'my' or 'mine' and then 'I want that.' This causes all the trouble. Thinking 'I,' we will also think 'you.' When we think 'you' we think 'yours' and then the trouble begins. We think, "I want your things. You are different from me." The reason for thinking 'I,' even from the moment of birth, is ignorance. At the beginning, ego-clinging is neither very strong, nor very developed, but as the infant grows, this tendency becomes stronger and stronger. We even receive specific training in developing our egos so that when grown-up, we become full-fledged ego-people unable to be satisfied no matter how much we receive.

Towards one's peers, one feels jealousy and envy. One despises and scorns those who are lower than oneself and will criticize and make obstacles for those with higher positions. In short, an ego can find no satisfaction.

The ego or 'I' has no basis for its label. It merely seems to be, but without true existence. At birth, one has no name. This is given later on, so the name and the person are two different things. Subsequently, one becomes accustomed to the name and holds on to it, becoming angry when the name is wrongly accused. We hold on to the idea that we and our name are one and the same. If we really examine phenomena, we discover that the labels put onto things have no real basis. From the way things appear, or from the way in which they are grossly experienced, we assign a name onto a conglomeration of things. Flesh and bones for example, take on a specific name.

The trouble only occurs as long as we don't examine. When we begin to look carefully into what phenomena actually are, then everything becomes clearer.

STUDENT: The text, at one point, seems to criticize experiences and at another point says that experiences are a sign of realization. I can't seem to distinguish the two. Rinpoche, can you explain this?

RINPOCHE: The basic difference derives from whether or not one has the inclination to try to hold on, to fixate, or to modify the experience. That is the error, the sidetrack. Without holding on to or fixating on the experience, there is no mistake. The phrase 'ordinary mind' is very important. 'Ordinary' means not distorted, not corrected, and totally not fabricated; simply leaving it as it is.

STUDENT: Rinpoche, how does the vipashyana experience of looking for the meditator differ from *unsupported shamatha*?

RINPOCHE: First of all, shamatha, supported or unsupported, with or without focusing on an object, is still shamatha. It is still the mind dwelling on something, remaining calmly on an experience. Whether or not it has a support, it remains basically the same. Vipashyana, on the other hand, is looking into, "What is it that meditates?" Without receiving the pointing-out instruction one won't be able to reach any significant conclusion. Merely thinking, "Who is it that meditates?" is by itself, just another thought. It is nevertheless not pointless, because the moment of looking into "What is it that meditates?" can be of further use. For example, we first rest the mind on the HRIH in the heart center, and then we look into what is meditating. At that point everything simply disappears. That occasion, then, is important for pointing out the nature of mind. There's a big difference between 'looking into' and just simply 'remaining.'

STUDENT: When you spoke of path Mahamudra, you quoted Milarepa as saying that although Mahamudra is causeless, still, strong faith and devotion cause it to be recognized. Can Rinpoche explain how that works?

RINPOCHE: The Kagyü tradition in particular is called the transmission of devotion. Devotion, or strong yearning, is important because Mahamudra cannot be recognized through studies and intellectual learning alone. Regardless of one's diligence, one cannot recognize Mahamudra through meditation alone, nor through simply accumulating merit and purifying obscurations. How is Mahamudra recognized? The Mahamudra masters, and, in particular, the Kagyü teachers say, "At the moment of strong devotion towards someone one can trust and rely on completely, there comes an opportunity for recognizing Mahamudra." Faith and devotion are therefore very important.

Through devotion one can receive the blessings. 'Blessings,' in this context, does not have the sense of a concrete thing passing from one person to another, but we must call it something. We say 'receive the blessings' because a transmission of wisdom mind takes place. We are not handed a 'thing' from the master, but at that moment of devotion, all concepts and disturbing emotions spontaneously vanish, and recognition of mind essence is therefore very easy. The opportunity for recognition is what is called 'blessings.' But not only faith and devotion can bring this about. Strong compassion provides the same opportunity as does shock or sudden fear. The latter can be dangerous, since one can be hurt if one's mind is not really strong. With devotion and compassion, however, there's never any danger.

STUDENT: If compassion and emptiness or luminosity and emptiness are the fundamental source from the point of experience or awareness, do the manifestations of both conceptual mind and the material world arise from that? Does form or manifestation arise out of the emptiness?

RINPOCHE: [Laughing for a long time] First of all, to discover how our basic situation really is, you must look into the question and check for yourself "What is it that is experienced or manifests and what is it that experiences? How is there an experience of something that is manifest?" If you really look into this, then, as it is, all manifestation is beyond arising — not arising, not abiding anywhere, and not disappearing either. But individuals appear to exist as those who experience manifestations. It seems that something is being experienced and that the act of experiencing is taking place. As we progress further in practice, this will become clearer. Just because something is being experienced, it doesn't follow that it also exists. For example, pressing your eye, you can see double. But there are not in fact two objects. Dreams are the same way. Whatever we dream about needn't exist. Also, if we take different kinds of drugs, we may see various manifestations, but that doesn't mean that these exist either.

In short, the experiencer is something mistaken, the experienced is something mistaken, and the experience itself is also mistaken. As in a dream, all three aspects are mistaken. It's mere delusion. While dreaming, you feel you experience something. You do feel something, but there really isn't anything, even though things feel very real. If you are crossing an abyss in your dream, you hold on tightly and try not to fall. If someone appears and tries to hit you, you'll fight back. Sometimes it feels like you're being hurt. So, while dreaming, it seems that something is experienced, there is someone who experiences, and experience is taking place.

But, looked at from the point of view of the waking state, the dream lasts only a very short time and can easily be dismissed as unreal, as not really happening. Yet, what proof do we have? Were we to dream for months and months, then how would this seem to us?

STUDENT: Towards the end of this song, mention is made of repeatedly recognizing dreams. Can Rinpoche tell us what that means?

RINPOCHE: There are different ways of sleeping at night. Some people sleep in a completely stupid and dull state, noticing nothing whatsoever. Others sleep more lightly. They experience different kinds of paranoia, running away from this and that, repeating daily experiences. It's all just confusion, called 'double confusion' because the waking state is confused, and dreams are doubly so. But with some stability of practice in the waking state, one can, at nighttime, mingle the sleep with luminosity and sleep within the state of luminosity. This is difficult to discuss as it is connected to one's own level of experience in practice.

STUDENT: Rinpoche, you said that devotion, compassion, or shock are the three ways of recognizing Mahamudra. You explained how devotion works, but I'm wondering about compassion. How does compassion work and can we practice compassion so as to make this happen?

RINPOCHE: This teaching is for someone who already has a qualified master, not just anyone with a little faith or compassion. Without having received the pointing out instruction, both devotion and compassion are mere thoughts. They need not be an opportunity for realization. For one who has received the proper instructions, realization can occur in a moment of intense compassion.

STUDENT: What kind of shock can bring realization about?

RINPOCHE: Electric shock. [Laughter] Really! Try it. [Laughter] No, no! I'm just joking. This is dangerous to get into and belongs to the function of a qualified master only. If we try to scare each other, we might get into a lot of complications.

For example, there are stories from the past about a certain practitioner who slaved through years and years of practice, making millions of prostrations and having nothing in particular happen. His master who was no ordinary teacher, but could know the minds of others, saw that the time was right for the student to go and stay in the mountains alone. Meanwhile, the master also sent someone else up the back way to suddenly jump out and say "boo" or something. The master went there too, and immediately gave the pointing out instructions saying, "That's it! Now, you've got it." If ordinary people try to do this, it is called a dog imitating a lion's leap. A lion can leap from one precipice to another, over an abyss, arriving safely on the other side with great dignity and majesty. If a dog sought to emulate him, he'd only fall down, howling all the way, break his back, and die.

STUDENT: You talked before about dreams. If we have the experience of knowing that we're dreaming and the thought arises, "Well, now that I know I'm dreaming, what should I do? I can do anything." Is there something in particular to do?

RINPOCHE: First of all, when we recognize dreams, it's usually just a thought. We think we are recognizing the dream, but actually it's just another concept. It's just part of the dream, not really recognizing, or being aware of dreaming. It is just dreaming that we are recognizing. [Laughter] Actually, it's quite difficult to truly recognize and be able to do whatever one wants—totally free, and probably quite impossible without training first in the Six Yogas. At that point, if one practices the Six Yogas, there are steps which are called creating and transforming apparitions.

STUDENT: You often mention 'disturbing emotions.' Are there non-disturbing emotions?

RINPOCHE: Yes. They are called *virtuous mental states,* such as faith, devotion, and compassion. Abhidharma talks about the eleven virtuous mental states, but there are many others. In the context of Mahamudra and Dzogchen, a good thought is also just a thought. We have to take things in their proper context.

STUDENT: Of the five disturbing emotions, it seems to me that pride, because of its subtlety and the thought behind it being "I am better than everyone else," prevents us from combating the other negative emotions because we don't really believe that we have them. Rinpoche, can you tell us how to combat pride?

RINPOCHE: We mentioned previously that among the five disturbing emotions, although, at first glance it seems that attachment, anger and delusion are the worst, actually the worst are pride and jealousy, because they are the easiest to have and the most difficult to identify and give up. There is no way other than what we call learning, reflection, and meditation. There's nothing else that can help.

STUDENT: The text says, "At the time of practicing the main part, stillness is to abide totally free from thinking, occurrence is when the mind wanders through the ten directions without staying still, and awareness is to notice whatever takes place, be it stillness or occurrence." I was wondering whether this stillness is the stillness of shamatha or the stillness of vipashyana that Tulku Urgyen teaches?

RINPOCHE: What is the difference between stillness and ordinary mind? The three instructions on stillness, occurrence, and awareness are according to the Mahamudra system, a teaching given before the mind essence is pointed out. It is a way of becoming clear about what one's mind, or one's consciousness is. Usually ordinary people just think, "Yes, I have consciousness and mind," but there's no precise idea about what it is and how it is. To investigate the stillness, occurrence, and awareness is a way to find out what the mind is like. One does this after being told, "First let the mind rest. Does it stay still? Find out. Does it think? Is there occurrence? Let it think but observe how it is during this time. That which notices the stillness and the thought occurrence is called awareness. So, now look at what the mindfulness or awareness is like." One looks into all of this, trying to investigate, and asking oneself, "What is it that notices?" It becomes impossible to find any clear answer. It's impossible to pinpoint 'mind' as being such and such. It is at that point, that the master points out ordinary mind.

STUDENT: So, it's that act of trying to be aware that is the turning point when we start to get the deeper teachings?

RINPOCHE: It's not enough just to notice stillness and thought occurrence, but to rest in the equanimity of the essence of this noticing. That is what is called dharmakaya or ordinary mind.

STUDENT: Dharmakaya...

RINPOCHE: Yes, there are three kinds of dharmakaya, the dharmakaya of ground, of path, and of fruition. At this point we can only call it 'ground dharmakaya.' We can't call it the 'dharmakaya of fruition' because the enlightened qualities are not yet present.

STUDENT: My next question is, what's the difference between the space you find in your mind through these higher teachings, the dharmakaya, and ordinary space. We already know that ordinary space is expansiveness and dharmakaya has cognizance. Somewhere in between, when meditating, we're developing our meditation to a point where we're finding 'space' or ground dharmakaya, so what is it exactly?

RINPOCHE: All things fall into just two categories, *compounds* and *noncompounds*. Space is a noncompound because it cannot be classified as being anything whatsoever, as having a certain shape, color, form, or concrete substance. There's nothing at all we can pinpoint or point out. Still, we talk about space as though it were some 'thing' that existed and, in a way, it does exist because it accommodates everything else. We talk about 'inner space,' the empty aspect of mind, and secret space, the recognition of the essence of mind.

However, whether recognized or not, all sentient beings possess the enlightened essence, what is called ground wisdom or basic wakefulness. But, due to the beginningless momentary obscuration, we are not aware of it. This basic wisdom is not something that can be pinpointed or identified, grasped or characterized as either existing or not existing. It is like space, but not the same as space. Ground wisdom has tremendous qualities, however unmanifest at present. As we practice on the path and finally attain fruition, inconceivably great enlightened qualities will manifest. That is the major difference.

STUDENT: Would it be correct to think of space in the mind as the place that accommodates thoughts?

Rinpoche: We could say that, since we say that the essence is empty, the nature is cognizant. There's a lot to understand about cognizance, *salwa,* in Tibetan. Space and mind are both empty in essence, but the mind's nature is cognizant while space has no self-nature. Therefore, the purified mind-nature is the state of enlightenment; when not purified, it is the state of a sentient being caught in samsara.

Student: Can you further clarify the difference between shamatha and vipashyana?

Rinpoche: Generally, it is said that if shamatha turns into a dull and oblivious state where one doesn't notice anything, as though having, in a sense, fainted or totally blacked out, then even though the mind is completely still, this is a great defect. But if it is such that, although totally absorbed in the tranquillity, one can still, through the occurrence of either a sound or smell emerge from that, then it is alright. Basically, shamatha practice is the sense of resting, totally calm and still, without any disturbance or thought activity. Vipashyana on the other hand, literally means 'seeing clearly,' 'seeing vividly.' In this context, that points to a presence of wakefulness or cognizance or wisdom. Mahamudra teaches that vipashyana cannot be developed without the basis of shamatha. First practicing shamatha, one is later introduced to vipashyana. According to Dzogchen, various ways exist, but shamatha is generally not emphasized much.

7
The Song of Enhancement

> Although the master and your own mind may be
>   inseparable in essence
> And 'one taste' as the emptiness of dharmadhatu,
> Visualize above your head the master as Amitabha,
> The unobstructed expression of awareness and supplicate
>   him.
> By the power of blessing, you will then have progress in
>   your realization.
> For this reason, practice daily the guru yoga.

The first line of this verse means that the realization in the mind of one's personal teacher and what, through his kindness, has been pointed out and recognized by oneself as the view, the natural state of mind, are in essence, totally inseparable, not different in any way. The wisdom of all the buddhas and bodhisattvas, the wisdom of one's master, and the wakefulness that one has recognized, are of 'one taste' as the emptiness of *dharmadhatu,* totally beyond all mental constructs.

There is a big difference between empty and emptiness. A cup without tea is empty; the sky or space is empty; but, the nature of mind is emptiness, the unified state of being both cognizant and empty. In essence, one's mind and the mind of the master are truly inseparable. On the level of manifestation however, he should be visualized above one's head as the unobstructed expression of one's awareness, and supplicated in the form of Amitabha, the Buddha of Boundless Light.

As mentioned previously, Buddha Amitabha has a red complexion. Seated above oneself upon a lotus flower and a moon disc, he is dressed in the yellow robes of a nirmanakaya manifestation. With his hands in the gesture of equanimity, he holds a begging bowl filled with nectar. One should visualize the master like this and supplicate him wholeheartedly. Through the coincidence of the power of the blessings and one's own devotion, realization will progress. For this reason, it is important to practice guru yoga daily.

Although many guru yoga practices of various lengths have been taught, simply imagining the inseparability of the body, speech, and mind of the Buddha and one's own body, speech, and mind will suffice for receiving all the empowerments, for purifying one's nature, for receiving all the various blessings, and for gaining progress in one's understanding.

> Although you may have realized that the yidam
> Is the manifestation aspect of your own mind,
> Visualize your body in the form of your yidam, the Great Compassionate One,
> And recite the six syllables.
>
> That is the coincidence for planting the seed of the rupakayas
> And the Secret Mantra teaching of unity of development and completion.
>
> Although the six classes of beings may lack concrete existence,
> With spontaneous, immense love and compassion
> For sentient beings, who without understanding
> Are wandering through samsara,
> Inhale with your breath the misdeeds and sufferings of the six classes of beings
> And dissolve it all into yourself.
> Contemplate that all sentient beings are then separated from suffering.

This section concerns the *sending and taking* practice, *tong-len* in Tibetan. As a prelude to this practice, do the following: Visualize Buddha Amitabha in the sky before you, a little above your head. Visualize yourself in your ordinary form, looking as you usually do. Buddha Amitabha is red, adorned with the major and minor marks of excellence, the protuberance at the top of his head, the designs of the *dharmachakra* in his palms and on the soles of his feet, and so forth. His hands rest in the gesture of equanimity, holding a begging bowl of nectar, and he wears the three robes of a *bhikshu*. Avalokiteshvara and Vajrapani stand at his right and left sides respectively, and he is encircled by many other bodhisattvas.

Next, make the pledge to attain enlightenment for the sake of all sentient beings. This can be according to the traditional liturgy of a practice text or simply by making the wish. At this point, you are still in your ordinary form. Make the strong wish and supplication for the blessings to be bestowed so that great compassion will dawn within you, and that you may be able to alleviate all the suffering of sentient beings and benefit them all.

The Buddha and the bodhisattvas then dissolve into you and you take the form of Avalokiteshvara, the Great Compassionate One, seated with crossed legs and having four arms. At this point you are ready to begin the sending and taking practice. Imagining yourself in the form of Avalokiteshvara, your mind becomes inseparable from Avalokiteshvara's mind, the unity of compassion and emptiness, and your speech becomes the speech of Avalokiteshvara, his six syllable mantra.

> Together with the exhalation of your breath,
> Let all the merit and roots of virtue you have accumulated
>   dissolve into all beings,
> And contemplate that all beings are endowed with
>   immeasurable happiness and well-being.
> The indispensable means for attaining buddhahood
> Is the visualization of this 'sending and taking,' the essence
>   of the profound teachings.

While maintaining this mindfulness of your inseparability from Avalokiteshvara, imagine that rays of light stream forth from you. This light represents all your merit, wealth, happiness, virtues, and good qualities. It shines forth in all directions and gently dissolves, like falling snowflakes, into all sentient beings, benefiting them. Combine this with the exhalation of your breath, breathing very gently.

Exhaling slowly, imagine that your virtues and happiness gently dissolve into all sentient beings, endowing them with happiness and freedom from all types of misery or suffering. Do this with great compassion and loving kindness, imagining that they obtain the two accumulations of merit and wisdom. After establishing sentient beings in the state of happiness, inhaling slowly and gently, imagine that all their misery and pain, negative actions, obscurations, and sicknesses are totally absorbed, immediately, into yourself.

As you are already in a pure form blessed by all the buddhas and bodhisattvas, the form of Avalokiteshvara, the personification of emptiness and compassion, don't worry that this practice, of giving away your merit and good qualities and taking upon yourself the illnesses, negative actions, and obscurations of sentient beings will cause you to become defiled or obscured.

The incredible merit accumulated by first supplicating all the buddhas and then practicing generosity towards all sentient beings will increase your experience and realization further and further. This realization results from having accumulated the merit of devotion, compassion and generosity. Imagine that your wakefulness and awareness have become much deeper, sharper, and clearer than ever before. Simply rest in this open and free state.

Practice this repeatedly, while exhaling and inhaling. With each completed cycle, imagine that your form as Avalokiteshvara, empty and yet apparent, becomes increasingly more brilliant, majestic, and splendid than before. Repeating this practice one hundred times a day, or at least a number of times corresponding to your age, is best. If one is 35 years old, attempt to do it 35 times.

If you wish that the confused karmic experiences of sentient beings all become completely purified, and if you generate profound compassion for all sentient beings, wishing them happiness very intensely, your hair will sometimes stand on end, you may experience goose-bumps, or your eyes may fill with tears. You may feel tremendous devotion towards all the enlightened beings, the buddhas and bodhisattvas, and your root guru. This unfabricated devotion and compassion, combined with the correct view of emptiness, can bring real progress in your experience and realization.

Gampopa once asked Milarepa, "My devotion and compassion seem artificial and contrived. How can I have genuine, natural compassion and devotion?" Milarepa replied, "That's how it is right now. But continue generating devotion. Once you truly realize Mahamudra, the ultimate truth, you will perceive me, the old father, as a buddha in person. At that time, you will have genuine and natural devotion."

Right now, to have genuine compassion is very difficult because we don't really feel what other beings feel, their suffering. Feeling true devotion is also very difficult because we don't really perceive the enlightened qualities of the great masters or the buddhas. We actually have very little idea about what being enlightened means. Sometimes, if we suffer an ordeal of great pain or a serious illness, then we know what suffering is like. Some people, having experienced these things themselves, can feel compassion for others experiencing great pain. When someone has been very sick, he will say, "You can't believe how terrible it was! There was such pain!" Then, he has some understanding of what suffering means.

Approaching insight into the nature of mind, you will perceive some fraction of the enlightened qualities and your devotion will automatically grow. In this instance, you will understand the immensity of the enlightened qualities that the buddhas and your own master possess. Material wealth can only be kept for a few years and is ultimately left behind at the time of death. The introduction to the nature of mind, on the other hand, does not only benefit this lifetime, it is the authentic cause of enlightenment. Understanding this great kindness, our devotion and appreciation of the teachings will grow so tremendously that we will automatically feel great faith and yearning towards our spiritual teacher.

At the same time, when reflecting upon the state of sentient beings, genuine compassion will automatically arise when you realize the terrible waste caused by sentient beings' inability to acknowledge their own true nature, and, how they, therefore, through confusion, wander in the different realms of samsara. Creating negative actions without wanting to experience the resulting unhappiness, they don't know how to create happiness for themselves. How terrible! This insight brings about genuine, unfabricated compassion, and at this point, devotion and compassion can become overwhelming, almost unbearable. We usually associate the term 'unbearable' with anger, saying, "I can't bear this." Compassion and devotion can also become something like that.

Westerners talk a lot about this practice of tong-len, but it is, in short, simply what has just been taught. At the end of this practice of giving and taking, look into who gave and who took. Then, simply rest in the natural state without any fabrication.

The Buddha taught his disciple Kashyapa saying, "What is ultimate bodhichitta? It is truly free from all mental constructs, like space; it cannot be indicated by any analogy whatsoever. It falls into no extreme or category; it is beyond mental constructs. It is the unity of emptiness and compassion; it is empty like space. Yet, it is loving and compassionate, open and clear. That is ultimate bodhichitta."

Many teachers and various practice manuals teach the importance of practicing sending and taking and of examining who it is that gives, and who it is that takes. Rest then, without trying to fabricate, without accepting or rejecting anything. Practicing like this, beginners will gain some understanding of the view, and those who have already recognized the correct view, will have great enhancement. Tong-len practice is also very beneficial for temporary situations, such as illness, feeling uncomfortable, mental anxiety, and paranoia. Some people feel quite nervous and cannot sleep, as though deeply disturbed; yet, through this practice, their discomfort can be dispelled.

Mahamudra and Dzogchen each has its specific view, meditation, action, and fruition. According to Mahamudra, the essence is nonarising, the expression is unceasing, and the manifestation is the unity of these two. According to Dzogchen, the essence is empty, the nature is cognizant or luminous, and the compassion is the unity of these two. The correct view is pointed out, and can be called Mahamudra or Dzogchen, but it is actually one's own enlightened essence. In order to recognize mind nature, it must first be pointed out. After recognition, one must train on the path in order to stabilize the realization. Finally, one achieves the ten or *thirteen bhumis*.

This initial understanding can be deepened or expanded in various ways while training, and here we need to rely upon oral instructions. According to Mahamudra, the six yogas of Naropa constitute the meditation necessary to improve the view. These six yogas, such as dream yoga, illusory body, bardo teachings, and so forth, were transmitted through Naropa. When practicing these, merely doing the yogic exercises of the nadis and pranas is not enough. This practice must be embraced with the view of Mahamudra, which one has recognized, and then these exercises can be used to enhance that view.

The Dzogchen view is called Trekchö or cutting through, and what is pointed out is the primordially pure essence, also called self-existing wakefulness as well as other names. The meditation is called Tögal. This text teaches the Trekchö view throughout, but the Tögal meditation is usually kept secret. Having not yet recognized the view, we can still apply this practice of Avalokiteshvara with compassion and combine it with shamatha and vipashyana. Finally, through the vipashyana practice, we will be introduced to the view of nonconceptual wakefulness.

A practitioner traditionally begins by contemplating the general outer preliminaries, the four mind-changings. Following this, to the best of one's ability, one practices the special inner preliminaries of four times one-hundred thousand: prostrations, Vajrasattva recitation, mandala offerings, and guru yoga. After that, one practices the yidam in order to receive the blessings of the lineage so that the view of the main practice can be pointed out. After attaining stability and proficiency in the practice of the view for some time, then comes Tögal practice.

> By gazing with semi-closed chakshus toward the surya rays
> In the morning and in the afternoon, there will manifest
> Rainbows, lights, rays, big and small circles, syllables, and the forms of deities.
> Look, while mingling the practice with mind essence,
> And you will perceive the sambhogakaya realm of unified luminosity and emptiness.
> Without letting the view remain as a mere assumption,
> The profound point of Dzogchen is to be able to see directly.

[Note in the root text: At the time of putting Tögal into practice, one should keep it secret and practice only after having received empowerment, reading transmission, and oral instruction from a qualified master. If this practice is explained to faithless people with perverted views, it is said that the protectors will send out punishment. So, keep it secret].

To put Tögal into practice, one must first receive the instructions from a qualified master, having already achieved some stability in the view of Trekchö. One must receive empowerment, transmission, and continual oral instruction. There is a reason for these essentials. To apply the practice of Tögal without stability in the view of Trekchö is quite pointless and there will not be any progress in that practice. The detailed information on Tögal should be kept away from faithless people, and from those who have not received the proper transmission. So, it's important to keep Tögal teachings private and secret.

QUESTIONS AND ANSWERS

STUDENT: Must a beginner accept the entire body of teachings before taking refuge? I personally find it difficult to accept certain aspects of Buddhist metaphysics, yet I feel very drawn to practicing Dharma. Feeling this way, can a mild skeptic take refuge? If he does, what can he do to remove his doubts in order to develop and reach realization?

Rinpoche: Any particular point of metaphysics?

Student: The principle of karma, for example, and reincarnation. But I'm still attracted to the dharmic discipline.

Rinpoche: The main point of Dharma is altruism, benefiting others, what is called bodhichitta. All the teachings can be condensed down to that. Benefiting others is the core of the Buddha's teachings. Metaphysical sub-points are not something a person comprehends immediately, as a beginner. Yet, with study and practice one will understand more and more. You don't start out knowing the whole thing. Just as at dawn, when the light is first appearing, we can not say that the sun has risen yet. It comes slowly, slowly.

Student: So, is it okay for a mild skeptic to take refuge?

Rinpoche: If you think that compassion is pointless and that having devotion towards enlightened beings is useless, that doing good actions and avoiding negative actions is also without a purpose, then it's better not to take refuge. But, on the other hand, if you think that developing love and compassion and benefiting others, avoiding negative actions and cultivating positive ones is meaningful, you have then actually taken refuge already. Refuge is included within that. Do you know anything about hypnosis?

Student: Not really.

Rinpoche: Maybe study a little about it and then get back to Buddhism and what it says about karma and reincarnation.

Student: What is the connection between hypnosis and Buddhism?

Rinpoche: It's just a small point. I've heard a lot about hypnosis and I also saw a film where a person in a hypnotic trance, sixty years old, was asked to be six. He began to talk and act like a six year old. When asked later on, "What was it like in your mother's womb?" He crawled into the position of a fetus. When asked "What was it like before entering the womb?" the person suddenly began speaking a language he claimed to be native to his past life homeland, describing the money, where he lived, his house, etc. I don't know whether one should believe in these things. I have a different system of proving reincarnation, past and future lives.

STUDENT: What's your system? [Laughter]

RINPOCHE: [Laughing] It's very secret. There are different kinds of perfect measure. The perfect measure of the words of an enlightened being and the perfect measure of one's own reasoning.

STUDENT: Can Rinpoche say more about the five buddha families?

RINPOCHE: Beginners may find this subject a bit difficult. However, Trinley Norbu Rinpoche has written two books discussing this, *Echoes* and *Magic Dance*. Trungpa Rinpoche's *Cutting Through Spiritual Materialism* and *Journey Without Goal* are also quite good.

STUDENT: Rinpoche, many of us are trying to develop a life-style which will keep us out of samsara and bring more and more realization. The other day you spoke of the three kinds of practitioners: the one who lives in the world and does his practice, the one who lives in a monastic setting, and then the lonely meditator. Because many of us have wants and desires cultivated in the part of the world from which we came, how can we best choose a path? For myself, I find appealing the idea of a family that could be Dharma oriented, but, on the other hand, sometimes I think that a three year retreat is what I need. These are seemingly two very different directions.

RINPOCHE: True. First of all, we can conceive of our body as the place of retreat and our mind as the meditator, the person in retreat, and for the time being try to put more perseverance and practice into our present situation and see what happens. If, through perseverance in our present practice, we reach a point where it seems we can't get any further, then think about physical retreat. I think this is best.

STUDENT: Rinpoche, you mentioned that for temporary problems like sickness, tong-len practice could help somewhat. Is that true even if we don't yet have natural compassion, but just a fabrication? Does the practice still benefit the other person or are we practicing simply to develop our own compassion?

RINPOCHE: The best, of course, is to have love embraced by the understanding of emptiness, but love and compassion have great power even without any profound understanding. Selfless love, without expectation of reward, has great effect. The power of substance is inconceivable, the power of sound or mantra is inconceivable, and the power of concentration or samadhi is inconceivable. Love and compassion are higher than mantra. They belong under samadhi and thus definitely have great power.

STUDENT: What is the main reason for the use of musical instruments in Buddhist rituals? Does the sound have a deep meaning as an invocation, or is it just an offering?

RINPOCHE: Using music as part of ritual has many purposes. Music is said to bring greater blessing into the practice of Vajrayana. Music functions to make one's fixating thoughts and concepts collapse quickly. Music also enhances the practice itself. Of course, it is also an offering, of which there are outer, inner, and innermost aspects.

STUDENT: We've heard about love, compassion, and wisdom, all gentle qualities. Chenrezig is a peaceful deity, but why are there wrathful deities in Buddhism?

RINPOCHE: Do you have love and compassion for your baby?

STUDENT: Yes.

RINPOCHE: And are you always only kind and gentle towards him?

STUDENT: No.

RINPOCHE: What do you do sometimes?

STUDENT: I don't feel kind and compassionate. I feel aggressive or angry.

RINPOCHE: You haven't touched upon the experience I hoped to get to yet, because your baby is too small. [Laughter] When the baby is a little older and does naughty things that are improper, like not wanting to wear warm clothes in the cold or not wanting to eat and so forth, some parents show an angry face and perhaps give a slap or two at the right time. This is not out of aggression or hostility, but if one examines it, one sees it is out of kindness. To the baby, however, it looks wrathful, as if the parent is angry. [Rinpoche laughs]. It's not the same anger one shows towards one's enemy, which is real aggression. Showing anger towards a child, if it is to benefit the child, is out of kindness and love.

Likewise, when the buddhas, out of their wisdom and skillful means, consider sentient beings, they see that some are tamed through loving kindness and some through wrath. Wrathfulness is not anger, but is intense compassion, because buddhas show themselves in various forms according to the needs and dispositions of beings. The wrathful form is said to manifest from the realm of dharmadhatu out of intense compassion, not anger.

STUDENT: In order to realize our own emptiness, do we identify ourselves as an imaginary creature, such as a yidam? The Hindu tradition also includes a technique of imagining that one is everything. What is the difference?

RINPOCHE: To imagine oneself as being the yidam deity is only a technique, not the ultimate in itself. Right now, we have a solid physical body, but if we instead imagine ourselves in the form of something insubstantial like a rainbow, our clinging to things as being real will diminish, and we will also receive great blessings. If one thinks that it is the ultimate view, to be a yidam, then that is wrong.

STUDENT: A few days ago, Rinpoche said, "Knowing one frees all."

I think you were talking about Milarepa's instructions to Gampopa. Can you explain what this means?

Rinpoche: The traditional axiom is "Knowing a hundred things but missing one. Knowing one, frees all." Imagine that you're traveling in a place like Tibet with many mountain streams, perhaps one hundred, which you must cross. You can either wade through or try to jump across each of them, but this is quite difficult and bothersome. Yet, lower down in the valley all the streams flow together, and there may be a bridge. Crossing this single bridge will free you from many hardships. You will quickly reach the other side of the river, safe and dry. In the same way, although many teachings exist, the most profound, the Mahamudra or Dzogchen teachings, comprise all the other vehicles. It contains them all, so you needn't depend upon other teachings to clarify confusion and deal with the various negative emotions. There are said to be five or six poisons, even up to 84,000, but for one who has recognized and knows how to sustain the self-existing wakefulness or ordinary mind, everything is complete within that and nothing else is needed. This is the meaning of "Knowing one frees all."

The lower vehicles contain different kinds of remedies for each of one's mind poisons. For example, to avoid attachment one should examine the object of attachment. If it's a nice piece of chinaware, examine it, thinking, "What is it actually?" Just some fired clay, soil, with some paint and glaze on it. If one examines it minutely one finds that it is not so perfect; it may be dirty and stained. In this way, one's attachment diminishes. Likewise, when examining a person of the opposite sex, think about the fact that the attractive body actually consists of skin with flesh and bones underneath, intestines, lungs, heart, veins, and arteries. If all this is laid out on the floor, will one's attachment remain or not? Through this kind of careful examination, one's attachment will diminish. According to the lower vehicles, to clarify delusion, one contemplates the twelve aspects of interdependence; to counteract anger, one cultivates love and compassion. Yet, in Dzogchen, one needn't scrutinize like this.

STUDENT: In the meditation practice to generate compassion for other beings, you think of their suffering, which works, but also, I find that I get quite depressed and heavy with that. Am I doing something wrong?

RINPOCHE: That's very good! It's a sign of taking upon yourself the suffering of others, of not being just a Dharma parrot. It is the basis for compassion. Through compassion, one takes the suffering of others upon oneself and, having been able to do that, one should feel happy that they are free from suffering.

STUDENT: To what extent should teachings be kept secret?

RINPOCHE: The common or general teachings are something we can always discuss or tell others about, but the special teachings like Trekchö, the view of the natural state of mind, Tögal, the ejection of consciousness, and so forth, are topics we should not teach to others because if we haven't really realized the practice ourselves, the effect will not be very good. Especially *phowa,* the *ejection of consciousness,* can be dangerous if discussed openly.

STUDENT: Other texts, like the *Rain of Wisdom,* talk about the good experiences of bliss, clarity, and nonthought. Can Rinpoche elaborate?

RINPOCHE: First of all, the experiences of bliss, clarity, and nonthought are all temporary experiences. They will not last. Being too fascinated with these experiences, one risks becoming attached and clinging to them. This itself is a sidetrack, straying into the three god realms. If one does not cling to these experiences at all, there is no danger. Concerning thoughts being dharmakaya, recognize the difference between thoughts being dharmakaya and the essence of thoughts being dharmakaya. To say, "Thought is dharmakaya," is a little too pretentious. We can say, "The essence of thought is dharmakaya," because the essence of even the mind poisons, like desire, stupidity, and so forth, is dharmakaya.

STUDENT: Rinpoche, you've encouraged us to practice both shamatha and vipashyana. I had thought that vipashyana was something that just happens to you after practicing shamatha for a while. Can you discuss the difference between vipashyana and shamatha and how to practice vipashyana?

RINPOCHE: As you say, vipashyana does not take place by itself, but occurs after practicing shamatha. It doesn't happen, however, without mind nature being pointed out. According to the Mahayana teachings in the traditional path of shamatha perfected by a Hinayana practitioner, it is said that at the end of the path, while remaining for a long time in the state called cessation, rays of light radiate from the crowns of the heads of the buddhas in the ten directions which reawaken the practitioner, who then enters the Mahayana path and attains complete enlightenment.

According to the Vajrayana, especially Mahamudra, one practices shamatha as a basis for later practices; but, if it is too intense, the shamatha state becomes an obstacle, a hindrance. In the beginning, one practices either supported or unsupported shamatha, or one alternates. For example, one can concentrate on a pebble, something concrete, but if one fixes the mind too intensely on that, such fixation can also become a hindrance. Therefore, one alternates between unsupported shamatha, resting with the gaze in space, using space as an object, and supported shamatha, meditating upon a concrete object. Through gaining some stability in shamatha or stillness, one will be able to gain control over one's mind and mental activity, and at that point, in the Mahamudra system, one is introduced to the vipashyana aspect.

STUDENT: Then one needs a qualified teacher to point out the vipashyana experience?

RINPOCHE: Generally, a qualified master points out the mind essence, but the biographies of past teachers contain stories about it happening in other ways, too. In these cases, different emanations or apparitions created by their root guru, like beggars or other people whom they came across, suddenly gave the pointing out instruction, but they usually felt that these were not just ordinary persons, but apparitions made by their teachers. A qualified teacher is not limited only to being someone with the title "His Holiness."

STUDENT: Sometimes, when we practice meditation here and I hear the instruction to generate bodhichitta, I feel very confused. I know one can use many techniques, like exchanging oneself for others but I really don't know quite what to do. It's similar to being confronted by a beggar in the street. I don't have enough intelligence to know whether I should give him money or whether this may not help him. I want to generate bodhichitta, but I also want to generate wisdom. Is there something simple to do?

RINPOCHE: You should study more about that. There are many details on how to develop the mind of bodhichitta which are good to study further. Your understanding will become clearer. In essence, the very simple way is to just think, "May all beings be happy. May they be free from suffering." Since the only way to be free from suffering is through complete liberation, also think, "May all beings attain complete enlightenment." Concerning the beggars, give what you can, whatever seems appropriate; otherwise, at least refrain from getting angry and remain indifferent.

8
The Song of Taking Death as a Path

What follows now in the final song is phowa, ejection of consciousness. Various kinds of phowa exist: dharmakaya phowa, sambhogakaya phowa, and nirmanakaya phowa. We'll briefly touch on this topic now.

We are taught the importance of following a qualified master, but what is a qualified master? Speaking of the holy, sacred or perfect master, he has nine qualities or characteristics, called the nine ways of perfection. Such a master should be skilled in expounding the teachings, in composing, and in debate; he should be learned, noble, and have pure conduct; he should have perfected the three aspects of study, reflection, and meditation. The most important aspects among these is that his mind should possess love and compassion, bodhichitta and insight into the nature of emptiness. A master possessing these attributes will be able to point out the essence of realization and be an unfailing guide in leading us out of samsara. He should be free from faults that can lead a follower to the lower realms. We must search for such a master.

The Hinayana, Mahayana, and Vajrayana teachings recognize various kinds of teachers as well as various precepts and vows that masters should possess, but at best, a teacher should possess the *pratimoksha* vows externally, the bodhisattva trainings internally, and the vidyadhara samayas innermostly.

Yet, simply following such a master will not suffice. We must receive the teachings; merely to meet or be with a master is not enough. We need to be able to assimilate the qualities of his wisdom into our own mind. These days, it seems this cannot be done without using words, verbal teachings. But just to hear the words and say, "Now I have received the teachings. He taught, I heard it!" and just leaving it at that will not do. We must actually absorb the teachings into our own being, truly taking them to heart so that at the time of death, we have the true confidence of knowing clearly and exactly what to do. Hearing the Dharma teachings has great benefit, but without applying them to oneself, aside from the blessings and accumulation of a bit of merit, we will not progress toward enlightenment. However, by hearing only one four-line teaching, taking it to heart and assimilating it, great benefit will result.

>Emaho!
>The purpose of the master's teachings and one's practice of the sacred Dharma
>Is because there is a need to clearly know exactly what to do at the time of death.
>Without that, there is no certainty whatsoever as to the state of mind of beings.
>Always keep in mind the uncertainty of the time of death.

We take to heart the master's teachings and practice the sacred Dharma in order to know clearly and precisely what to do at the time of death. Since everyone here is going to die, we must learn these things right now.

At the time of death, the best is to practice dharmakaya phowa, next, sambhogakaya phowa, and then nirmanakaya phowa. Since there is no certainty about the time of death nor about what will happen at that time, we should be prepared right now. The three kinds of phowa apply to the individual's level of practice and cannot be specified in public. Yet, one thing is certain: if, at the moment of death, we have any attachment to our possessions, even to a mere needle and thread, then having successful phowa at that time will be difficult. Being totally free from holding onto anything, it is very easy to accomplish.

At the time of death, if we can apply the phowa, 'ejection of consciousness,' either dharmakaya, sambhogakaya, or nirmanakaya phowa, great benefit will result. But, in order to do this, we must know right now exactly what to do.

After death, we will experience the bardo, the intermediate state. We can study many detailed texts about the bardo state. In the bardo, we could experience great fear and terror. Sounds, colors, and lights manifest. A person lacking the proper pure karma, who hasn't developed the knowledge that realizes egolessness, will, due to past propensities and tendencies, probably take rebirth in one of the various types of samsaric life-forms, like an animal and so forth.

While in the bardo state, the manifestations of the five poisons can cause us to feel as though we are being pursued by a mass of fire, or as though we are falling into a deep abyss or sinking into an ocean. Many kinds of frightening experiences occur. The sounds, lights, and colors will be hundreds of times more intense than what we experience while alive. These karmic phenomena all seem to be quite unpleasant. We may hear voices shouting, "Kill him! Beat him! Catch him! Chop him into pieces!" While extremely terrifying, these are merely karmic phenomena. Not much that is pleasurable happens in the bardo, yet, at this time, if we can remember the teachings and rest in the equanimity of the view, we will have quite good results. Recognizing the essence is said to be very difficult at this point, but if we can recognize it, we will swiftly perfect the training and attain stability. However, because of the strong panic and fear, remembering to recognize the essence and remaining in composure is especially difficult. Just as right now, remembering emptiness and compassion seems to be quite difficult when we become very upset and angry, doesn't it?

When everything is fine, when our stomachs are pleasantly full and the sun is shining, we feel warm and contented. It is very easy to remember emptiness and compassion and sit and meditate with a pleasant smile. Similarly, when our teacher or master is kind, giving us material things and speaking nicely, teaching what appeals to us, we feel strong faith and devotion. If he doesn't treat us very kindly or if he says something we don't like, we nearly lose faith immediately. If other people are kind and helpful towards us, we feel great love and compassion for them, but if someone treats us badly, we become angry, forgetting completely about compassion. So it seems that right now we already find maintaining the view difficult. It is even more difficult to recognize the essence during the bardo.

The dharmakaya phowa is performed by a person who has received the perfect teachings from a perfect master and has practiced them perfectly; in other words, someone who has had the view of either Mahamudra or Dzogchen pointed out and has attained stability in that recognition in this very lifetime. Then, at the moment of death, there is no one moving from one place to any other place; no transference of some concrete thing from one realm to another. One simply merges with dharmadhatu. Hence, dharmakaya phowa is called 'free from transference and something transferred.' It is simply resting in the equanimity of dharmadhatu.

When someone has attained the dharmakaya phowa at the moment of death, external signs occur. The sky overhead will be totally clear without a trace of clouds. The internal sign is that the body will not lose its luster or radiance, nor become bloated or stiff. The innermost signs will be relics or what is called ringsel left behind in the cremation ashes, as well as self-appearing designs, such as the symbol AH, on the skull or bones, signifying the realization of the nonarising dharmakaya. [At present, a disciple of Tulku Chökyi Nyima in the Kathmandu valley possesses a skull with a clear, self-appeared image of the syllable AH.]

The signs of attaining sambhogakaya phowa are the appearance of rainbows and different lights in the sky. Regarding the body, a tiny hole on the crown of the head will ooze a little lymph and drops of blood, by a mere touch. The hair around this part will fall out very easily. At times, a protuberance even appears at the top of the head. As the innermost sign, relics of the five rainbow colors and various kinds of images of deities and attributes of the buddha families may appear on the bones and the skull.

The external sign of attaining nirmanakaya phowa at the moment of death is that sunshine and rain will occur at the same time, large raindrops gently drizzling down, called a shower of flowers. The inner sign is a few drops of either lymph or blood dripping from the left nostril, which indicates that the person has departed for the benefit of beings. Many small pill-like objects, *ringsel,* will be left in the cremation ashes, and signs like wheels or sword designs will appear on the bones indicating activity for the benefit of others.

Deliberate phowa or transference is done when we are absolutely certain of having arrived at the moment of death. Different indications signify that death is approaching. Certain specific experiences accompany the dissolution of the elements, such as the experience of the earth element dissolving into the water element and so forth. When totally sure that we are about to die, we should perform phowa. Otherwise, to perform phowa before the actual moment of death can result in a very great negative effect.

Ejection of consciousness is of great importance since we can easily do it by ourselves. If necessary, a qualified master can do it for us at the moment of death. If done correctly, even though we have not attained stability in the proper view, performing this practice and ejecting the consciousness at the moment of death assures that we will not take rebirth in the three lower realms.

The final type of ejection of consciousness into another body is called *drongjug* and though we still have the written text, the transmission for the application of the teaching has been lost. It had been given the seal of secrecy to be passed only from one person at a time to another. After Marpa the Translator returned to Tibet, he passed this transmission on to his son, Dharma Dodey, as the sole successor to this lineage. One day there happened to be a festival in the nearby village and Marpa was invited to attend. Though he and Dharma Dodey were in the middle of a three-year retreat in Marpa's home, Dharma Dodey decided to go anyway. Just as he was leaving the house, his mother intercepted him and begged him not to go. He insisted upon going to represent the family, and his mother finally relented, but admonished him saying, "All right, go if you must. But promise me this: don't sit at the head of the table, don't make any speeches, don't drink any wine, and definitely do not participate in the horse racing."

Of course, he did all these things. First, he was repeatedly requested to sit at the head of the table until he finally consented. Then, he was asked to drink the wine and drank quite a bit. Finally, as a favor to his mother's uncle, he agreed to ride in the horse racing. Unfortunately, on his way home, he was thrown from his mount, fractured his skull, and later died. Since he had the teaching on the 'drongjug' transference of consciousness and knew the practice, shortly before his death, Marpa's disciples tried to find another body for Dharma Dodey to use, since his own was dying. But no human beings had died at that time and they returned with the body of a recently dead pigeon. He entered the bird's corpse and remained with Marpa for a few days until Marpa gave him some final teachings and last advice and sent him flying off to India. Though Dharma Dodey took a human body when he reached India and later became a great yogi, the transmission was not passed on and, hence, was lost.

> Without discrimination as to how much one is attached,
> One still dies, though trying to hold on.
> Since even the flesh and bones one is born with must be thrown away,
> It is pointless to be attached to relatives and wealth.
> Therefore, offer mentally your friends, relatives, and wealth, along with your own body,
> To your master and the Three Jewels.
> Having offered it, there is no point in worrying about who will take it
> Or to whom it will belong, just as with something without an owner.

Rich people hold on to their possessions, their houses, their gold, and whatever else they may have accumulated, and poor people hold on to their old leather bags. We all hold on to something, but success in phowa, it is taught, is hindered if the mind clings to possessions.

The possessions and wealth you have accumulated in this life will certainly be left behind at your death. Even your body, born from your mother's womb, which seems like your second nature, will be left behind to be either buried, consumed by fire, tossed in the river, or whatever. So, it's silly to be attached to the body or to our relatives, wealth, and possession. At the moment of death and even before dying, it is quite important to mentally offer to your master and the Three Jewels, all of your relatives, friends, wealth, and your own physical body, holding on to not even a needle and thread. You shouldn't worry about what will happen to these possessions after your death. Let whoever wants take them, like objects without an owner.

> Visualize your body to be your yidam, the Great Compassionate One.
> Imagine that above your head is your master,
> As Lord Amitabha, who embodies all the Precious Ones, and supplicate him.
> Block each of your eight openings with the syllable HRIH.
>
> Within your body is the central channel, the size of an average bamboo arrow.
> In the heart center is your mind as a white letter HRIH.
> Eject it repeatedly and dissolve it into the heart center of Amitabha.
> Perform this visualization one hundred or twenty-one times.
> Following that, without thinking of anything whatsoever,
> Rest vividly awake in the practice of mind essence.

At the moment of death, visualize yourself as your yidam, the Great Compassionate One, Avalokiteshvara. Think of your body being hollow, made of rainbow light like a tent of light with a single pole inside, a hollow bamboo stick placed as the central channel. It is open at the top and closed at the bottom. At your heart center, it narrows a tiny bit and there is a lotus flower. Above this lotus is a small sphere of prana, with the letter HRIH, symbolizing your consciousness. The prana-sphere and your mind are very buoyant and light, like gas, and are ready to fly up. This so-called bamboo tube is also made of light. Narrow at the bottom, it is wider at the top where it opens up at the crown of your head.

When beginning the practice, first emanate many HRIH letters to block all your body's apertures, the nostrils, ears, mouth, and so on, to prevent your consciousness from exiting through any opening other than the one left open at the crown of the head. Then you are ready to do the practice. Details of how actually to do the practice can be obtained individually when one is ready to do the practice itself. Various systems exist. Sometimes, there is a certain shout like PHAT or HIK or HRIH. Then, the syllable in the heart flies up and touches Buddha Amitabha's feet where his two big toes are closing the aperture on the crown of the head. He sits above one's head with his feet resting on the crown aperture. The syllable lifts the feet up a tiny bit, but they push it down again so that it doesn't fly out. That's very important. This is repeated many times. The practice can take from one to three weeks, but a good meditator can perfect it very quickly, even in two days, so that a certain sign occurs. People with strong concentration will have a few hairs and a few drops of pus fly off by themselves. Otherwise, a lama or your master can check to see if a tiny opening has been made where a tiny straw could fit. After that, you are assured of being able to perform phowa in the same way at the moment of death.

You will also be able to help others at the time of death, making it easy for them to be successful in phowa by combining your own visualization with theirs and guiding their minds at the moment of death. To do this, certain oral instructions must be received. For instance, methods differ according to certain illnesses. For contagious illnesses, to mingle our mind with theirs is not good. Instead, we must visualize another body beside the ill person and do it together with this body. That prevents the disturbance of the sickness from inflicting itself upon you. Furthermore, the visualization given here differs from the one done at the time of death, like dissolving into the heart of Amitabha, so you need the precise oral instructions to be able to do the practice.

> No matter what occurs during the dissolution stages,
> Be it 'appearance,' 'increase,' or 'attainment,'
> You don't need to identify it individually,

> Since nothing will appear which is not your own mind.
> Just look into the essence of whatever may manifest.

Following this visualization, again rest vividly awake in the practice of mind essence, without thinking of anything whatsoever. This is also done at the end of the practice. At the time of death, no matter what occurs during the dissolution stages: *appearance, increase,* and *attainment,* we needn't identify each of them individually since nothing will appear that is not our own mind itself. Just look into the essence of whatever manifests.

> When the external breath has stopped, but not the inner one,
> The ground luminosity, like a cloudless sky,
> Will dawn upon you, so rest in the continuity of that.
> If you remain for a long time, that is called 'taking hold of the practice.'
> As a sign of that, your complexion will be nice and your eyes half open.
> And, it is taught, your mouth will appear as though smiling.

It is said that when the external breathing has stopped but the inner breath remains, that is the easiest moment for ejecting the consciousness. As the text says, at that time, *ground luminosity, like a cloudless sky, will dawn upon you, so rest in the continuity of that.* Remaining in this for a long time is called 'taking hold of the practice,' which means remaining in the equanimity of the view. The external sign is that one's complexion will be nice, not pallid, and one's eyes will be half-open, neither glaring nor closed. Some people look as though they have died in panic or great fear or despair, but in this case one's mouth will appear to be smiling, one's face will appear very kind and compassionate, and one's countenance will be peaceful. This is the external sign of having taken hold of the practice.

The posture of squatting, sitting cross-legged, or the sleeping lion posture —
Whichever way the funeral servant may place you —
Actually, there is no difference between lying down or sitting up.

If one has not taken hold of the practice or if one has no assistance,
There is great benefit if your consciousness can leave through the 'opening of Brahma,'
By performing the visualization of ejection at the moment of death.
Since this is the same principle as the 'dharmakaya ejection,'
There is no contradiction between the two, so this is the most stable method.

After that, even if you have to wander in the bardo,
By looking into the essence of whatever occurs
It becomes simply the empty forms of your mind's confusion.
There does not truly exist even a single peaceful or wrathful deity, nor a Yama.

If, after that, you still are about to take rebirth,
You have from beginningless samsara until this moment
Circled through the six realms taking one rebirth after the other.
Birth, old age, sickness, and death have followed each other like beads on a string.
Therefore, it is better to be weary and to decide that you've had enough of samsara.

The suffering of the lower realms is unbearable.
The births and deaths of gods and humans spin like a wheel.

Your posture when dying is not important, sitting up, squatting, lying down etc.; the state of mind is what is important. A funeral servant or a relative might pose the body in various positions, but that is not essential.

Having died, if you failed to perform the ejection of consciousness, even if you must wander through the bardo, look into the essence of whatever occurs. The appearances of the bardo state become simply the empty forms of your mind's confusion. Not a single wrathful or peaceful deity truly exists, not even Yama, the Lord of Death. Still later, if you haven't recognized all these manifestations as your own mind, a time will come when you are about to take rebirth. Certain experiences will precipitate this event, such as seeing an empty house that you feel compelled to enter or seeing cracks in rocks into which you feel forced to go. Various kinds of indications occur which mean you are about to enter a new rebirth. When this happens, reflect in this way, "Since beginningless samsara until this moment, I have circled through one birth after another throughout the six realms, experiencing birth, old age, sickness, and death, one following after the other like beads on a string. Therefore, let me be weary and fed-up and decide to have had enough of samsara. The suffering of the lower realms is unbearable and the birth and death of gods and humans spin like wheels one after the other."

> Thinking, "Now I shall go to a blissful place free from misery,
> I shall go to listen to the sacred Dharma from Amitabha
> In the realm of Sukhavati in the western direction!"
> You should abandon all attachment and clinging and go.
> It will not be necessary to travel by walking,
> Nor will you need to fly there like a bird by its wings.
> Your mental body will arrive at the very moment of intending to be there.
> When born there, it is perpetually blissful without any misery,

> And you will even be able to accomplish the benefit of
> sentient beings.
> Having accomplished the levels, you can fulfill the aims of
> others through emanations.
> When dying, dissolve therefore into the heart of
> Amitabha.

In order to reach Sukhavati, you needn't travel on foot nor fly on wings like a bird. In the bardo state, we don't have a physical body, but a mental body, and at the moment of thinking of a place, we immediately arrive there. Therefore, the mental body will arrive in Sukhavati in the very moment of intending to be there.

When born in Sukhavati, you take birth by suddenly appearing in a lotus flower in the presence of Buddha Amitabha. After that, you can receive the teachings and progress through the bodhisattva levels and the five paths and finally attain complete and perfect enlightenment. It is perpetually blissful without any misery and you can even accomplish the benefit of sentient beings. Having achieved the bhumis, you can achieve the aims of others by sending out emanations. Therefore, when dying, dissolve yourself into the heart of the Buddha of Boundless Light.

> As a response of gratitude for an offering of paper
> From the faithful tradesman Budu,
> These small songs on practice in eight chapters
> Were based on notes of short teachings explained in the
> course of three days.
> They were completed in writing by Raga Asye
> On the second day of the fourth month of the Year of the
> Tiger. Mangalam.
>
> Since I simply wrote down whatever arose in my mind,
> just at that very moment,
> If there are any mistakes or contradictions,
> I confess them in the presence of all the learned ones.

By the merit of this, may all attain rebirth in the blissful realm of Sukhavati.

This completes the teachings on Karma Chagmey's Union of Mahamudra and Dzogchen. If we actually practice these teachings there will great benefit. So, please practice!

QUESTIONS AND ANSWERS

STUDENT: We talked before about Westerners coming here to study Dharma. Is the method of teaching you present here dramatically different from the way Tibetans learn the Dharma?

RINPOCHE: Dharma studies have not been a great problem for Tibetans because they speak the language and can ask masters and receive teachings easily. Traditionally, one begins with the general preliminaries, the four mind-changings, and then practices the special preliminaries, and slowly gets to the main practice, step by step over a very long time. But, for Westerners who come to the East, this is a little complicated because first you come from far away and it may be hard to stay very long. Not speaking Tibetan, it may be very difficult to take teachings from the various important masters without finding an interpreter. Also, to practice the teachings step by step in the old way can take many years. What to do? You should read the many fine translations already in English. Study these very well and make a list of important points you are not clear about. Have these clarified by qualified teachers; ask questions about what you don't understand and become clear about what the teachings are and how to practice. Receive teachings given by the many qualified master as often as possible. But theoretical knowledge is endless; as much as you want to learn, there will never be an end to it. The Dharma teachings are extremely extensive and very vast. What is important is to take it to heart, to assimilate what you have already learned, and to put it into practice. This is the real way to progress and attain enlightenment.

A story is told about a frog, who lived in a well, and a sea tortoise, comparing the size of their homes. The tortoise said that he lived in a very large place, so the frog said, "Maybe it's just like a corner of my well." The tortoise replied, "No, it's much bigger." "Then maybe it's half the size of my well." "Nope, it's much bigger still." "Oh, then maybe it's almost the same size as my well!" "No, no. It's much, much bigger." The frog said, "It's not possible! How can there be a place bigger than what I'm used to here?" The tortoise answered, "Why don't you come and see?" Together they trekked down to the seaside and when the frog saw the vastness of the ocean, he had a heart attack and died. Theoretical knowledge has no end. Take to heart and practice what you have learned.

Five Songs by Chökyi Nyima Rinpoche

SPONTANEOUS SONG OF EXPERIENCE

In the essence of realization of the buddhas, the lords of the three times,
The natural state of the Dharma of the definitive meaning,
There are no divisions as to buddhas and sentient beings.
Sugatagarbha is present in everyone.
Reflecting on this innate state, I feel great joy!

All beings are fooled by the thought of ego-clinging.
Reflecting on this delusion, I feel deep despair!
The lord guru has pointed out the natural face of awareness.
Reflecting on this liberation, I am filled with amazement!

This is not far away; it is right before you.
It is not too difficult; it is too simple.
What a great loss not to recognize
The fact that your present ordinary mind
Is the self-existing buddha!

Don't cover your naked empty awareness
With layers of indecisive meandering!
Don't veil your natural face
Within the grip of a meditator and his object.
Now is time for direct experience!

The sign of experience is your nature turning gentle.
Faith and devotion spring forth spontaneously.
Love and compassion naturally well up.
The ocean of understanding and experience overflows.

Vital it is to practice the view, meditation, and action
Condensed into a single key point!

Seizing the stronghold of your innate mind
You have captured the illustrious kingdom of dharmakaya.
With no need to hope for a future result,
Disciples! Aren't you filled with joy?

This inexpressible nature, self-existing wakefulness,
Is claimed to be understood by almost everyone,
But rare is it that someone is free from mental fabrication!

You may have the drive of wishing to meditate,
But unless you give rise to experience from your heart,
Halfway understanding will fail to liberate you.
What certainty is there, without realizing the true nature!

Resolve the view definitively!
Refine the practice repeatedly!

By the singular kindness of my gracious father root guru, I felt that my being was slightly liberated through learning, reflection, and meditation on the definitive meaning, and so, in the presence of the Mahabodhi Stupa at Vajra Seat, the eminent site where our teacher reached true and perfect enlightenment, I, Dharma Surya, offered this earnest wish in order to remind myself and inspire others in the year of 1990. May this be a cause for fulfilling its intended purpose!

SPONTANEOUS SONG OF THE ULTIMATE

Homage to the ultimate nature!

This present ordinary mind,
Subject neither to confusion nor liberation,
Neither exists nor not exists.
It isn't real and it isn't unreal.

A thought cannot grasp what it is and what it isn't.
Words cannot explain how it is and how it isn't.
Isn't 'suchness' just a label we use
For this innate nature, beyond thought and description?

There is no basis for this name and also no one to label it.
That is why we call it self-existing wisdom.

There is no one to cultivate it and also not a 'thing' to be cultivated.
To hold notions, assuming it is this and not that,
Aren't these the views of eternalism and nihilism?

In the genuine and real natural state
No notion is held, so deluded experience caves in.
With no distraction, there is no meditation.

With nothing to keep and nothing to clear away,
Sustain this continuity in short moments, repeated many times.
Isn't this what destroys your ego-clinging, disturbing emotions, and deluded experience,
All at once, from their very root?

To aim at a superior view, meditation, and action,
So eminent and impressive,
Isn't that just fooling yourself?

While the buddha is within yourself,
How tiring it is to search elsewhere for the qualities of knowledge, compassion, and ability!
Do not exhaust yourself pointlessly!

Meditator and the act of meditating dissolve into space.
And yet, since it is you who must take care of yourself,
Be certain to resolve the true state
And let the qualities of the paths and bhumis arise.

To do that, exert yourself right now!
Strive on, strive on, everyone!

Undistracted, unfocused, and unmistaken,
Unerring and undeluded, practice like that!

These words are from my heart, dear friends!
They are pith instructions, the jewel of my heart!
Don't let this jewel go to waste!
Treasure it, and your wishes will be fulfilled!

Nourished on nothing but the blessings of my root gurus whose kindness is incomparable, this was written by Dharma Surya to remind myself and to help others like me. May it be meaningful!

SPONTANEOUS SONG

Homage to the ultimate essence!

Watch the deluded experiences of the world,
Dualistic fixation linked with karma and disturbing emotions;
The clinging to things as being real and permanent is so tight.
Hope and fear, pleasure and pain, alternate.
Anxiety and falsehood, are beyond count.
Seeing this, sadness and anguish well up within me.

While wondering what to do, what to do,
The sun of this life is about to set.
Now, give thought to this!
All the things you see are impermanent.

Spinning around in the machine of karma and disturbing emotions
Through samsara's birth and death, joys and sorrows,
This endless roving about in cyclic existence
Is a calamity wreaked upon us by ourselves.

It is I, myself, who whirls around in samsara.
And this fiber of thinking me and mine,
A delusion both innate and conceptualized,
Is ignorance, the seed of dualistic experience.

The chief force that drives beings around in the six realms,
The basic component of all suffering,
Is this uptight ego-clinging.

Awareness is the innate natural state,
Free from arising, dwelling, and ceasing.
Unimpeded openness, inexpressible empty cognizance —
Your primordial essence is beyond conceptual mind.

This is the path journeyed by the buddhas of the three
   times,
The realization of Mahamudra, Dzogchen, and the
   Middle Way,
The nature of wisdom, compassion, and power.
Let this buddha rise from your natural seat!

With ineffable and fearless courage
Awaken the six classes of beings of the three realms
From the deep sleep of ignorance
And lead them to this primordial kingdom.

Effortlessly, within the self-existing essence,
The three kayas dwell as your innate possession.
Act for the welfare of all beings
And your wishes will be spontaneously fulfilled.

This was freely written by Chökyi Nyima, someone who has one-pointed devotion to the wisdom that lies at the heart of the root and lineage masters, and who after understanding the reason has gained steady faith.

THE DREAM SONG

In all the awakened ones, I take refuge;
Please watch over me with great love and compassion.

Due to ignorance, karma, disturbing emotions, and
    habitual tendencies,
I and all others who roam through samsara,
Unbearably and pointlessly,
Suffer again and again
The myriad miseries of the six classes of beings.
How sad is this self-wrought tragedy!

Alas! To be free from this mire of deep sadness
We need a teaching so simple and effortless,
A secret key point that is easy to apply and most effective;
We must realize the knowledge of egolessness!

Once we realize it, our fixation on joy and sorrow
As being real and permanent falls away.
We will also understand how to abandon, transmute, and
    take as path
The disturbing emotions of the five poisons.

Faith, diligence, and discriminating knowledge overflow.
Overwhelming love and compassion well up.
The great strength of wisdom of the twofold knowledge is
    perfected.

All the Buddha's teachings and their commentaries
Are means for learning, reflecting, meditating, and
    practicing in order to realize this.
Your essence can never be obscured by these methods;
Indeed, it cannot be realized without them.
So, don't separate means and knowledge.

The one who correctly practices this meaning
Upholds the essential teachings.

To myself and others, I say "uphold them!"
May the goodness of fulfilling all wishes be present!

In the early hours on the tenth day of the second month in the Year of the Iron Sheep, I, Chökyi Nyima, dreamt of writing this. When awakening, it remained fresh in my mind, so I wrote it directly down on some sheets of paper.

SONG FIVE

Homage to all-knowing wisdom.

Not understanding the nature, exactly as it is,
Of the root of our mind, is the inner basis for confusion.
Without this, you may take much support from scriptures and reasoning
To describe in dry words, as existing or not existing,
The myriad outer appearances of reality, our deluded experiences.
But how can that destroy your rigid fixation
On a permanent, enduring and solid reality?

Reflect on this, and remain evenly
In the basic state of your innate nature.
Besides this vital point, I have nothing more important to say.

Dear friends, please keep in your hearts
These words spoken with pure intention!

This was written with affection by Chökyi Nyima Rinpoche on the 8th day of the third month in response to several devoted and loving students. May it be meaningful.

The Bardo Guidebook

*A Commentary by
Chökyi Nyima Rinpoche*

Foreword by Kyabje Tulku Urgyen Rinpoche

Dedication

This book is dedicated to the memory of my mother, Kunzang Dechen, whose life and death were an inspiration to us all. It is my sincere wish that the reader takes to heart the precious teachings presented herein and uses them to attain liberation.

Chökyi Nyima Rinpoche

Contents

Editor's Preface	259
Foreword by Kyabje Tulku Urgyen Rinpoche	261
Introductory Teachings	267
The Natural Bardo of This Life	279
Dharma Practice	301
The Painful Bardo of Dying	315
How to Die	325
The Luminous Bardo of Dharmata	339
Direct Instructions	347
The Karmic Bardo of Becoming	367
Afterword	381
Notes	383

Editor's Preface

Marcia Schmidt

Following the advice of Kyabje Dilgo Khyentse Rinpoche, Tulku Chökyi Nyima Rinpoche agreed to teach on *The Mirror of Mindfulness,* a classic text on the four bardos by Tsele Natsok Rangdröl, a master of the Practice Lineage of Vajrayana Buddhism.

Rinpoche offered a series of ten talks during the 1987 autumn seminar at Rangjung Yeshe Institute, Boudhanath, Nepal. During that precious time, everyone present was impressed by the profundity of the subject and the insightful brilliance of Rinpoche's presentation. Inspired by the richness of the material, many students helped in transcribing the talks. Later, the English oral translation was carefully checked against the original Tibetan oral teachings. Seven months after the seminar, those of us involved in the project became painfully aware of the significance of our work following the tragic death of our dear friend Gilda Goldman. No longer were 'the stories of the bardo' a distant tale: we understood that these experiences await unexpectedly every individual.

Motivated by our sense of loss and the desire to help other people, we redoubled our efforts. What followed was a careful condensation and selection of the most pertinent material. Tulku Chökyi Nyima often stated that he wanted these teachings to be a practical guidebook, easily applicable. We hope we have succeeded in offering such a guidebook. I would like to extend my thanks first to Erik Pema Kunsang for translating and carefully checking the manuscript, to the transcribers, particularly Marilyn Montgomery and Elizabeth, to Tara, who helped check tapes, to Kathy Morris for editing the rough manuscript, to Mim Coulstock for fine editing, to Kerry Moran for copy editing, to Phinjo Sherpa for entering the corrections, to Abraham Zablocki for proofreading and of course to Chökyi Nyima Rinpoche for making it all possible.

Foreword

Kyabje Tulku Urgyen Rinpoche

For the moment of death, there is an instruction described as a child jumping onto his mother's lap. A child recognizes his mother and without any doubt jumps straight onto her lap. 'The child without doubt' is an analogy for a person who has received oral instructions on *Trekchö* or Mahamudra from a qualified master and has recognized 'his mother', primordial purity. The uncompounded essence of the present consciousness, free from mental constructs, is the empty luminosity of primordial purity. When dying we should recognize this empty essence. The one who recognizes such a state of empty awareness at the moment of death attains enlightenment in dharmakaya.

Our body was initially produced through causes and circumstances, namely, the white and red elements from our father and mother. Within our body is the central channel called avadhuti, that is like a pillar within a house. At the upper part of the central channel dwells the white 'bindu' or essence inherited from our father. It has the nature of the letter HANG, white and blissful to the touch. At the lower part of this channel is the red element obtained from our mother. The red element is located at the juncture of the three nadis, four fingers below the navel. Its shape is called ATUNG, meaning flame-shaped. It is red in color and hot like fire. Between them is the life-wind, the life-prana, that keeps these two essences from meeting. When the last breath is expired and the life-wind ceases, then the white and red elements meet in the middle of the heart. During this process three experiences occur.

The first experience is called 'whiteness' and takes place when the letter HANG, the white element from our father, slowly descends. That experience is like the white moon slowly sinking in the sky. Then from below the navel the red element from our mother ascends like a sun. This experience is called 'redness' and is red like the rising sun. When these two essential elements meet at the level of the heart, the experience is like the meeting of the sky and earth. This experience of blackness is the moment when a normal person falls unconscious.

During the white experience the thirty-three thought states caused by anger cease. During the red experience the forty thought states caused by passion cease. When the two essences meet, the seven thought states caused by stupidity cease. It is said that when the black experience occurs, normal people and inexperienced practitioners will faint and remain oblivious in the state of the all-ground. At that moment they become unconscious with tears streaming from their eyes; all the eighty kinds of thought states have completely ceased.

Someone who has not received instructions on how to recognize mind essence falls unconscious for three and a half days. After this period, it is as if the sky and the earth again separate. When awakening, the consciousness can leave the body either through the top of the head, the five sense organs, or through the lower openings of the body. If it leaves through the lower part of the body one goes to the lower realms.

When the consciousness leaves the body the deceased feels confused and thinks, ... "What shall I do now? ... Am I alive or dead?" The spirit will go to its former home, to its family or to its father and mother. The spirit of the deceased will pat them on the shoulder and say ... "Don't cry, I am not dead, I am right here," but they will not hear anything. Finally, the dead person will become panic-stricken and realize ... "Oh! I am dead."

When the spirit of the deceased walks on sand he doesn't leave footprints. The dead person can freely traverse through solid matter and may think: ... "Before I could not pass through walls. What has happened to my body? The body we have at this time is an illusory body, the same body we feel we possess while dreaming; an imagined body. Of the five aggregates, the aggregate of form is absent but the other four aggregates of sensation, perception, conception and consciousness are still present, connected to a mental body.

Because of the force of conceptual thinking, also known as the karmic wind, the spirit is unable to remain still for even an instant. It constantly moves around. At this time there are the six kinds of uncertainties. The dwelling place is uncertain, the support is uncertain, and behavior is uncertain. Food is uncertain, one lives on different smells and odors. Companionship is uncertain and experiences are uncertain; one floats about like a feather moved by the wind.

In this state, one is threatened by the three abysses corresponding to the three mind poisons. There is the pitch black abyss of stupidity, the deep abyss of aggression, and the vast abyss of desire. Also, at this time one hears loud sounds caused by the four elements of earth, water, fire and wind. There is the sound of an avalanche continuously falling behind one, the sound of a great rushing river, the sound of a huge blazing mass of fire like a volcano, and the sound of a great storm. Moreover, there is no perception of the sun and moon, which can only be seen when we have a physical body. For forty-nine days there is neither night nor day. These are some of the experiences we undergo.

To reiterate, according to our master's instructions, we should recognize our nature as primordial purity and maintain awareness free from the thoughts of the three times. In the moment of recognizing awareness not a single one of the 84,000 negative emotions is present. To recognize awareness during the three experiences, the whiteness, redness, and blackness, when all the emotions have completely ceased, makes it possible to attain stability in the state of primordial purity. Sentient beings who do not recognize mind nature fall unconscious, whereas those who do recognize mind nature and have practiced do not faint. The moment of the three experiences is the time to apply the teaching of the child jumping onto his mother's lap. The awareness that our teacher pointed out is like the child. The primordial purity itself, the basic luminosity, is like the mother. This recognition at the very moment of death, in the bardo of dying, will ensure liberation.

After the dissolution of the five elements and the three experiences of appearance, increase, and attainment, the unfolding of the bardo of dharmata begins with what is called 'consciousness dissolving into space.' Then follows 'space dissolving into luminosity,' 'luminosity dissolving into union,' 'union dissolving into wisdom,' 'wisdom dissolving into spontaneous presence,' and finally 'spontaneous presence dissolving into primordial purity.' The moment the luminosity dissolves into union, the one hundred peaceful and wrathful families manifest. When one does not recognize the essence of the peaceful deities, then the wrathful deities appear. Not recognizing the essence of the wrathful deities triggers the reoccurrence of habitual tendencies, and the bardo of becoming begins. On the other hand, if we do recognize mind essence, we attain enlightenment in the sambhogakaya level during the bardo of dharmata.

When one realizes one is dead, one should observe the six recollections, such as remembering one's practice and yidam. If an individual knows how to recognize mind essence and does not have any broken samayas, it will be possible to take birth from the bud of a lotus flower in one of the five emanated buddha fields, in the five directions. If one has broken samaya, the experience at this time will be like walking in darkness, as if in thick mist. One will be totally lost.

In the bardo of becoming the eighty innate thought states commence again. One starts to think … "Where can I take birth?" and begins to search, experiencing immense suffering and worry. If one is going to be born in the three lower realms one's head will not be facing up but will be facing downwards due to the power of karma. If one is going to be born in one of the three higher realms then one will walk upright, one's head held up. One searches for a place to be born, until one comes to the place where one's future mother and father are having intercourse. At the entrance of the womb there will be many beings waiting, hovering like flies on a piece of meat.

If one is going to be born as a male, one feels aggression toward the father and passion toward the mother; the opposite is true for a female. Through the power of this passion and aggression one immediately enters the womb. The consciousness is like a fly and the red and white elements from the father and mother are like glue; one's mind sticks to that glue.

Once one has entered the womb, one lacks the ability to leave; the freedom to say … "I don't like this place." During the consecutive seven-day periods that follow, one's body develops from a tiny embryo and grows bigger and bigger. First the central channel is created, joining the navel to the eyes. Slowly, slowly, every seven days a major change occurs until finally after nine months and ten days, one takes birth from the mother's womb. It is said that our kind mother carries us for nine months and ten days. During this time the breath of mother and child is the same. When the mother is active there is much discomfort to the child. When she eats the child experiences the terror of being pressed under a big mountain. When approaching the end of these nine months and ten days, through the special prana the baby turns upside down.

During birth, one suffers pain that is similar to flesh being peeled from one's bones. The actual moment of birth is like falling from the sky and crashing down on the earth. When one is born and draws the first breath, only then is one independent from the mother's breathing.

At present we are in the bardo of this life, which lasts from the moment of taking birth until the beginning of the death process. In this bardo we should practice what is called the bardo of meditation, through the instructions of a master. As I explained before, at the moment of death there are the three experiences of whiteness, redness, and blackness. If, through the instructions of our master, we can recognize the mind essence without fainting, then recognizing, training, and attaining stability is like three snaps of the finger. We attain complete enlightenment.

Introductory Teachings

Out of his great skill, wisdom and compassion, the perfect teacher, Buddha Shakyamuni, gave 84,000 different kinds of teachings according to the various dispositions and capacities of sentient beings. All these teachings can be condensed into the twelve aspects of excellent speech, or simply into Sutra and Tantra. The extensive Sutra includes the three sections of Vinaya, Abhidharma, and Sutra. The profound Tantra comprises the four sections of tantras.

The Mirror of Mindfulness belongs to the profound teachings of Tantra, yet it is a combination of both Sutra and Tantra. This text is applicable not only to people who are advanced practitioners but also to beginning Dharma students. It explains the nature of mind and how our minds act in different situations.

The teachings on the bardo are not only for Buddhists. Both Buddhists and non-Buddhists find themselves in various states called 'bardo.' Here bardo literally means a 'period of time between two events.' Right now, we are in the bardo that began at birth and ends with death. After this bardo, others will follow. Therefore, whether Buddhist or not, it is important to study the teachings on the different bardos.

We can study and learn many different philosophies. In Buddhism, the main topic is the inner science of spiritual practice. Basically, Buddhism is concerned with investigating how and what the mind is. What is the fundamental situation of what we call 'mind?' What are its positive aspects, what are its negative sides? Through spiritual or meditative practice, how can we defeat the negative aspects and increase the positive ones?

How do we approach this inner science? We begin by studying the Dharma, the Buddha's teachings. But simply studying the teachings is not enough to cut our doubts and gain complete clarity. We must think them over. That is called 'reflecting upon' or 'contemplating' the teachings. Still, only studying the teachings and thinking about them is not sufficient. At that point our understanding is merely theoretical. In order to experience the truth of the teachings we need to rely on a third point: actual meditation practice. By applying the teachings to our own experience, we can gradually conquer the negative aspects of our minds. Once the obscurations of dualistic knowledge and disturbing emotions are purified, the wisdom of knowing the nature as it is and the wisdom of perceiving all that exists will arise. Finally, we will be rid of all defects and will have perfected all the qualities.

It has happened in the past that the master simply rested his or her mind in the natural state without saying anything. The student, by simply being in the teacher's presence, would experience the same realization, without a single spoken word. Sometimes just a few words would pass between them. The student might say, … "How is it?" and the master would say, … "That's it." That would be enough to transmit the realization. Sometimes the transmission of insight would take place through a hand gesture or by showing some symbolic object. But in the present age, this transmission does not seem to happen so often without the student having studied, reflected, and meditated. We must depend upon teachings, think about them and put them into practice. Why is that? It is because these days people are more confused and quite different from people who lived in the days of the Buddha. Although our minds may be sharper, they are more fickle. We have less faith and confidence. Because of our sharp but unstable intelligence, it is hard for us to develop real faith. It is very difficult for us to generate devotion, compassion and complete trust in our teacher, while it is easy to find fault with and criticize him. Nowadays it is very rare to find people who have totally realized the absolute state. Good qualities do not arise spontaneously. We must develop the three kinds of knowledge through studying the teachings, reflecting on them, and putting them into practice.

Knowledge purifies the stains of lack of understanding, misunderstanding, and doubt. Whether we are studying, thinking about or practicing the teachings, it is always important to be free from misunderstandings, doubts, and ignorance. By listening and studying attentively we can make sure that we are free of these three defects. First, get a clear picture of what is being said or written. Next, keep it in mind, do not forget it immediately. Afterward, try to go over it another time: What was actually presented? What was the main topic? Was it correct or not? Is it beneficial; is it reasonable? Reflect on it. If there is a point you are not clear about, discuss it with your Dharma friends. In this way, it is possible to gain a clear comprehension. If we are simply physically present during a Dharma talk but our mind is wandering and we do not really cognize or remember what is being said, it is not a very effective method for reaching understanding.

The Buddha taught in accordance with the nature of how things are. The teachings are true. An intelligent person will study and think about them, and the more he or she does that, the more confidence and trust in the Buddha's teachings will arise as well as great delight in practicing them. Therefore, it is important to be free from the three stains: lack of understanding, misunderstanding and doubt. The way to be free from them is to study, reflect and practice in the correct way.

Furthermore, to engage in the proper learning, reflection, and meditation practice of the Buddha's teachings, we need to have gathered conducive conditions. The most vital of these is to connect with an authentic teacher. Traditionally a teacher should have experience as well as realization of the three aspects of learning, reflection, and meditation. Six additional qualities are used to determine a qualified teacher: being skilled in exposition, debate and composition as well as being virtuous, noble-minded and knowledgeable.

The qualities a teacher should possess vary according to Hinayana, Mahayana or Vajrayana. For example, a Hinayana teacher should have abandoned what should be abandoned and realized what should be realized according to the teachings of that vehicle. Essentially, a competent master of Mahayana needs the quality of having realized the unity of emptiness and compassion. If he does not have that, then there is no benefit in following him. A teacher who has such realization cannot possibly give mistaken or misleading teachings because his motivation is pure. If students follow such a teacher, because of his or her compassion he or she will not deceive or cheat them or lead them in a wrong direction. Therefore, a teacher must have this most important quality.

Our present situation is indeed very fortunate. We are human beings. We can receive, understand and practice the teachings. We are also able to meet a qualified teacher. We do have some favorable karma. But on the other hand, we do not have the best fortune because there have been many buddhas and enlightened beings in the past, and for some reason or another, we did not connect very well with them and we did not reach perfection. Until now we have not been liberated. It seems as though we have been left behind. In that sense, we have not had the most eminent karma of meeting a fully enlightened buddha.

However, we do have the fortune of meeting some of the present spiritual teachers. It is not that our personal teacher is superior to or stands above the buddhas of the past. It is because the Buddha appeared and taught that there are teachers today who we can meet and from whom we can receive teachings. But, in our own experience, since we have not met the Buddha in person, then our own teacher is extremely compassionate. Thus, in some sense, the personal teacher is even more important for us than a buddha who appeared in the past. Actually, the essence of all the enlightened beings, the buddhas and bodhisattvas of the three times, and the mind of a qualified master are inseparable. In that way, our teacher is the embodiment of the Buddha.

Our lama's mind is the Buddha because the teachings given stem from the Buddha's realization and are in accord with his words. The master's voice is the Dharma. She is also the embodiment of the Sangha. Since she manifests as a person who is a great practitioner, her body is the Sangha. In that way, the Three Jewels, the Buddha, Dharma, and Sangha, are embodied in a qualified master.

While the qualified teacher is a primary condition, the student also should be a proper recipient. What qualities should a practitioner, the student, possess in order to receive the teachings? There are many different categories of qualities that we should have such as devotion, sincere interest, diligence, intelligence, and so forth. But the most important quality is our basic motivation for engaging in practice. We should firmly decide and pledge, … "I will practice in order to get rid of all disturbing emotions!" We should think, … "I will do whatever is necessary to conquer the root of disturbing emotions that cause me to wander in samsara. The precious Dharma is the remedy to vanquish these disturbing emotions." All the teachings that we hear and understand should be put directly into practice. They should not be left as mere theory, mere words; we should apply the teachings directly to our personal experience. Through the strength of this intention we come to really know the Dharma. Without doing that our Dharma practice is not genuine but will on the contrary further enhance competitiveness and pride. In this case the Dharma will not be of much help.

To illustrate this point: if we pick up a stone that has been lying in a riverbed for hundreds of years and split it, we will find that although the surface is wet it is completely dry in the center. That is the example for the person who has studied, reflected upon, and meditated on the precious Dharma without assimilating it into his being, and therefore is unable to conquer the disturbing emotions. If we are unable to conquer these emotions, we are like the stone that is wet on the outside but dry within. The excellent thought to bear in mind is the motivation to practice the Dharma as a remedy against our own disturbing emotions. We should begin to cultivate this motivation right this instant, not in a month or a year from today.

Whatever we do, whether we walk around or sit quietly, we should watch ourselves. We should be our own teacher. If we practice Dharma like that, even if we have only studied four lines of teaching, there will still be great benefit. If we fail to truly assimilate the Dharma into our being it becomes empty words, though we may be very skilled at talking about it or writing it down in an eloquent style. Since the Dharma has not really penetrated our hearts and we have not been able to tame our own minds, all our Dharma practice becomes pointless.

Another aspect of motivation is developing the enlightened attitude of bodhichitta, which is the wish that our Dharma endeavors may benefit all sentient beings. The two main types of bodhichitta are called the bodhichitta of aspiration and the bodhichitta of application. 'Bodhichitta of aspiration' means to aspire to attain enlightenment for the sake of all beings. 'Bodhichitta of application' means to actually apply that aspiration and engage in virtuous actions of thought, word, and deed, such as the six paramitas, the vast actions of bodhisattvas. When we embrace any act with these two types of bodhichitta, the effect of that act multiplies and will bear extremely beneficial results. To recite even one *mani becomes a very beneficial act. Without this motivation of bodhichitta even a great virtuous act will not be ultimately beneficial.

Of the six paramitas, the first five--generosity, discipline, patience, diligence, and concentration--are called conditioned or conceptual virtues. Conditioned means that by engaging in these, one gathers the accumulation of merit with a reference point. The sixth paramita is 'prajnaparamita,' transcendent knowledge, and cultivating it ensures that one gathers the accumulation of wisdom.

By embracing any of our actions, in this case studying the Dharma, with these six paramitas, we thereby gather the two accumulations. This gathering of merit facilitates our understanding and realization of the two levels of truth through which we will attain the two kayas. We should keep the orientation that the ground, the starting point, is the unity of the two truths, that the path is the unity of the two accumulations, and that the fruition is the unity of the two kayas.

For example, when we make an offering or present a gift after receiving a teaching, that is the first paramita of generosity. We can offer flowers or any material thing or we can offer a mental creation such as a mandala offering of the whole universe, Mt. Meru and the four continents. That is all included in the paramita of generosity.

Secondly, making sure that we have the correct motivation for studying and forming the proper frame of mind is called the paramita of discipline.

The third, the paramita of patience, is not attaching much importance to our physical state. Sometimes we may be a little too cold or too hot, or our seat may be uncomfortable, or the talk may last a little too long. Nevertheless, do not give in to weariness but understand that the teachings are more important than such temporary discomforts.

Fourth, the paramita of diligence is that we take delight in and exert ourselves in absorbing what is being taught. We examine the meaning of the words, wondering … "Do I understand this? Will I remember it?" To have an acute desire to understand and a sense of delight with the teaching constitutes the fourth paramita.

Fifth, the paramita of concentration ensures that we are not carried away by other sense impressions such as distracting sounds, physical sensations or wandering thoughts. We need only to listen with our ears and try to understand the meaning of what is being said. Nondistraction is the heart of the fifth paramita of concentration.

The sixth, prajnaparamita or transcendent knowledge, means that at best, we should listen while understanding the unity of the two truths. In other words, we should understand relative truth as dependent arising and ultimate truth as emptiness. If we cannot do that, at least we should have the intention, … "I will try to study, reflect, and meditate within the state of realizing the view of emptiness." Embracing our act of studying with the six paramitas will be extremely beneficial, and that benefit will extend into all aspects of our Dharma practice. If we can embrace both the relative and ultimate aspects of practice with the six paramitas, we will be able to quickly progress through the five paths and the ten bhumis, like flying in the fastest airplane.

The key point of any practice is to unite skillful means and knowledge, prajna and upaya. The combination of means and knowledge is the swiftest way to liberation and is therefore extremely important.

In short, the perfect condition for spiritual practice and true understanding is the meeting between an excellent teacher and a qualified student. To approach this from another perspective, according to Mahamudra, Dzogchen, and Madhyamika, the basic view of emptiness is totally free from any mental constructs and is realized through two methods: devotion and compassion. For that reason, it is extremely important to engender devotion to the root teacher from the core of our heart in order to receive blessings. The second method is through compassion for those who have not realized the nature of their minds and therefore wander through the different samsaric existences. When considering these beings who are not aware of their mind essence and roam in samsara only to experience suffering, we cannot help but feel compassion.

There are basically two possibilities: either one is realized or one is confused. If one is realized, then one is a buddha; if one is confused, then one is a sentient being. What are the benefits and reasons for realizing the unmistaken view? Being realized means that one has understood the nonexistence of an ego, so that clinging or fixation on a self-entity falls away. Therefore, everything connected with that, the disturbing emotions and karmic actions that compel one to continue in samsara, cease. Realization means that one is liberated from samsara and at the same time, one is endowed with many sublime enlightened qualities. An enlightened or realized person becomes an example of that toward which others can then strive, have respect for and learn from. That is why the Three Jewels are considered something to take refuge in, objects worthy of trust.

On the other hand, beings who are confused, unrealized and holding on to the idea of a self, will consequently give rise to disturbing emotions and karmic actions, thus creating suffering to be experienced in the different realms of samsaric existence. Reflecting on this, we cannot help feeling compassion. All the phenomena of samsara and nirvana are ultimately, primordially and utterly pure. In the natural state or in the essence, there are no such things as birth, life, death, joy, sorrow and so forth. Needless to mention, ultimately even these words are totally nonexistent. All sentient beings are deluded. They do not realize the natural state of emptiness, free from fabrication, beyond arising, dwelling and ceasing. Their minds are caught in fixation, endlessly imprisoned by this hollow dualistic experience. Thinking of this, we cannot help feeling compassion for the suffering beings who wander in samsara.

Due to the karmic deeds we have created we are reborn into different realms. In all of them some misery is experienced. You have probably heard about these realms. It is said that there are six realms of samsaric existence: in the hells one suffers from heat and cold, as a hungry ghost from hunger and thirst, as an animal from slavery and stupidity. In the human realm, there is the suffering of birth, old age, sickness, and death. In the realms of the gods one suffers from death and transmigration and among demigods from fighting and strife.

In general, there are the three major sufferings: the suffering of change, the suffering upon suffering and the all pervading suffering of formation. Then there are the lesser pains of not getting what one wants, meeting with what one does not want, being separated from loved ones and encountering enemies.

No matter where one is born in the six realms there is automatically suffering. Thinking of how sentient beings experience so much misery, we feel compassion for them from the core of our heart. The object of our compassion is sentient beings who have at some point in our past lives been our own mother or father and shown us immense kindness. How can we liberate our 'old mother' sentient beings? How can we lead them to the state of enlightenment, the level of buddhahood?

Out of the wish to liberate all these sentient beings the buddhas have taught countless different skillful means, such as the aforementioned Hinayana, Mahayana, and Vajrayana vehicles. In particular, it is said that the Vajrayana teachings have many methods, few hardships and are meant for people of the sharpest faculties. Among the Vajrayana teachings, the forefathers of the Practice Lineage have given many instructions that summarize all the essential key points. Just as butter can be extracted as the essence of milk, the teachings on the four bardos can be extracted from the profound tantras, the extensive sutras and all the 84,000 different teachings of the Buddha.

In general, when people hear the word bardo they think it means only the period between death and the next rebirth. When a person has passed away people say, … "Now he is in the bardo." It is considered a terrifying, painful, difficult period. Therefore, we should generate compassion toward, offer prayers for and perform virtuous actions to help the person who is in that state.

But the after-death state is not the only meaning of bardo. Bardo means the period between two events. According to *Liberation Through Hearing in the Bardo,* there are six bardos. All aspects of life and death can be categorized as different bardo periods. In *The Mirror of Mindfulness* by Tsele Natsok Rangdröl, there are four: The natural bardo of this life, the painful bardo of dying, the luminous bardo of dharmata, and the karmic bardo of becoming. Tsele Natsok Rangdröl mentions that the two additional bardos, the bardo of the meditation state and the bardo of dream, are included within the bardo of this life.

These four periods form a complete cycle. Each will be explained in succeeding chapters under three points. First, each bardo is identified briefly and precisely. Second, an explanation is given of what one experiences during that state. Third, clarification is given regarding the instructions on how to deal with those experiences. Furthermore, Tsele Natsok Rangdröl explains how the bardos appear to an ordinary person who has never practiced, how they appear to a practitioner who has some degree of experience, and how these bardos appear to a person who has perfected the practice.

In *The Mirror of Mindfulness,* Tsele Rinpoche clarifies the general points of these bardo experiences. His style is 'general' because it is not one specific type of bardo system, but a gathering of all the various teachings transmitted orally from teacher to student as well as those that were hidden as concealed treasures or terma. The text clarifies these instructions by arranging them so they can be used as a basis for a learned person to give a detailed explanation. In addition, a beginner can read the text and find it comprehensible. For the practitioner, *The Mirror of Mindfulness* is written as a practical guidebook, an instruction manual.

The English translation of *The Mirror of Mindfulness,* I believe, is quite honest and straightforward, so the main body of the text is not hard to comprehend. In the following chapters I will therefore focus on the vital points within the eminent instructions of Tsele Natsok Rangdröl and the topics that are the most difficult to understand.

Please keep in mind that this teaching is not merely a description of the bardo states. It is a guidebook on how to apply the instructions of the buddhas in this life and the next. Depending on the individual, different experiences will occur. Therefore, one must know the different practices to apply, what benefits will arise from doing so and what consequences will come from failing to practice. Precious teachings abound for those on the path. The beginner should be instructed in the methods to be applied when arriving at the bardo of dying and dharmata and prepare for that right now.

Ordinary people spend their lives pursuing happiness and pleasure. They try to gain fame, power, influence and material wealth in any way possible. They are preoccupied with creating a situation that they imagine will bring contentment. That is the aim of the ordinary person. But a practitioner aims for liberation during any of the four bardos. Therefore, he will already prepare during this lifetime to be liberated right now. If he fails in that, then at least he will be liberated at the time of death or in one of the other bardos. To do that a practitioner must acquaint himself with the practices that are applicable to each bardo.

The Natural Bardo of This Life

Depending upon the context and the recipient, there are many ways to expound the Dharma. The main reason to explain the Dharma is to help the practitioner actually practice. There is a certain way of teaching for simple practitioners and meditators. One style is called the 'old lady's pointing-out instruction,' which uses simple words as well as hand and facial expressions to point directly to the heart of the matter.

Traditionally, certain methods of teaching existed in India. For example, the Buddha himself taught within the context of the five perfections as well as by means of his miraculous powers of body, speech and mind. A bodhisattva's way of teaching is through the six paramitas and a shravaka's or arhant's way of teaching is called the three aspects of purity. In the great monastery of Nalanda, the pandita's way of teaching treatises was through what is called the five major indices of exposition. In other monasteries such as *Vikramashila,* panditas would traditionally teach in accordance with the three aspects of purity. But here in this book, I am mainly concerned with teaching directly, in order to immediately benefit the reader's mind. This benefit does not depend so much on eloquent expressions and poetic analogies, but on communicating in a straightforward way what is important.

The first of the four bardos explained in *The Mirror of Mindfulness* is called the bardo of this life, which in Tibetan literally means the bardo of taking birth and remaining alive. Regarding taking rebirth, there are traditionally four types of birth: one may be born from a womb, from an egg, from heat and moisture, or instantaneously born. With a few exceptions, people in this world are born from the womb of their mother. The bardo of this life lasts from the moment we are born until we meet with one of the 404 types of illness or 80,000 negative influences that are the causes of death. The period from birth until one meets the circumstances for death defines the bardo of this life.

How people experience and spend their time in the bardo of this life depends upon their different ways of experiencing what they consider to be reality. We all have various ideas of what things are, how we experience them, and who we are as the perceiver. In Buddhism there are several levels of schools of thought. The four Buddhist philosophical schools have specific ways of defining the two truths, subject, object and reality. According to their individual systems, different things are accepted as real and true. Each school examines viewpoints inferior to its own, finds and rejects faults and then establishes certain statements which that school claims to be true. Since all the phenomena of samsara, nirvana and the path is included within the categories of the two truths, relative truth and ultimate truth, the distinctions between the schools are merely how they define the two truths. A person who has not adopted a philosophical view does not think too much about the difference between the two levels of truth. As soon as we start to study philosophy, we gain some idea of what is not merely apparent reality, how things seem, but of the real situation, of what is really true. Depending upon the degree to which we understand ultimate truth, there are different kinds of experience and different levels of realization.

Let us examine the exprcrience of the bardo of this life for the person of the highest caliber, with the greatest degree of intelligence. A person who has spent much time studying, contemplating and practicing the unity of the two truths can rapidly progress on the path of gathering the two accumulations. Therefore, realization will be attained more swiftly and this person will quickly realize things as they are. For the most fortunate, meaning the person of the greatest capacity, the world and its inhabitants are seen as a spontaneously perfect mandala. What does that mean? According to the general Mahayana teachings all sentient beings have buddha nature, sugatagarbha, and everything is pervaded by the nature of the three kayas. According to the Vajrayana system, all that appears and exists is of a divine nature, all sounds are mantra, and all thought occurrences are the display or expression of innate wakefulness. The person of the highest intelligence realizes that this is how it is. It is not that he must create the mandala of deities, mantra and wisdom through some mental construct or visualization practice. On the contrary, he realizes the all-encompassing purity. The realization of the superior type of person is simply a matter of understanding things as they truly are.

Take the example of Milarepa who said, … "When ordinary people look at me they feel pity, but when the enlightened masters regard me, they are overjoyed." Such a person who has reached a high level of realization through practice may look like an ordinary human being but his mind is not different from the mind of the buddhas. Tsele Rinpoche describes realized beings by saying, … *Their thoughts manifest as the play of dharmata, everything is the nature of the three kayas.*[1] Milarepa had realized that. According to Dzogchen, this state of realization is called the all-encompassing purity of appearance and existence. Another term used is the 'wisdom continuity of individual experience.'

From birth until death an ordinary person is continuously under the power of ignorance, negative tendencies, deluded experiences, and solid fixations. What does that mean? Before birth one already had inherent ego-clinging. Holding tightly to the idea 'I am,' ego-clinging creates a solid fixation on reality, on oneself as the perceiver and other things as the perceived. This becomes a chain reaction that draws one through life after life, birth after birth in the six realms of samsara: through the hell realms, through the realms of hungry ghosts, animals, humans, gods and demi-gods. This vicious circle goes on endlessly. That is how the bardo of this life is experienced by an ordinary person. In this way, through the force of karma, one continues until attaining liberation through practice.

Tsele states that … *Ordinary, ignorant … people regard the unreal to be real and expect the impermanent to be permanent.*[2] There is a lot one can say about this statement. Most people do not pay attention to anything other than what is superficially real, such as what we perceive with our eyes, ears, nose, and tongue. Since we are caught up in the web of what is apparently so and do not think much about what is true and real, we rarely perceive the ultimate truth. Our scope is limited to superficial reality. But by examining things using reason and quotations from the scriptures, and by analyzing the perceived objects and the perceiving mind, we can arrive at the understanding that all things are without true existence. The main difference between buddhas and sentient beings is that a buddha has realized that all phenomena are totally devoid of arising, dwelling, and ceasing and have no true existence, whereas sentient beings believe everything to be real and solid. Another difference between buddhas and sentient beings is that buddhas understand that things are nonexistent whereas sentient beings believe things exist.

Through understanding the two truths, we understand the nature of both the outer perceived objects and the inner perceiving mind. We understand that everything in the world is without substance and lacks true self-existence. Things do not exist concretely and independently. There is no external creator who created them.

In short, examining things more closely, we can discover that outer phenomena lack true existence. Even the old culprit of ego-clinging, holding on to the thought 'I am,' can be found to have no real basis. We can gain some understanding of the nature of things, but such understanding is nevertheless still theoretical. It is not sufficient to just have the idea that all things, including oneself, are empty. We must experience it directly. To gain real experience, we must go to a teacher who has this experience himself and knows how to simply rest in the natural state without forming mistaken mental constructs; someone who perceives things as they are--empty and without solid reality.

Moreover, we need to combine our own reasoning with the statements of the enlightened ones and with the oral instructions of a qualified teacher. A qualified teacher is one who has compassion, understanding and experience. When receiving the oral instructions, we should be open-minded, have faith and devotion, and also be intelligent and industrious in applying these teachings afterward. Through personal experience we will discover what is called egolessness, according to the general teachings, innate wakefulness according to Mahamudra, or in Dzogchen terms, the single sphere of dharmakaya.

Let's examine more closely this statement that we as ordinary people expect the impermanent to be permanent. Everybody has some coarse understanding of impermanence, but seldom is it on a subtle level. We regard a thing as permanent until it is destroyed. For example, a person is permanent until he or she dies; a cup is permanent until it falls and breaks. That is a coarse understanding of impermanence. Through understanding subtle impermanence, we realize that everything changes from instant to instant, moment to moment. Every micro-second a person is changing.

We can give aging a pleasant gloss by saying that a child is growing up and getting bigger, but actually, from the moment he was born, the child ages every day and grows closer to death. The same pertains to the seasons and all other things. We say, … "Now it is summer," and we have the idea that although summer is impermanent it seems uninterrupted. Summertime is suddenly gone and we call it autumn. Actually, things change with every instant; even the most subtle particles in concrete matter change continuously. Nothing remains stable from one moment to the next. That is subtle impermanence.

Impermanence is a fact we should become accustomed to and not forget. Let us make the understanding of impermanence grow in our minds. By so doing we will have less attachment to the things of this life, and our ability to understand the teachings, to put them into practice, and to rest in the equanimity of meditation will increase. Training the mind in understanding impermanence will make it easier to practice meditation. It is said, … *If you cling to this life, you are not a practitioner.*[3]

By being attached to the things of this life and feeling that what we have is not enough, we waste our time and slowly our life runs out. There are four main aspects to impermanence. The first is that everybody who is born will die. It is one hundred percent certain that one who has taken birth will die. There is no question about this; it is just a matter of time.

Second, people who come together will separate. Consider the yearly seminar at my monastery in Nepal. It is a group of eighty or ninety people. After a few weeks, they separate. After a few months everyone leaves the place and several years in the future they all will be living in different places in the world. Some of them will have already died and most of them may never meet again. After one hundred years, everyone will be dead, some cremated and some buried under the ground. After one thousand years their names and all trace of their existence will have completely disappeared. That is a fact of impermanence.

Third, everything that has been gathered will be dispersed or depleted. No matter how much wealth and material possessions we may amass, it will all be used up sooner or later. Finally, everything that is constructed will be destroyed. No matter how solid the material, be it steel, iron or whatever, sooner or later the object will fall apart and disintegrate. Those are the four facts of impermanence. Just as it is the nature of fire to be hot and of water to be wet, all phenomena are by nature impermanent.

In addition to mistaking the impermanent as permanent, we also confuse the painful and pleasant. We persistently create the causes of suffering and completely waste our lives with the futile, deluded and attached activities of the eight worldly concerns, such as subduing enemies and protecting friends. Ego-clinging, this delusion that we are born with, the concept of a truly existent 'I,' creates the disturbing emotions of pride, jealousy, aggression and attachment. We instinctively feel that our opinion is quite important, while the opinions of other people have less value. Due to this habitual tendency we do not attach much importance to what other people feel or say. We try to override them and gain the upper hand through our words, attitudes and physical actions. This is called the 'activity of subduing enemies.'

There are many ways we can subdue enemies or people we dislike. We can physically kill them. We can undermine them by slander or criticism, trying to turn others against them. We can show an angry face or glare in an unkind way. We can feel irritated when other people have a good time or things go well for them. All this comes from attachment and aggression in our own mind. These disturbing emotions arising from ego-clinging are the root cause of disagreement between people, and on a larger scale between countries.

Someone skilled in politics never subdues the opposition directly, but rather works behind the scenes, having other people say to them what he would not say directly. When meeting face to face with his opponents he will shake their hands, smile and speak of friendship and co-operation while plotting strategies to undermine them. There are many ways to subdue enemies, either directly, indirectly or in a concealed manner.

In any case, our main obstacle is ego-clinging, the tendency to think that what 'I' feel and need is extremely important. Because this ego-clinging holds such a persistent, tight grip on our minds, we are never really satisfied. Whatever situation we find ourselves in, it is never perfect. There is always something missing, something extra that we need. If we get what we want, we find that we need twice as much. If we have one dollar, we need two; if we get two, we need one hundred or one thousand. Sometimes even that is not enough. We need ten thousand or one hundred thousand dollars.

The same applies to other possessions. At first it is difficult to obtain our heart's desire but once we acquire this treasured object, it is difficult to keep it. Maybe it breaks, maybe it is stolen, maybe it wears out. Next it is difficult to increase what we have. And finally, the more possessions we have, the greater our anxiety. A poor person doesn't worry about losing things he does not possess. In the old days one worried about cattle and servants because they had to be fed and cared for. These days we worry more about our technical gadgets and household utilities. It is annoying when our things break down and have to be repaired.

As ordinary people, our minds are preoccupied by the eight worldly concerns: attachment to pleasure, praise, good reputation, material gain, and aversion to their opposites. As well, we have the pain and worry of losing what we have and not getting what we want. In short, most people who are not practitioners spend their lives concerned with mundane aims, thinking of themselves, helping their friends and subduing their enemies. They waste the bardo of this life immersed in the eight worldly concerns. That is quite sad.

At night during our sleep we are unconscious, like someone drunk or drugged. Unless this state is embraced by the key points of meditative practice, we are not much different from a breathing corpse. Someone very drunk or drugged may become extremely unpleasant and obnoxious although when sober he may act dignified. In the same way, someone sleeping deeply appears very dull and stupid and we don't recognize the intelligent person he usually is.

During the dream state, most of the time is spent reacting to our experiences with either attachment, aversion or indifference. Sometimes dreams are very unpleasant, we may have nightmares and try to run away. In this way, the bardo state of dream and that of meditation are also included within the bardo of this life.

Tsele quotes *the Sutra of the Noble Source of the Precious Ones*, in which the Buddha said, ... *By the power of attachment to wrong thinking, all beings are completely tossed about in this [samsara]*.[4] Wrong thinking refers to our way of perceiving things — to perceive without the understanding that everything is unreal and lacks concrete substance. One way to understand this is through a type of logic called the reasoning of interdependence. Understanding this reasoning, we understand that things are unreal, that they only have dependent existence. Without that understanding our thinking is incorrect and in contradiction with the way things are. Attachment to that kind of wrong thinking, and attachment and aversion in general, are what cause beings to be completely tossed about in the six realms of samsara.

Conversely, the sutra continues, the person who understands the equal nature of things sees the self-existing tathagata, the true buddha. He or she will attain the supreme qualities of peace, which means he or she will attain realization of the way things are. Understanding and not understanding the nature of things is the difference between buddhas and beings.

Now I have discussed the bardo of this life both for people who are realized and those who are not realized. However, hearing such a description is not sufficient. We need to know what to do ourselves. If we think of our lives, what have we done up to now? Think ahead; what we will do in the future? What would be the most valuable and important way to spend the rest of our lives? At this point Tsele Rinpoche says that one can use different frames of reference: either the teachings of an enlightened buddha or one's own intelligence. We should not blindly believe what others say, not even the Buddha, but personally examine the teachings. Only then can we discover the truth of how things seem and how they really are. Gaining confidence in that truth, we should receive oral instructions from a teacher and learn how to put his teachings into practice.

In Tibetan Buddhism there are four different schools or lineages, each with particular qualities and different emphases. There is a saying that the Gelug School inherited the Sutra teachings, the Sakya School inherited composition, the Kagyu School inherited practice, and the Nyingma School inherited Mantra, meaning the Vajrayana teachings. The Gelug and to some extent the Sakya schools emphasize study and reflection on the teachings. They consider it very important to gain a complete comprehension of the Buddhist teachings, mainly of what is called the Five Great Treatises, five major scholastic works. They spend a great deal of time studying these. After gaining a clear understanding of these teachings they go on to actual meditation practice. In the Kagyu and Nyingma traditions the emphasis is a little different; they stress immediate application of whatever teachings one has received. Of course, we should study and reflect on the teachings, but not for too long because life is short. We must gain some degree of intellectual understanding, but it also must be put into practice. Personal application is the focal point. Unless we wish to become a teacher, someone who benefits beings in a vast way, we need not acquire detailed intellectual understanding of the teachings.

The Mirror of Mindfulness mentions that, according to the Nyingma system, we should be like a swallow entering its nest. To enter its nest a swallow first makes sure that the position of the nest is safe and secure. Being free of all doubts, it enters directly and without hesitation. This refers to the approach in the Kagyu and Nyingma Schools. We must gain sufficient conviction in the main point, the empty nature of things. To do that, one must first find and study with a qualified teacher.

Traditionally it is said that, at first, one should be skilled in examining the teacher, next one should be skilled in following the teacher, and finally one should be skilled in absorbing his or her understanding, assimilating her wisdom. To do that one must first seek out a genuine teacher. Finding a charlatan, following him blindly, taking perverted teachings and then becoming a charlatan oneself would be disastrous. It is important to find a qualified master and receive the teachings in a proper way, following them correctly oneself. We should follow the teacher sincerely, please him in many ways and be free from deceit in thought, word and deed.

We also should receive the three sets of precepts: the Hinayana vows of Individual Liberation, the Mahayana training according to the bodhisattva path, and the Vajrayana samayas. Regarding the vows of Individual Liberation, the highest degree means full ordination as a monk or nun, next best as a novice, or at least, as a male or female lay person, someone who has taken refuge. Moreover, corresponding to the level of vows we have taken, we should keep the precepts of Hinayana, Mahayana and Vajrayana. As Tsele mentions about these vows, ... *One should observe them without being tainted by even the tiniest stain of violation, breach, fault or downfall.*[5] If the vows and samayas are broken, mend them immediately.

...*Studying and reflecting upon all the stages of the Sutra and Tantra vehicles without prejudice, one should cast away any partiality and clinging to a certain school of thought.*[6] This means that while engaging in Dharma practice, do not hold onto any idea such as ..."I am a Gelugpa, ... "I am a Nyingma...I do not like other teachings." It is very important to be free from such prejudice. Learning and studying should be unbiased because we need to understand what is what, both in the Buddhist and the non-Buddhist teachings. Understand the different views taught, and then you will know what is correct or incorrect. Without having studied, how can one recognize correct teaching from wrong view, true from untrue? The same applies to the non-Buddhist philosophies and schools: we need a thorough knowledge of them to understand whether they are right. It is not valid to say that everything non-Buddhist is wrong. It is quite foolish to hold such an attitude, even though according to Buddhism all 360 non-Buddhist schools of philosophy are said to hold incorrect views. Why is that? It is not because they are non-Buddhist but because their tenets cannot ultimately withstand the scrutiny of reasoning and logic. Wrong views are incorrect in the sense of not being in accord with the nature of things. Only for that reason are the non-Buddhist schools of thought called wrong views. This is important to know. Avoid sectarianism.

A good example of someone possessing learning free from prejudice is the present Dalai Lama, who studied and received teachings from masters of all the different lineages, not just from his school. In Tibet, the non-sectarian *Rimey* tradition was promoted by Jamyang Khyentse Wangpo the First and such lineage-holders as Khyentse Chökyi Lodrö. The present Dilgo Khyentse Rinpoche studied all the teachings of the different traditions and is respected by all schools as an incomparable master in expounding teachings and practices. His is a good example to follow.

…If one goes astray, becoming attached to great learning, one will merely pursue words of sophistry without understanding the actual meaning. One should, therefore take to heart and apply to oneself whatever one has learned.[7] Our studies of the Dharma have become perverted once we deem it sufficient to be able to explain to others the stages of the path and all the details of the teachings. What is the whole point of study? The vital point is to gain some understanding that can give rise to direct experience. To treat the Dharma merely as intellectual theory is to waste the teachings.

One of my teachers, Kunu Lama Tendzin Gyatso, was an Indian. He was born in Himachal Pradesh and learned Sanskrit and Pali. In Sikkim he started to study the Buddhist sciences and later went to Tibet where he studied at Sera and Drepung monasteries. Finally, he went to Kham. He was quite learned but also very proud and thought that no one in Kham could match him. Arriving at Katok Monastery, he met Katok Situ Rinpoche but was not particularly impressed. He thought … "How can such an ignorant lama have so many monks and be the abbot of this huge monastery? What is going on?"

Kunu Rinpoche loved books and wanted to stay in the library to do what is called a 'library retreat.' That means a scholar locks himself up for a certain time and reads all the books, finding out who wrote what and so forth. When he asked permission to do that, Katok Situ Rinpoche responded, … "Our library is not very impressive, but we do have a few good books. To examine them all will take you a few years. Still, you might be able to cover most in five or six months."

Inside the library Kunu Rinpoche found many original Indian manuscripts in Sanskrit and Pali, written on palm leaves. He also found many books of which he had never heard. The Sanskrit spelling, he later said, was terrible but the meaning was intact. Discussing this with Katok Situ Rinpoche, he discovered that the Rinpoche actually knew Sanskrit very well and was familiar with all the teachings and meanings contained in the books. At this point Kunu Rinpoche's faith and devotion started to take root.

Because of Kunu Rinpoche's nonsectarian attitude and his all-encompassing knowledge, if you ask anybody nowadays what school Kunu Rinpoche belonged to, the Nyingma followers will say he is Nyingmapa because he received many teachings from Nyingma masters; the Gelug followers will say he was Gelugpa because he followed the Gelug teachings, receiving them and passing them on to others. You can ask almost anyone from any school and receive a different answer because Kunu Rinpoche studied everywhere. But if you asked Kunu Rinpoche himself, he would say … "I am just a Buddhist. I practice the unity of Sutra and Tantra." It is best if we can emulate him: study with all the schools and be completely without prejudice. If we cannot do this, at least we should refrain from disparaging other traditions.

We may not have the time or intelligence to absorb the entire body of Dharma teachings, so we should just follow the teaching we ourselves have received, put it into practice, and at the same time refrain from criticizing other traditions. The oral instructions of one's master alone embody the essence of all learning and reflection. We should take these oral instructions to heart without any doubt. Even if we have received only four lines of teaching, it should be assimilated in our heart and put into practice. Otherwise there is no point in having received any teachings.

The Buddha gave many teachings and the commentaries on them abound. Unless one has the highest degree of diligence and intelligence, one cannot examine them all and gain understanding. Therefore, it is most important to put into practice the oral teachings of the master with whom we study. Our teacher can condense the body of teachings into a form we can apply. Do not stop at just having received teachings; take them to heart.

The process of understanding and becoming free from doubt is like refining gold: the useless parts are filtered out and we are left with pure gold. Having received the teachings and put them into practice, we gain some understanding but also some doubts. To increase this understanding, clarify doubts with your teacher repeatedly. By repeatedly practicing and receiving teachings, our understanding becomes more and more refined until finally, we are free from doubt. To make water drinkable in places like Nepal, we boil it for a long time to get rid of all the microbes until finally we have pure drinking water. Our understanding of the teachings should be equally refined.

When we do not abandon worldly pursuits, we squander this life. Sometimes people say, … "I have no time to practice." What is the main reason for saying that? It is because they are too preoccupied with preparations for a comfortable life. Sometimes people do not even find time to eat their meals or sleep properly because they are so busy working, making arrangements, or striving for some aim. My teachers often said, … "Human life is spent preparing. While preparing for the future one's life flies by. One dies with preparations still unfinished." People pursue material things; they buy what they want to possess and enjoy. But, often it happens that they pass away before finding time to wear all their clothes, spend their savings or enjoy their gadgets.

Tsele Rinpoche addresses people who consider practice the most important part of their life. Basically, there are three types of practitioners: those who stay alone in secluded places, those who take ordination and live monastically, and those who try to practice within the context of ordinary life. In the past in Tibet and India, it was impossible to count the people who made practice the most important part of their lives and eventually reached accomplishment. Many, many people, like the flow of a huge river, attained enlightenment by abandoning all worldly concerns and focusing exclusively on practice. The best known was Jetsun Milarepa, who was completely unattached to the fleeting objects of mundane pleasure. For example, if invited to a five-star hotel, he would not be fascinated but think, … "How futile! How pointless to believe that these luxuries bring any lasting pleasure. They are all completely impermanent." He might even be saddened by seeing the futility of such aims.

Most people are preoccupied with subduing their enemies and protecting their friends. They regard the false as true and the impermanent as permanent. They are bound by the five poisons. Through the eighty-four thousand types of disturbing emotions, they accumulate karma due to attachment, anger and delusion. Even if they go to a secluded place, they may stay for a couple of months or a few years and then give up. Their reason for going into retreat may have been that they were tired of life's hassles. Maybe someone close to them had died, or maybe they did not get along with their spouse, boyfriend or girlfriend. Something had happened to make them feel tired of mundane things and want to practice. Nonetheless, not having completely cut all ties and attachments, after some time they return to civilization and live among other people. They return to their past habits. This is not good. It is better to completely cut attachments.

Why should one go to a secluded place? From solitude comes silence, and from silence comes mental quiet. Only when undisturbed by mundane concerns do we have the free time to concentrate one hundred percent on practice. The practitioner should stay in a clean, quiet, secluded place. Many great practitioners said that the mind becomes clear and realization is easily attained in a clean place with pure water and air. In such an environment experience and realization have a chance to increase quickly, whereas progress is much slower when one is involved in many business dealings and activities.

Often it is said that the foremost practitioner is someone who abandons the world and lives in secluded mountains. The Buddha abandoned his kingdom as though it were a heap of straw or a nest of snakes. Yet unlike the birds and animals in secluded places, he exerted body, speech and mind in spiritual practice. Although it is said that the foremost practitioner gives up all worldly concerns and stays in mountain dwellings, just to physically stay in a secluded place is not enough. Our frame of mind is most important. On the other hand, if we can practice in an ordinary life situation without being carried away by the disturbing emotions that arise, we will progress even faster than in a retreat situation. Still, there is great benefit in abandoning all worldly concerns and giving up attachment to material goods.

It is difficult for us to abandon everything immediately, and even the attempt to practice in a mundane situation brings incredibly great benefits. Actually, the person with the highest intelligence and diligence can practice in any situation. Many animals and birds live in mountain caves; there is in itself nothing special about physical seclusion.

The main point of all the teachings is to understand the unity of emptiness and compassion, often called 'emptiness with a core of compassion.' Once you realize this vital point, enlightenment can be reached even without vast learning. But without realizing the unity of emptiness and compassion, to have studied a lot, to be able to expound all the teachings, or to write many books is not enough to attain enlightenment. Ultimately such activities are not sufficient, and one will continue to wander in samsara. Buddhahood means that faults are exhausted and enlightened qualities perfected. The word buddha is not applied to people who have gathered a lot of information. Buddhahood is attained through meditative experience and not only through study and reflection.

One might think, … "Where do wisdom, faith and devotion belong if it is only necessary to realize the unity of emptiness and compassion?" Actually, all those qualities are embodied within that unity. How are these qualities contained in emptiness with a core of compassion? In the state of having realized emptiness and compassion as inseparable, compassionate wakefulness is already present. Through recognizing that, devotion and faith become unshakable. There is no longer any room for doubt.

At present while we are not fully realized, our devotion to a teacher is shaky and fluctuates like the moon waxing and waning. When the teacher is kind and speaks pleasingly, we feel tremendous devotion. But the moment he criticizes us or says something that we think is not good, then our faith immediately vanishes. We feel irritated and are ready to criticize and disparage him. We may even get angry and argue with him. That is the nature of our fickle faith. Why is this? It is because of lacking real insight into emptiness. The greater our understanding of emptiness, the more devotion and confidence we will naturally have in realized beings and in the Buddha, Dharma and Sangha. Right now our view of emptiness is merely a mental construct, nothing more than an idea; our compassion and devotion are also fabricated and artificial. Yet, the moment realization of emptiness with a core of compassion dawns within us, all these qualities become genuine. Just as water is naturally wet and fire is hot, true insight into emptiness is naturally compassionate.

Although we may understand the nature of emptiness, we should not belittle the consequences of virtue and evil but have firm trust in the unfailing interdependence of cause and effect. We must train ourselves in a combined view and behavior that accords with the words of the Victorious One. Understanding the correct view of emptiness is not sufficient; it is only the starting point. We must journey along the path and progress through the bhumis. If the view of emptiness is emphasized too much at the outset of our practice, we may intellectually convince ourselves: … "Everything is empty. There is no cause and effect! Reality is totally beyond these superficial appearances!" Based on such convictions devoid of direct experience we may overlook the importance of how we treat others. Our practice becomes distorted. Intellectual conviction may be accompanied by meditation experiences such as bliss, clarity and nonthought. One may suddenly feel quite enlightened, that one has already gone through the whole path and that there is nothing more to do and develop. This kind of false conviction becomes a strong hindrance to further progress. It is essential to respect the law of cause and effect.

We must know the difference between negative and positive actions, because everything does exist on a superficial or relative level. We do experience pleasure and pain; we have past and future lives and our negative and positive actions bear fruit. Whatever we have to go through is true on the superficial level. At the same time, on the ultimate level all phenomena, both subject and object, are only the nature of thatness, totally free from the constructs of arising, dwelling and ceasing. This is truth on the ultimate level, but the superficial is also true. Therefore, since all things do arise interdependently, as long as we are not completely enlightened, we must carefully consider negative and positive deeds, and gather the conceptual accumulation of merit and the nonconceptual accumulation of wisdom. We do this by avoiding negative actions, especially the ten nonvirtues and adopting positive actions, the ten virtues. Why? Just as a child is not an adult and a sprout is not a flower, intellectual understanding of the view doesn't equal enlightenment. This understanding is the seed that will grow into the fully blossomed flower, but it is not yet matured. The plant grows due to a combination of different conditions: there must be a seed, fertile ground, moisture, light, warmth, space and fertilizer. Time must pass. When these conditions come together a plant has no choice but to grow. If one condition is lacking, the plant itself lacks the power to grow.

Until a crop has fully ripened, it is essential to guard it carefully. There might be hail or severe winds; there might be too much water or too little. A skilled farmer will protect against these negative conditions. It can be quite difficult. The most crucial aspect for growth is the place of planting. The ground should be stable, not eroded or shaky. For practitioners like ourselves, this means beginning with a quality of steadiness and constancy. We also need the moisture of compassion and the warmth of devotion. When these conditions are met, there is no way to avoid the blossoming of the flower of emptiness. This is a vital point.

Different religions have their own definitions of good and evil. According to Buddhism, one creates positive and negative karma through thought, word and deed. How to avoid the negative and adopt the positive is defined according to the following levels of teachings: the moral codes of the Hinayana precepts of Individual Liberation, the Mahayana trainings of the bodhisattvas and the Vajrayana samayas of the knowledge holders.

I will now explain the basis of all vows, which is to abandon the ten unvirtuous actions. First, the negative actions of body are killing, taking what is not given and sexual misconduct. The opposite of killing is to save the lives of other beings; the opposite of stealing is being generous; and the opposite of sexual misconduct is leading a decent and proper life. There is great merit in avoiding what is negative and adhering to what is right.

There are four negative actions committed through speech. During a single day, we can commit the negative actions of lying, divisive talk, harsh words and idle gossip. We might not notice, but it is not difficult to twist words a little bit to become a lie. When passing on information it is very easy to add something totally pointless that disturbs others. It is common to say derisive words that separate people. Be careful about these actions. Any attempt to avoid them brings great merit.

Most destructive are the negative actions of mind: ill-will, covetousness and wrong view. All religions agree that ill-will and covetousness are misdeeds. Covetousness is to desire the possessions of others. When perceiving other people's enjoyments, merit and wealth an uncomfortable feeling arises. The opposite of covetousness is to rejoice in whatever others have. Ill-will means the intention to harm others. This can be counteracted if we try to develop the intention to benefit others. Defining what is a wrong view causes some complication. What Buddhists consider a wrong view may be regarded as a correct view by other religions. Because this is a subtle point, we will spend more time examining wrong view, the tenth negative action.

What does wrong view actually mean? Wrong view means to misapprehend the four noble truths. By studying and understanding the four noble truths, wrong views are automatically cleared away. The four noble truths are not beyond our understanding. Anyone who contemplates these topics can understand them. One need not be a philosopher and study innumerable books to gain a comprehension of the four noble truths: suffering, origin, cessation and path.

The first noble truth is to look at living beings and understand that they experience pain and suffering. The second noble truth is to search for what actually causes beings to suffer and feel misery, and to find it is the disturbing emotions and the resulting actions, called karma. The third noble truth is the fact that avoiding the causes that create suffering brings happiness. In Buddhist terms this cessation of the causes of suffering is called enlightenment, either the state of an arhant or a buddha. The fourth noble truth is the path, how to reach enlightenment. Can we reach the roof of a house in one instant or must we walk up the staircase? Obviously, we must take certain steps to reach a certain point. In Buddhist terms, this is called following the path to enlightenment. Understanding the four noble truths we will be concerned about the law of cause and effect, and this concern will impel us to engage in Dharma practice.

We should train ourselves in a combined view and behavior that accords with the words of the Victorious One, the fully enlightened Buddha Shakyamuni. Some people deem the view less important, while considering one's conduct of extreme importance. To value conduct above the view is not the road to quick progress. That would be like being blind with a strong body. Walking fast but blindly, one will not reach the destination. On the other hand, having the eye of knowledge as well as a good body, we will reach our destination very soon.

Right now, we are in the bardo of this life, the period between birth and death. How long will this situation last? That is uncertain; there is no guarantee how long we will remain alive. Already a good part of our life is behind us. We have grown up and we probably will not remain here much beyond the age of sixty or seventy. Therefore, we should start counting our days.

Once ego-clinging is exhausted, all dualistic and confused experiences collapse and there is no need to go through any of the succeeding bardos. Nevertheless, as long as we retain ego-clinging, the idea of 'I' as a self-entity, there is always the idea of 'other,' of 'them' or 'that', and confused experience is perpetuated.

The most important bardo is that of this life. Everything that comes after depends on this life. The most important achievement in this life is liberation, enlightenment. If we cannot attain that, we should try to reach halfway; at the very least, we should have entered the path because then there will be more chances for liberation at the time of dying.

During the bardo of dharmata and the bardo of becoming we have additional opportunities for liberation. It is like the end of a football game with five minutes left. We still can score one more goal. But when the last second is up, then that chance is gone. Life is like that. We must be very careful how we spend the time we have left in the bardo of this life. Often people ask, … "What should I do in the bardo? What practice should be done when I arrive in the state after death? The bardo of dharmata sounds especially interesting!" To pile up these teachings while not applying them in this life is totally useless. To gain some degree of mastery over our mind, some stability in practice right now is the key point for attaining liberation at the moment of death. Without having any practical experience during this life, the chances for liberation in the bardo of dharmata and especially in the bardo of becoming are very slight. Tsele Natsok Rangdröl emphasizes that what comes after death, the next three bardos, depends totally upon what one does in this life. If we attain the best results in practice right now, we will not have to worry about going through further bardos. If we have some degree of experience, we have a strong chance of becoming liberated at the moment of death or in the bardos thereafter. Therefore, the bardo of this life, our present situation, is utterly crucial.

People tend to plan their Dharma practice, and especially like to dream of making a long retreat. We plan how the retreat hut should look, its shape and where it should be positioned; we plan the time to start our retreat, maybe one, two or three years from now. It is very easy to make such plans, but it is more difficult for these plans to become reality. Therefore, it is more realistic to engage in Dharma practice today, right this moment, not tomorrow or next year. Practice now in whatever situation is at hand. Otherwise, your life can easily run out while planning to practice later. Do not make long-term plans.

There is a saying, ... "The Dharma belongs to none but the diligent." Honestly, we are never prevented from practicing the teachings. It is totally in our own hands. Any moment of the day we can embrace Dharma practice, even when eating or going to the toilet. Having spent one's life planning while never applying the practice, it suddenly becomes too late. When the time of death comes, the one who had interest in Dharma practice but never did anything will be filled with regret. Some people on the verge of death even beat their chests in remorse.

Padmasambhava once said, ... *Those who feel as though they have plenty of time get busy at the time of death. They then feel strong regret, but it seems far too late*.[8] This means that it is futile to feel regret when it is too late. Therefore we must train ourselves in the ability to attain liberation in the bardos from this very moment.

Many think that the bardo is only what comes later, that it refers to the intense and terrifying experiences after death. Actually, we are already in a bardo state. Train in the practices now. It is of vital importance to study, reflect, meditate and gain direct experience. Especially, train in the awareness that recognizes emptiness.

The Buddhist teachings that were propagated in Tibet are known as *the Eight Great Chariots of the Practice Lineage,* each applying practices in a system that is the unity of Sutra and Tantra. These days the four schools of Kagyu, Nyingma, Sakya and Gelug still survive and flourish.

The essential meditation practice is Madhyamika, Mahamudra or Dzogchen. We should apply the essential teachings before it is too late. Tsele Rinpoche says that having received the oral instructions, whatever Dharma practice one chooses, one has entered the door in accordance with one's particular karma and potential. Our practices should therefore bring our being to maturity and liberation. The meaning is that we should practice whatever we have received teachings on; it does not matter whether it's Hinayana, Mahayana or Vajrayana. Focus on the teachings you have received and on applying them personally.

Dharma Practice

The previous chapter emphasized three points: how to identify the bardo of this life, how this bardo appears to ordinary deluded people who have not engaged in much practice, and how the results and benefits of spiritual practice during the bardo of this life are experienced by people who have perfected the path through learning, reflection, and meditation. In the course of these explanations I briefly mentioned the instructions on how to practice during the bardo of this life. I will now explain these instructions in more detail.

In order to gain liberation in this lifetime through Vajrayana practice, three things are indispensable: the ripening empowerments, the liberating instructions, and the supportive reading transmissions. In this context, reading transmission means the full permission to use a certain text that is obtained when a lineage holder reads the text aloud.

Concerning the ripening empowerments, Tsele Rinpoche scolds both the teachers and practitioners of his day and age. He first describes the teachers, saying, *… Empowerment, as most of the masters of the present dark age perform the ritual, rarely accords with the tantras and the tradition of the vidyadhara forefathers.*[9] There are superior, mediocre, and inferior masters. Tsele Rinpoche is saying that inferior teachers only give empowerments for personal gain, such as material wealth, reputation, prestige and so forth. Furthermore, the students who request empowerments very often want them only for worldly purposes. They hope to gain protection against the temporal harms of sickness or demonic obstacles, or to gain status, companionship, wealth or long life. Many people receive empowerment only for the prestige, to be regarded as a member of a certain class of practitioners. They may wear a special kind of dress, carry a rosary in their hand or don a peaked hat, but in fact their aim is not really to apply these teachings. Some attend empowerment gatherings to find a girlfriend or boyfriend; some merely come to see what is going, who the teacher is, how he looks, how many people come, what they wear and so on. Some come just for entertainment, as if an initiation is a theater performance. There is not much benefit in such motivation.

We need to adopt the right motivation: with strong faith from the bottom of our heart we should wish to attain liberation from samsara and the omniscient state of buddhahood in order to ripen the unripened and to liberate the unliberated. We should attend teachings and empowerments out of the wish to attain enlightenment quickly for the benefit of others. This should be our sole intention.

For real empowerment and transmission to take place it is crucial that both the master and the disciple be qualified. Disciples must possess certain characteristics to be worthy recipients of the teachings. They must be sincere; it is not enough just to pretend to be worthy. The disciple must have genuine faith and devotion. Concurrently, the master must have realized whatever appears and exists, the world and beings, to be the mandala of the deity.

Transmission means that something is passed on from the master to disciple; it is not a physical or concrete entity that is handed over, but something more subtle. It is like when two candles touch; if one is already ablaze, the other ignites by merely touching the flame of the first. To be a worthy recipient we must be like a candle that is ready to catch fire, not one with a wet, weak wick. All the conducive conditions should be present. Transmission automatically takes place when those conditions coincide during empowerment.

What is the real purpose of empowerment? Empowerment means that some realization occurs in the student. If no insight takes place or if some degree of understanding fails to dawn in the mind of the student, then there is only the blessing of having participated in the empowerment. This type of benefit can only dispel the obstacles of temporary circumstances. Insight is what empowerment is really about.

Unless some degree of insight takes place during the empowerment, the ritual is just child's play. Tibetan children put things on their heads and pretend they are giving empowerments to each other, but when grown-ups look at this, they see it is just a game and silly to regard it as real. Similarly, an empowerment ceremony in which both master and disciple are involved in deceit or parody is obviously not an effective means for ripening a person's mind.

The four empowerments introduce four levels of insight. Usually these four are given gradually, over the course of several years. Some people, however, need not be given the four empowerments separately, as they are capable of simultaneously realizing the understanding introduced in them. This was the case with King Indrabodhi, who is the example of 'understanding and liberation occurring simultaneously.'

The first empowerment is called the vase empowerment. At the time of receiving the vase empowerment, we should recognize appearance as inseparable from emptiness. This means to realize that whatever appears, all experience, is unreal and illusory. Receiving the second empowerment, the secret empowerment, we should gain some insight into the unity of clarity and emptiness. The third empowerment, the wisdom empowerment, is given by means of a mental consort or karmamudra, by which we realize the unity of bliss and emptiness. With the fourth, the precious word empowerment, we should totally merge with the single sphere of dharmakaya, the real Mahamudra or Dzogchen, the natural state in which all phenomena of samsara and nirvana, whatever appears and exists, is totally beyond arising, dwelling and ceasing.

It is the tradition to arrange a perfect shrine with various symbols of enlightened body, speech and mind to be used during the empowerment. Nevertheless, when a qualified student and a perfect master meet, it is not crucial to have the correct ceremonial articles present. When the ritual objects are placed upon our head, we usually think, … "Now, I receive the empowerment." But if we somehow missed the bonk on the head from an object, then we feel, … "I missed something. I did not completely receive that empowerment." While this is often the case, the real transmission of the view of Mahamudra or Dzogchen does not depend upon whether the articles touch our head. There is something more important. What is that?

To begin with, the whole point of receiving the empowerment is to gain insight, traditionally called 'realizing the wisdom that is the nature of the empowerment.' Unless that insight takes birth in our being, unless some understanding arises, the empowerment is not truly received. One may receive millions of empowerments and still fail to connect with the main point.

According to tradition, during the empowerment ceremony the master should sit on a lofty brocade-covered throne and be dressed in very elegant clothing. The disciples should have washed themselves and wear their best clothes and adornments. They should enter, prostrate and make offerings. There is often a traffic jam of offerings passing one way and ritual implements coming the other. The ceremony proceeds and reality is pointed out. I am not saying there is anything wrong with that style of conducting an empowerment. But if we miss the main point, the recognition of the insight that should occur during this elaborate affair, then the whole thing is just a charade. The main point is gaining insight, recognizing the wisdom that is the nature of the empowerment. Whether the empowerment is magnificent or plain is of secondary importance. If it must be elaborate to facilitate the occurrence of insight, then that is fine, but it is not the main point. There are stories from the past about great siddhas, such as Tilopa and Naropa, Marpa and Milarepa, who received empowerment in untraditional ways. We should read these in the English translations of their life stories.

One of my favorite stories is about Naropa and his teacher, Tilopa. When meeting Tilopa, Naropa was already a great scholar. He had studied a tremendous amount and acquired vast learning, but he felt that his understanding of Mahamudra was only intellectual and lacking direct experience. Repeatedly he begged Tilopa … "Please give me the transmission. Please give me the pointing-out instruction, the empowerment of Mahamudra." Tilopa responded by completely ignoring him. He paid no attention to Naropa. In fact, he treated Naropa terribly and put him through extreme hardship. Several times Tilopa sent Naropa into situations where he was beaten by other people. Then one day Tilopa took off his sandal and unexpectedly slapped Naropa across the face. Naropa was stunned for a moment but when he regained his senses his realization was equal to Tilopa's. That is one example of how empowerment can be transmitted without many elaborate articles. This story proves that transmission does not depend on a complex ceremony involving prostrations, supplications, a mandala on the shrine, and so on. Similar stories are found in the Nyingma lineage. When Shri Singha gave the transmission to Vairochana, it was in a more pleasant way. He handed Vairochana an apple rather than slapping him with a sandal. It is said that Vairochana obtained the entire Dzogchen empowerment known as the 'expression of awareness' simply through that gesture of being handed an apple.

Then there is the story of Gampopa's meeting with Milarepa. Milarepa was a yogi while Gampopa was a monk keeping monastic precepts. When they met for the first time, Milarepa forced Gampopa to drink *chang* from a skull-cup. Gampopa hesitated, thinking, … "I am a monk. If I drink alcohol I break my vows. People are watching. What will they think? What will they say about me afterward?" But Milarepa just kept saying … "Drink! Drink!" Without further thought Gampopa drank the chang, leaving no remainder, and in the same moment gained tremendous insight. Thus, you can see there is no fixed rule as to how a qualified master should give empowerment to a qualified disciple. Empowerment does not depend upon a vase touching the top of our head or on being blessed with any special representation of enlightened body, speech or mind.

There is another story about Paltrul Rinpoche, some of whose teachings you have probably read. He was very learned and always engaged in practice. But people did not know that he was a great practitioner because he was often seen sleeping. He seemingly did nothing at all, was quite eccentric and often acted in unconventional, even outrageous, ways. Though he was realized, he would often come to another master's teachings incognito and sit in the back of the room. Most of the time he would lean back or lie down with eyes and mouth open. Often, he would lie down outside, look up into the sky and do nothing.

On one occasion he was passing through the monastery in eastern Tibet known as Dzogchen Gompa, where a learned khenpo lived who had yet to experience deep confidence in the view. The khenpo asked Paltrul Rinpoche for the pointing-out instruction. His insistent requests were only met with Paltrul Rinpoche's feigned ignorance. The khenpo begged many times, saying, … "Please give me empowerment. Please give me teachings!" Paltrul Rinpoche's response was simply to say, … "Yeah, yeah. We will see!" Then he would then lie down outside and look into the sky. The khenpo thought, … "I regard him as my teacher and want to receive teachings. Maybe I should just act like him." So at the close of day he also went out and lay down and looked up at the sky with open eyes, open mouth, arms and legs spread out, completely relaxed. Then Paltrul Rinpoche said, … "Hey, Khenpo! What do you see?" The khenpo said, … "I see the sky." Paltrul replied, …Yeah, yeah." After some time Paltrul Rinpoche asked, … "What do you see in the sky?" The khenpo replied, … "I see the moon." Paltrul Rinpoche said … "Yeah, very good!" After a few minutes Paltrul Rinpoche asked, … "Do you hear the dogs barking at Dzogchen Monastery?" The khenpo said, … "Yes, I hear the dogs barking too." This exchange of a few sentences was enough for the khenpo to receive the full transmission of the view. Afterward, he attained very high realization.[10]

Having genuinely obtained the ripening empowerments, we also should receive the liberating instructions. They include the teachings on the four mind changings, the general instructions on how to turn one's mind away from samsara. These are followed by instructions on the special inner preliminaries. Afterward, we receive instructions on how to practice the development and completion stages.

The four mind changings are essential for the practitioner. If we do not grasp the reality that samsara is pointless, we will be carried away by attraction to samsara's deluded experiences. Without wearying of samsara, we cannot engage in authentic practice. We must turn away from samsaric aims by taking to heart the four mind changings: reflecting on the precious human body, impermanence and death, the cause and effect of karmic actions, and the defects of samsaric existence.

The first of the four mind changings, reflecting on the importance of the precious human body, stresses the difficulty of obtaining a human body. The human body is the best possible support for practicing the Dharma. It is incredibly difficult to get a human birth and therefore very precious. Merely having obtained a human body is in itself not enough; it is impermanent and does not last for very long. Birth certainly is followed by death. Right now we treasure our body, we give it the best food and adorn it with nice clothing. Yet when the energies that sustain the body disappear, it is declared dead, begins to smell revolting and is disgusting to people. Nobody wants to touch our dead body; it will be disposed of as soon as possible. It's certain this physical body will die someday.

By reflecting on impermanence and death, we lose the confidence that we will live for a long time and feel the immediate need to practice. As a result, we will not make long-range plans but try to use our time effectively.

What about karma? When we die our breathing ceases, the body is discarded and our possessions taken by others. All we retain is the karmic results of our past actions. What is the cause and effect of karma? What are the results of good and bad actions? These we must learn about. By understanding the relationship between the cause and effect of karmic actions, positive and negative deeds, we will be unmistaken about the way to practice the Dharma. That is called utilizing the law of cause and effect.

Where will our consciousness go after death? In which of the six realms will we be reborn? As long as we are encased in the habitual patterning of a deluded state of mind, no matter where we are born within the six imperfect realms of samsara, we will never be beyond suffering. Beings in the three lower realms of the hells, hungry ghosts and animals, experience only misery and suffering. Even the higher realms of gods, demigods and human beings lack perfect happiness. The vital point is that as long as we retain dualistic fixation and ego-clinging, rigidly holding on to the idea of self, we are always involved in deluded experience which makes suffering unavoidable. That which truly brings an end to the causes that perpetuate ego-clinging and deluded experience is the practice of the sacred Dharma. Therefore, to practice the Dharma is crucial. To study and apply the teachings is called utilizing our precious human body.

Having taken to heart these general instructions on the four mind changings, we are ready for the special inner preliminaries of Vajrayana, known as the 'four times one hundred thousand practices' or preliminaries: refuge with prostrations and bodhisattva vow, Vajrasattva recitation, mandala offerings, and guru yoga. Vajrayana is the vehicle of methods that are both skillful and free from hardship. These preliminary techniques can very quickly purify our misdeeds and obscurations of our body, speech and mind.

The famous statement, … "When obscurations are purified, realization occurs spontaneously," reveals the whole purpose of purification practice, since that which prevents us from attaining realization is our karmic misdeeds and obscurations.

In Vajrayana, the vehicle of Secret Mantra, emphasis is placed on yidam practice. Through this practice, we approach the body, speech, and mind of a perfect buddha. In order to be free of ego-clinging, which is difficult to immediately discard, we visualize the deity as a body of rainbow light, recite the deity's mantra and rest in the equanimity of enlightened mind. By familiarizing ourselves with the immaterial mental image of the deity the habit of clinging to concrete reality is diminished. Through visualization practice we ultimately obtain a body that is the unity of emptiness and luminosity.

Visualizing the form of the deity, reciting the mantra that is the voice of the deity and resting in the equanimity of the mind of the deity, we realize the nature of things. Why is this? It is because right now our body, speech, and mind are by nature already the pure aspects of the three kayas, the state of enlightenment. We ordinarily perceive our body as a material form, our voice as a dualistic way of communicating, and our mind as structured by dualistic thinking. Through the yidam practice we are introduced to and have the opportunity to recognize the pure nature of our body, speech, and mind, which, although obscured, is already present. This is the whole purpose of yidam practice: to realize the three kayas by uninterruptedly perceiving our body as the unity of appearance and emptiness, our voice as the unity of sound and emptiness, and our mind as the unity of awareness and emptiness.

Having received empowerments and instructions from various masters, we may like to keep count and list our credentials. But just to think …I have received such and such, just to have the superficial confidence of having obtained a transmission, does not by itself bring liberation. The only reason for receiving teachings is to liberate our being. The ripening empowerments and liberating oral instructions should free our state of mind in the sense that disturbing emotions should diminish and the qualities of wisdom should increase. Take that as your infallible guideline. Our disturbing emotions do not diminish by collecting notes of the different titles of teachings and the empowerments that we received, while neglecting to put these instructions and transmissions into practice.

Liberation here means the abandonment of conceptual thinking, the collapse of deluded fixation. If we do not succeed in this, we are like tea poured into a cracked cup; after a short time, it leaks out. We must carefully investigate for ourselves the defects and suffering associated with ego-clinging and the grasping tendency of our mind. No one else can do it for us.

No matter what practice we apply, some signs should occur. In the context of ground, path and fruition, on the path, signs should manifest as a result of practice. After progressing on the path, the result of fruition should be obtained.

While the view of Vajrayana is very subtle and profound, we must also conduct ourselves carefully in all actions as well as in meditation practices. It is possible to go astray by misapprehending the teachings or becoming too fascinated by the various meditation experiences that may arise.

We can practice different levels of teachings, such as the three or nine vehicles, the four sections of tantra and so forth. A good analogy for this abundance of methods is to consider the different countries of the world. Each culture has its own tradition for preparing and making food. If the cook is skillful the dish will be tasty while an inexperienced cook may create awful food. When applying the different levels of teaching, if the teacher is competent and the student qualified, then even though the prescribed teaching may belong to the path of a shravaka, which takes a long time, the student will eventually attain the result of that practice, which is liberation from samsaric existence. On the other hand, if the teacher is unqualified and the practitioner is neither sharp nor diligent, then even if the student is given a Vajrayana practice, liberation can take much longer than if he were practicing Hinayana methods.

No matter which path or level of teaching one practices, the speed and efficacy depends solely upon the individual. Through perseverance in the teachings of the shravakas, the Hinayana system, one can certainly attain liberation. On the other hand, to practice Vajrayana with a view that is only theoretical, not directly experienced, while maintaining behavior that does not even approach the Hinayana standard, will produce a result that is immensely harmful.

The vital point in all the different Vajrayana practices is to recognize unconditioned wakefulness, the unity of bliss and emptiness. Although our physical body is material and composed of the five elements, it is possible to ripen these constituents into the pure rainbow body. Within this very lifetime it is possible to achieve the unified state of the two kayas that are of one taste in the nonarising, space of dharmakaya, the absolute essence of cognizance.

As the heart of all liberating instructions, the Dzogchen teachings include several sections: the outer Mind Section, the inner Space Section and the secret Instruction Section. In addition, there are subdivisions such as *Ati, Chiti,* and *Yangti,* each more profound than the preceding one. But all the key points can simply be included within two aspects: Trekchö and Tögal.

Trekchö, Cutting Through, means to cut through thought occurrnce, thereby revealing naked awareness. Trekchö is the practice of the unity of awareness and emptiness. Having gained some degree of stability in Trekchö, the practice of Tögal is added to enhance realization. Tögal, Direct Crossing, is the practice of the unity of appearance and emptiness. Through certain key points used in Tögal practice, visual manifestations begin to occur in one's experience. These manifestations will eventually reach a degree of fullness and finally completely disappear.

Dzogchen has two systems of transmission: the oral lineage called kama and the treasure lineage called terma. It does not matter which system we practice, because the teachings are the same. It is essential that we receive the instructions in their totality from a qualified master and then apply them assiduously in secluded places.

Essentially, the view of Trekchö is identical with the final view of Madhyamika that is totally free from the eight constructs and four extremes. By repeatedly resting evenly in the state without mental formulations or fixation, our mind's negative aspects of disturbing emotions and thought activity are slowly exhausted and the enlightened qualities begin to manifest and increase. The key point is not to follow after the thoughts of the three times, but to rest in vivid, naked awareness.

According to the Mahamudra system, by resting without rigidly meditating and without being distracted, our thoughts of the three times, deluded experiences and disturbing emotions that obstruct recognizing the nature of mind will gradually cease, and we realize nonconceptual wisdom. At that time, the enlightened qualities begin to increase.

Chokgyur Lingpa, a close disciple of Jamyang Khyentse Wangpo and Kongtrul Lodrö Thaye, succinctly said, … "When abandoning the watcher in awareness itself, there is utter emptiness free from color and shape." When we start to investigate and look into exactly what our mind is and what the watcher is, it is impossible to pinpoint any concrete thing with a particular shape or color; it cannot be identified or held on to in any way whatsoever. We cannot say that our mind exists; we cannot say it does not exist. We cannot say it is a combination of existence and nonexistence or that it is neither of these. It is impossible to make any final statement at all about it. Chokgyur Lingpa continues, … "When not fixating on the thought

'It is empty that is the moment of seeing the nature of mind." To retain the idea that we are experiencing the empty essence of mind is still a subtle, dualistic fixation. When that fixation has also been relinquished, when we let go of the idea … 'This is empty,' the moment of seeing the nature of mind emerges. This again is the view of Trekchö, Cutting Through.

The main term used in the Mahamudra system is 'ordinary mind.' It is a very important word. Why is it that we are unable to rest in the ultimate view, the nature of mind? It is simply because of our inability to sustain the innate stability of ordinary mind. Without training, we are unable to maintain unfabricated naturalness. What is it that obscures this ordinary mind, our buddha nature? It is our distracted thought movements. Thinking is the root cause for all dualistic clinging and disturbing emotions. In short, the view of Mahamudra, ordinary mind, is immediately realized the very moment we are free from mental fabrication.

While the approaches to the three views of Madhyamika, Mahamudra and Dzogchen are slightly different, their end results are identical. Mahamudra and Dzogchen emphasize the pointing-out instruction, the introduction to mind essence, whereas the Madhyamika system approaches ultimate truth through intellectual analysis. Having repeatedly examined the subject, object and mind and failed to find anything that is truly existent, the absence of true existence becomes evident. By resting in the nature of that absence of true existence, it is possible to arrive at the same realization as the other two views.

While one needs some degree of faith and open-mindedness in order to engage in the analytical meditation of a scholar, faith is indispensable in the Mahamudra and Dzogchen practice called the resting meditation of a simple practitioner. That is why the Buddha said in one of the Prajnaparamita scriptures, … "Shariputra, the ultimate truth is realized exclusively by means of faith." Ultimate truth is realized through strong faith and compassion.

The main point of the bardo of this life is to receive instructions in a proper way from a qualified master, no matter which lineage.

The proper way is to become totally free from doubts, misunderstandings and ignorance about the teachings. Do not let your understanding remain vague or uncertain. Clarify it again and again with your teacher and become clear about how to practice correctly and the purpose of practice. Having received the oral instructions in full you can then go to a secluded place and practice on your own. As I mentioned earlier, circumstances have an effect. One is influenced by living in a place where people are very attached. Living alone, no one can influence us; we may feel lonely, but that is all. In such a situation we can concentrate one hundred percent on practicing the oral instructions.

In short, all those who reached perfect accomplishment in one lifetime through the profound teachings of the Eight Practice Lineages that flourished in Tibet, such as Mahamudra, Dzogchen, Lamdrey, Jordruk and so forth, were liberated in that very body without having to go through any further bardos. They attained enlightenment in one lifetime. That is the actual measure for perfecting the practice of the bardo of this life. However, these days, very few people of this kind can be found in the New or Old Schools. In any case, since we indeed have buddha nature, if we practice one-pointedly according to these teachings there is little doubt that we can attain complete enlightenment within this very lifetime, just as many practitioners of the past did.

How much time do we really have? A short time actually; there is almost no time at all. So, what will be of lasting benefit? Only by remaining in the egoless state of nonconceptual wakefulness can we put a halt to circling in samsara, life after life, birth after birth, be liberated from confusion and attain the unsurpassable state of enlightenment. The cause for attaining this unsurpassable state of enlightenment is to cultivate insight into emptiness.

The time we have now is so very precious that we must use this opportunity while body and mind are still together. During this particular time, we control our destiny. Therefore, if we are diligent in practice, both body and mind will benefit. The more capable we are of sustaining insight into emptiness, the closer we are to accomplishing enlightenment. If we neglect this opportunity, then at death when our body and mind have separated, we will wander through the ensuing bardos and liberation will be difficult. Not trying to accomplish enlightenment now, when the body and mind are together, is a big mistake.

The Painful Bardo of Dying

What has been taught up till now? First, we examined the bardo of this life: what it actually means, how it appears to both ordinary people and to people who are practitioners. I also taught what we can do during this bardo, what instructions we must receive, and finally how to apply these teachings once they are received. To understand these vital points of advice and what they entail is called developing the knowledge that results from learning. Thinking about them and becoming clear about the pertinent instructions is called developing the knowledge that results from reflection. Once you apply the teachings in your own life and embody them in personal experience, you develop what is called the knowledge that results from meditation.

The second topic is called the painful bardo of dying. The bardo of dying is said to be painful because the process of passing away usually involves pain and suffering. Although the death process might sometimes be very quick and we may think that nothing much is felt, some pain is certainly involved. Even if one dies in a coma or during a faint, the mind still experiences subtle pain during what is called the interruption of the life-force. This term refers to the destruction of the life channel where the prana that supports the physical body dwells. When that circulation is destroyed, some degree of pain is felt.

This second bardo, the painful bardo of dying, will again be explained under three headings: first, what it actually is, next, how it is experienced, and finally, how to apply the instructions to deal with it.

There are countless causes and numerous circumstances of death. Sometimes the circumstances of death are negative, but sometimes even positive circumstances such as medicine being improperly administered can result in death. According to the Buddhist medical tradition, illness arises due to imbalances between the three components, wind, phlegm and bile. In such cases an illness or a combination of diseases can strike the physical body, sometimes with fatal consequences. The three disturbing emotions of attachment, anger and delusion can take on the form of evil influences that cause fear, discomfort and even death. Regardless of whether death results from an imbalance in the three basic components or the evil influences of the mind poisons, all these negativities are basically caused by ego-clinging, the tendency to hold on to the idea of self.

There are two primary causes of death: either our time has run out or temporary circumstances result in death. When our life span has reached its end, nothing more can be done; death is unavoidable. However, if a temporary circumstance threatens our life, we can resort to different remedies, such as following a medicinal cure or having special ceremonies performed. Through these we can sometimes avert death temporarily.

Sometimes when we are very sick, we may feel … "Now I am going to die!" We might interpret the different experiences arising from the illness to mean that death is approaching. Actually, certain texts exactly describe the definite outer, inner and secret signs that indicate the proximity of death. Most people do not really like to study these texts because they explain very clearly the signs indicating whether one will die after exactly six years, after exactly three years, after six months, or even during the coming month. We cannot look far into the future, but the next six years can be known quite clearly.

Certain outer, inner and secret signs indicate that death is imminent. First of all, since the body was formed by the five elements, a strong imbalance in these elements occurs at the onset of the death process and at this time no amount of medicine will help.

Some death signs are clearer on certain days of the lunar month. For example, usually when we press our closed eyelids a tiny bit of light and color appears. If on the first day of the month that has disappeared, it is an indication that death is coming soon. Furthermore, there is normally a kind of very subtle ringing sound or resonance in our ears. If that is no longer heard, this is another indication that death is approaching. There are quite a few other signs as well. Examinations that presage death can also be made based on examinations of menstrual blood or semen. Those are outer signs.

Inner signs occur in one's dreams. Dreams are usually unreliable and beyond credibility, but death signs are fairly obvious. Sometimes particular inauspicious dreams will occur again and again in the early morning. For example, night after night one may repeatedly dream of putting on black robes and traveling in a downward direction. One may dream of encountering and riding downhill on the back of a wild animal such as a tiger or leopard or entering a dark area where everything becomes black. These dreams foretell one's death.

Furthermore, if one is very sick and dreams again and again that the sun and the moon are sinking in the sky, that is a sign that one will die. But to experience such dreams while in good health is a sign that one's root teacher is about to die or that an obstacle has arisen to threaten the root teacher's life.

A secret sign of approaching death is that our disposition and character begin to change. Someone previously gentle and kind suddenly becomes very irritable and easily angered. Neither acts of kindness nor admonishments from others seem to help in such a case.

When such signs occur, a practitioner will understand that death is near. If he or she has not yet been liberated in the bardo of this life, the practitioner should then concentrate one hundred percent on practice, knowing that the time is up. Supplicate your root teacher and all the lineage masters, mingle your mind with their wisdom mind, generate compassion for all sentient beings, and then simply rest in the natural state. By doing so you will have a strong opportunity for liberation during the bardo of dying.

This practice of mingling the mind of the teacher with one's own has a profound purpose. The mind of a qualified master abides uninterruptedly in the nonconceptual state of wakefulness that is naturally endowed with great compassion. With the openness of faith, make this supplication: … "May the realized mind of all the buddhas and the mind of my teacher right now clear away the disturbing emotions concealing my nature!" Having made such a supplication from the core of your heart, you can certainly attain some degree of realization. This is due to the connection between the blessings of the master's enlightened mind, your own openness of faith and the truth of dharmata, which is the natural state of wakefulness.

What is the painful bardo of dying? The first section in the chapter is called identifying the essence. ...*It is the whole period from the time one is afflicted by the sickness that will cause one's death, whatever it may be, until the true luminosity of dharmata, the first bardo, has arisen.*[11] There is some discussion as to whether the true luminosity of the ground belongs at the end of the bardo of dying or at the beginning of the bardo of dharmata. In *The Mirror of Mindfulness*, the author follows the Dzogchen system in which this luminosity occurs at the onset of the bardo of dharmata. Here, however, we will consider it as occurring at the end of the bardo of dying.

The superior type of person mentioned above who is liberated in this lifetime need not go through the other bardos. The Dzogchen teachings state: ...*As space within and without mingle together when a vase breaks, so body and mind dissolve into the emptiness of dharmakaya.*[12]

In this example, essentially there is no difference between the space within a vase and the space without, except for the degree of vastness. If a practitioner has realized the view of simplicity, his physical body may very well be made up of flesh and blood, but in essence there is no difference between his realization and the state of enlightenment. It is only that the kayas and wisdoms are not yet fully manifest. When the vase breaks, meaning when the physical body disintegrates at the time of death, the wisdoms and kayas will manifest. The main point of a superior practitioner is that he need not undergo the dissolution stages.

...*The mediocre yogin has three ways of dying: like a small child, like a wandering beggar and like a lion.*[13] Like a small child means that there is no concept of dying or not dying. Dying like a wandering beggar means that one does not care about the circumstances of death.

Some people are extremely sad when passing away because they cannot bear to leave their relatives. Parents with small children especially feel like this. They are heartbroken because they are leaving their children forever, not just for a short time. The separation is permanent. Therefore, it is good to be like Milarepa and make aspirations as he did: … "When I die, may I die alone without anybody to cry, without any relatives to mourn. May I die in solitude so that no one will see the corpse afterwards." Having cut attachments to circumstances is called dying like a lion. When the lion knows it is about to die, it goes into solitude to die alone.

In the first two cases, superior practitioners and mediocre yogins, have recognized mind essence, have trained in it and have gained a full or partial degree of stability. When passing away they do not need anyone else. It is better for them to be without disturbances so that they can liberate their minds. But the least skillful kind of practitioner needs some reminder: at best, one's teacher should be present when we die so that he can say, … "This and this is happening. Do not be attached; do not be distracted," and so forth. Next best is to be with a Dharma friend with whom we have shared teachings and gotten along with very well. If someone we didn't like is reading the teachings aloud at our deathbed, we may become irritated and angry. Instead of benefiting, this will create an obstacle. It is better to have a person one has never met before read the teachings aloud. According to the Nyingma lineage, there are many instructions to be read aloud to a dying person such as *The Liberation Through Hearing in the Bardo*.

When the best practitioners are passing away, they do not give others a chance to read the teachings aloud. They remain alone to attain rainbow body. There is no need to remind them of anything. The next-best practitioners may be reminded or not, it does not really matter. Nothing changes the fact that they will be liberated. But the least skilled practitioner needs the benefit of instructions to remind them at the time of dying. These do not always have to be very elaborate. For some Dzogchen practitioners, it is enough to simply repeat the syllable *ah in their presence.

The Mirror of Mindfulness is aimed mainly at the inferior type of practitioner. The superior and the mediocre practitioners do not need this information. That does not mean that we must remain inferior practitioners. Having studied these teachings, we can of course progress. Let nothing prevent that. But we must always start at the bottom of the staircase and climb one step at a time.

...In general, the body of all beings is first formed by means of the five elements.[14] As the powers of the five elements develop, the embryo takes shape in the mother's womb. From a small blob, the head, arms and so forth are slowly formed. After one is born, one also subsists by means of the five elements. The reason why the physical body finally perishes is that the powers of the elements begin to subside. For example, if we lose a finger, the power or sensation that the finger once possessed has been withdrawn into the body. When the powers of the elements have fully dissolved, the body dies and starts to decompose.

The body possesses five main pranas or winds, as well as the different wheels or chakras in which these winds move. At death these pranas begin to disintegrate, one after the other. This process is accompanied by certain outer, inner and secret experiences.

One of the five main winds is called the equal-abiding wind. When that ceases to function, one is unable to digest food. At this time one can only drink liquids. The warmth in one's body also starts to disappear. This means that the body heat withdraws from the feet and the hands and one gradually becomes colder and colder until finally, warmth remains only in the heart. Even though the feet and arms might be cold, as long as one's heart remains warm, one has not yet died. When the heart grows cold then this life is over.

...The disappearance of the life-upholding wind makes one's mind unclear and confused.[15] When the life-wind begins to disappear, one starts to have different kinds of hallucinations and to feel nervous and frightened. One is extremely uncomfortable. This can also happen during normal life when extra wind enters into the subtle nadi at one's heart. Tibetan doctors call this *nying-lung* meaning heart wind. It tends to make people neurotic or fearful.

When the downward-moving wind begins to disappear, normal automatic body functions such as control over urination and defecation become difficult. One can no longer choose when to let go or not let go. This can be quite unpleasant.

The disappearance of the upward-moving wind, another of the five main pranas, makes one unable to swallow any food or drink. It becomes very difficult to consume liquids and one is short of breath. When people are about to die the breathing grows irregular and shallow. Exhalations are very long but it is difficult to inhale. A gasp or rattle, like a very short breath, develops.

When the pervading wind that gives the muscles power to move disappears, one's body becomes like a corpse even though one has not yet died. One cannot even lift an arm, and eventually not even one finger. One's body is paralyzed.

…*The beginning of the destruction of the nadi wheels is the disintegration of the nadi wheel of the navel. After that, step by step, the disappearance of the supporting wind makes the earth element dissolve into the water element.*[16] The supporting wind is that which creates physical vigor. Its disappearance is the first step in the dissolution of the elements and is accompanied by outer, inner and secret signs. The outer sign is the loss of physical strength. One becomes very heavy and cannot move. The neck can no longer support the head. The legs can no longer support the body. The hand can no longer hold a plate of food, and the skin loses color and radiance. The face becomes pale and takes on an ugly, moldy, colorless texture. Stains collect on the teeth. One cannot contain saliva and nasal mucus drips out. Another sign is that the nostrils draw inwardly and the face takes on a hollow appearance. The eyes that usually have some shine become lackluster.

The inner signs concern one's state of mind. The dying person becomes dull and feels mentally heavy and obscured. Thinking that this is caused by physical circumstances, he asks people, … "Please take the blankets off. Remove some of my clothes. Lift me up a little." He feels as if he is sinking into the earth.

In short, the dying person grows pale and feels great anxiety. His voice changes and talking is difficult. His eyes lose focus and roll back in his head, showing the whites. People present start to feel uncomfortable just looking at his face.

Practitioners watch for the secret signs, the visual experiences resembling smoke, mirages, fireflies and so on, and pay close attention to them, whereas ordinary people will not even notice. Although the secret signs of luminosity are vague, like a mirage, a practitioner will recognize them. Focusing on the practice in which he has trained during this life, he will now be able to progress.

The next nadi-wheel to disintegrate is that of the heart chakra. At the same time the radiance-producing wind makes the water element dissolve into the fire element. The outer signs of this are that one's mouth and tongue become dry. The mouth becomes clogged and the lips become pale, white and shrunken. Usually when we stick out our tongue we can see the tip, but now that is impossible. Normally when we raise our hand in front of our face, we can see a portion of our wrist, but at this time we will unable to see that. At this point death is quite near.

…*The inner signs are that one is bewildered and has various visions.*†[17] One's mind becomes very unclear and hazy. Sometimes one recognizes the people around one, but sometimes one blacks out and is unaware of what is going on. One feels … "I am still alive," but in the very next moment everything is vague and hazy.

The various hallucinations are in accordance with one's basic character: evil-minded people will perceive terrifying visions and become frightened, while practitioners who have better karma and a purer frame of mind might have very delightful visions. They might see beautiful scenery or their root teacher might appear before them as if in person and confer upon them the four empowerments so that they attain realization. Actually, this point indicates what kind of practitioner one has been during the bardo of this life.

The Mirror of Mindfulness (pages 28–31) clearly describes the dissolution of the elements and their corresponding experiences. The dissolution of the gross and subtle thoughts is a bit more complicated and warrants detailed explanation. To fully comprehend these experiences, one needs to become familiar with the terms appearance, increase and attainment, which are usually called the three experiences of whiteness, redness and blackness. A practitioner should know what these experiences actually are. Whiteness or appearance is due to the descent of the white element, obtained from one's father at the moment of conception. At that time there is a white, shimmering light like moonshine. The outer sign is similar to the moon descending or rising. The inner sign is that one's consciousness feels hazy like a mirage. This should be acknowledged as the experience of whiteness.

The experience of redness involving the ascent of the red element obtained from one's mother at conception is like sunshine in a place filled with dust so that the sun appears very red. The outer sign is a red sun either rising or setting. The inner sign is scintillating sparks that appear and disappear like fireflies. The experience of blackness is like the darkness of the night sky. At this point, one's consciousness alternates between being clear and hazy.[18]

The three experiences, appearance, increase and attainment initially take place when the consciousness is conceived, as the egg of our mother unites with the sperm of our father. When passing away, these are the last three experiences that occur before the consciousness detaches itself from the physical body. At this moment, we should recognize the essential nature of these experiences. When we fail to recognize their essence, their manifestations are the three poisons, attachment, anger and delusion, through which we fall unconscious and take rebirth.[19]

Moreover, the nature of the five poisons in their pure aspect is actually the five wisdoms. In essence, the white element can be equated with mirror-like wisdom. The red element can be equated with the wisdom of equality. The consciousness is accompanied by the movement of prana or wind, which in essence is the discriminating wisdom. All of these can be combined into one entity, the all-accomplishing wisdom. The complete body created through that is the dharmadhatu wisdom.

Lacking understanding of this, consciousness takes on a physical form and enters another impure rebirth in samsaric existence. But with understanding, one takes pure rebirth within the manifestation of the five wisdoms and gains liberation. To realize the pure aspect of things is the main objective of Vajrayana.

How to Die

We must acknowledge the impermanence of all conditioned things and especially that human life is fleeting. By doing so, we understand that it is crucial to prepare ourselves for death. What is it that dies at the moment of dying? It is our body and speech that die; the mind can never die. It is our mind that continues to wander through samsaric existences, not our present body or voice. Only that which benefits our state of mind can be of help at the time of death. To concentrate on what is truly valuable when dying is considered intelligent, whereas to only worry about physical comfort is quite foolish. By all means, make some preparation for the moment when your life has come to an end.

The worst misfortune is to know how to take advantage of one's present situation but fail to do so. We all know that there is an end to this life, but no one knows the exact moment when it will happen. The time of death arrives without warning. Of course, to have a guaranteed life-span of seventy years would be very convenient. We could plan to spend a certain number of years on mundane projects, thinking, … "After that I will focus on Dharma practice and everything will work out very nicely." But we do not know when death will come. The time of death can catch up with us at any moment.

Usually we think that only old people with a lot of wrinkles and grey hair are close to death, while youngsters with sparkling eyes and radiant complexions will not die soon. There is actually no such guarantee. Sometimes just the opposite happens: people who are already old remain for a long time while young people suddenly die.

What is of real value when we arrive at the moment of death? It is personal experience in Dharma practice: the practices of purifying obscurations, gathering the two accumulations, and especially our insight into egolessness and emptiness, our training in the view free from mental constructs. Other than that, whatever benefits we acquire such as money, fame and worldly accomplishments, or anything else that is greatly valued during this lifetime is totally useless at the moment of death. The chief support is our understanding of egolessness.

We should ask ourselves, … "What will help me when I die?" When we have difficulties now, we can turn for help to family and friends. When we are sick, we can consult a doctor. But at the moment of death who can we see? Who can we turn to for help? We should ask ourselves these questions. When we honestly think about this it becomes clear only the results of our Dharma practice will help at that time. We should immediately prepare for the moment of death.

We can spend years studying whatever religion or school of thought is of interest to us. Even within Buddhism different philosophies and different levels of teachings exist. But simply studying these teachings, thinking about them and clarifying them in our mind, is not enough to be of true value at the moment of death. Only the application of teachings in personal experience through meditation practice will help; words and theories have no great value when facing death. Give thought to that now and know that only practical understanding and real meditation experience can help you at the time of death.

A small child does not make long-term plans or look very far ahead. If his immediate needs are attended to, then the child is happy and content. The attempt to avoid seeing what will come is childish. But many grownups act in this way, concentrating only on fulfilling immediate needs, fickle-mindedly running after whatever is in front of their noses and giving no thought to preparing for death. Then death arrives suddenly and it is too late.

Even while engaging in so-called Dharma practice there are many ways in which we can deceive ourselves. We can fool ourselves by spending our whole life gaining an intellectual comprehension of the structure of the Dharma teachings, memorizing all the stages of the path, the bodhisattva bhumis and the different levels of meditation experience. We can become very learned in the details of the Four Tantras, such as the complete structure of the tantric approach and all the rituals. However, this type of intellectual understanding is of little value at the time of death. Furthermore, we may become very skilled in debate if we have a sharp mind and a good tongue. We can excel at challenging the different arguments, refuting objections to the teachings and so forth. But that kind of competence is also useless when it comes to dying. What is really important now is to practice in order to realize egolessness. Just being able to talk about egolessness without practical experience is to fool yourself.

Religious people might be very successful in gathering followers, building temples and representations of the enlightened body, speech and mind, taking care of many disciples and giving teachings. But if they lack personal conviction about the state of nonconceptual wakefulness, the very essence of Dharma practice, then at the moment of death they will still have doubts, regrets, grasping and attachment. Do not let that happen to you.

When death approaches, abandon all attachment to spouse, children and parents, friends and relatives, possessions and property. To ensure liberation, completely cut all ties of clinging to these things. That does not mean that we should cut off love for other people such as close relatives. Love is genuine when it is compassionate kindness embraced by bodhichitta and not strangled by attachment. Ordinary love that is mixed with attachment, anger and delusion is a cause for further entanglements and binds us to samsaric existence, whereas the love embraced by the great passion that is wisdom and compassion inseparable is a cause for liberation and enlightenment. This type of love is a million times more precious than ordinary affection for others. Ordinary love and affection is quite fickle, whereas the love that is embraced by bodhichitta and insight into emptiness is unchanging.

It does not matter what the object of attachment is. It can be attachment to ordinary things, even one's shoes; or attachment to one's body and life, country and home, or to gold and silver. Even attachment to religious objects such as one's statues and texts is still attachment. The main point here is to leave no object of attachment for your mind to fixate on at the time of death. It is better to give away whatever you have, either to poor people, friends, relatives or to your teacher. Make sure no material thing remains to which your mind can be attached. We should be without possessions when we know that the time of death is near. It is best to give away everything. That will make it much easier at the time of death as one of the main obstacles to resting in the composure of meditation will have been cleared away.

At the time of death, we should have exhausted all plans, whether virtuous or evil. For example, although we may not have succeeded in getting ahead of our competitors, we should not worry about that at the time of death. We should also give up any idea of seeing a particular relative or a close friend one last time. Maybe there is an enemy we would like to see in order to have the last word; we should completely abandon such aims. There are stories of people who could not let go and die because they wanted to witness one last attack on their enemy. Even half dead, they still would not let themselves die out of anger, spite or a grudge. They wanted a last chance to take revenge. Only after hearing that the other party had died could they finally relax and pass away. We should not be like that. Let absolutely nothing unfinished capture your thoughts.

At the moment of death our frame of mind or the thought that we hold can become extremely intense, much stronger than usual. In ordinary life we have outer sense impressions that distract us from our feelings of anger. A person who is insane can become completely engrossed in one thought or emotion and magnify it to a tremendous degree. The same can happen at the moment of death. Because we may experience an intense degree of resentment or regret, it is very important to clear the mind of anything that could cause remorse. For example, if one has broken the vows belonging to any of the three vehicles, it is important to admit and apologize either mentally or to an actual person. Rid your mind of any such regret so that nothing is left that can linger on. Do not be hindered by what you were unable to accomplish; then everything will be much easier.

The best circumstance is if our master can be physically present while we are passing away, because then we can take initiation or receive the pith instructions again, clarify any last point of uncertainty, and be totally confident about the correct view. Moreover, due to the link between the powerful blessings of the teacher's realized mind and our own genuine faith and unfabricated devotion, it is much easier to recognize the view, the natural state of Mahamudra or Dzogchen. Understanding this correct view ensures liberation. Having the correct view at the moment of dying is a tremendous advantage; in fact, it is the very best of circumstances.

If your teacher cannot be physically present, the next-best situation is to have a close Dharma friend with whom you share pure samaya, someone with whom you have good relations and in whom you trust. Such a Dharma friend can remind you of the practice as you are passing away and can give reliable answers if you have questions. A Dharma friend who has deep understanding himself would be of tremendous benefit. Avoid any ordinary person who is only selfishly interested in your death, who has a grudge against you, or who will only talk about ordinary and deluded topics. Also avoid the presence of people fond of wailing and sobbing as that will disturb your meditation state at the time of leaving this life.

People who are quite stable in their practice do not need this instruction. This advice is meant for those who have only a slight degree of stability. The company and the situation at the moment of death is crucial for practitioners who are unstable and who are still influenced by outer circumstances.

There have been some cases of great practitioners who pondered, … "Tomorrow I am going to die, so why not die in some special, unusual way?" For them dying was a kind of game. They would dress up and sit in some funny posture so when their bodies were found they would create a strong reaction in others. Other lamas with high realization when about to die said, … "Ha! ha! It is time to die. How should I die? What was so and so's posture when he died? Cross-legged? Okay, then I think I will die lying down this time," and doing so, would simply pass away.

For practitioners who possess the confidence of realization, dying and the bardos are like a game, a form of entertainment. But for those of us whose confidence is not that stable, these same experiences may be dreadful.

Furthermore, it is not always certain that the dissolution stages will happen in sequence. We cannot truly generalize about the manner in which a person will die or the experiences one will undergo. Sometimes the different dissolution stages of the elements occur in completely the opposite order. One aspect may be stronger or it may be very short. The dissolution stages depend upon the individual's physical constitution, the condition of his channels and the circumstances surrounding his death, i.e. whether it is due to illness, evil influences and so on.

It is good to become familiar with the different dissolution stages and the outer, inner, and secret signs of death, so that when they occur we will know what is happening. We will then be able to focus on what is of real benefit at that time. Although there are different techniques, the greatest benefit comes from simply resting in ordinary mind, in innate wakefulness.

The reason we continue to roam about in samsaric existence is, first of all, because we have not recognized ordinary mind, this unconstructed wakefulness that is already present in us. Also, we have not trained or gained stability in that recognition. The highest value during the different dissolution stages results from realization of ordinary mind. If we can simply rest in the nature of ordinary mind, it will make all the difference. At the time of death, we can no longer rely on credit cards, money or friends. We can only rely on ourselves. Again, this self-reliance depends upon our ability to rest in ordinary mind. When the dissolution stages are finished, it is possible that through resting in the state of ordinary mind, one can attain liberation during the event called the meeting of the luminosity of mother and child.

What is the best physical posture to assume while passing away? It is best to sit up in the meditation posture. Next best is to recline in what is called the posture of the sleeping lion; holding the thumb at the base of the ring finger on each hand and placing the left hand on the left thigh and the right hand under the chin in a particular manner. This has a special effect on the movement of subtle energy currents in the body. This posture also facilitates recognition of the luminosity of the path during the death process and improves meditation at that time.

Usually it is said the person who has trained in the luminosity of the path during his life will be able to recognize the luminosity of the ground at the moment of death. This doesn't mean that there are two different luminosities, one here and one there. But unless one has recognized the luminosity of the path and knows how to experience it during practice, one will have no idea about what the ground luminosity is when it manifests at the end of the dissolution stages. The experienced practitioner recognizes the ground luminosity at that point simply by thinking, … "Oh yes, that's it!" and then resting in equanimity. This is called the meeting of mother and child luminosities.

No matter who your teacher was or which practice he or she did, at the point of death the vital importance lies in feeling complete trust in him and confidence in your own practice. Mahamudra and Dzogchen use different terminologies to describe an identical experience. Innate wisdom can be called ordinary mind or it can be called the view of Trekchö. It is really the same; simply the recognition of the luminosity of the path. If we are able to recognize the luminosity of the path at the moment of dying, then regardless of what appears in the dissolution stages we will be liberated into dharmakaya.

The particular Dharma terminology we use to describe this does not really matter. The key point is our personal and practical understanding of Mahamudra or Dzogchen, our ability to simply relax and rest in the state that is empty yet cognizant, emptiness indivisible from cognizance. When resting like that, totally relaxed, free and easy, whatever occurs during the dissolution stages does not really matter. The experiences just pass by. That is the key point. No technique or further instruction is needed.

If we simply rest in this state of empty cognizance known as the luminosity of the path and are totally relaxed when the ground luminosity manifests, we are naturally liberated. There is no question, no doubt about this. We need not try to apply a special technique or trick. Liberation occurs automatically.

…One should confidently resolve that the gradual manifestations… are all nothing but the luminous dharmakaya manifestation of self-cognizance.[20] Earlier, the unity of being cognizant and empty was stressed. Here, in the case of a practitioner of Tögal, we must resolve that whatever manifests, all the different experiences in the dissolution stages, are the display of our mind. Yet, the main practice is simply to rest in the view.

One may have practiced *the Six Doctrines of Naropa*, the Mahamudra practice of bliss and emptiness, the Sakya system of *Path and Result* called *Lamdrey* or the *Jordruk* system of Kalachakra. Due to one's practical experience based on the channels, essences and energies, one will be able to recognize the subtle aspects of the dissolution stages as they occur.

What are the chief differences between the practices of Trekchö, Tögal and *the Six Doctrines*? In Trekchö and essence Mahamudra, the main point is to be able to rest in and sustain the continuity of the view. That is sufficient for achieving liberation. When practicing Tögal, while maintaining the view of Trekchö one uses whatever manifests as an adornment in the sense of acknowledging that all the different experiences that take place are actually the display or manifestation of innate wakefulness. One attains liberation through that recognition. According to the Six Doctrines, the key point is to acknowledge that our body, speech, and mind are in essence the vajra body, vajra speech, and vajra mind. As such they become a support for different yogic techniques and we thereby recognize the pure natural aspects of our body, speech and mind. Through that we are able to realize the view of Mahamudra.

Physical pain may arise during the process of passing away, especially at the moment called the interruption of the life-force. When the skilled practitioner is confronted with intense agony, he merely looks into the essence of the sensation of pain and the pain is no longer an overwhelming problem. The important point for people who are not stable in practice is not to get too carried away, not to put too much importance on the sensation of pain or physical discomfort during this time. Simply relax in the view, right up to the experience that is called the ground luminosity of full attainment.

If you are unable to do that, then visualize your root guru and with intense and deep-felt devotion make the aspiration to recognize the nature of luminosity. By combining the power of devotion with the blessings of an enlightened teacher at this point, it is possible to recognize the luminosity of the path. Therefore, when the ground luminosity dawns, one will be liberated. The crucial point here is one-pointed devotion. Unite your mind with that of your root teacher and develop powerful trust in order to realize the luminosity of the path. If you are unable to engender this confidence, one more chance remains which is the practice called *phowa*.

Phowa literally means to change place, to move from one place to another. Phowa can be explained under three headings: the type of person who practices it, the time to practice it and how to practice it. Practitioners who have a high degree of stability in Mahamudra, Dzogchen or Madhyamika practice and some realization will have the confidence to be liberated simultaneously with the final exhalation of breath. No subsequent bardos appear for them. They simply rest in dharmadhatu. Such people need not worry about the practice of phowa because they do not conceive of a real entity to be transferred and do not hope for a place to be transferred to. Such practitioners are totally beyond these concepts.

For practitioners of a lesser capacity who lack the confidence of the view of the natural state, there are many instructions on how to practice phowa at the moment of dying. Masters like Nagarjuna in India and Marpa in Tibet acted as if they were practicing phowa at the moment of death in order to show this path to others. For example, *The Mirror of Mindfulness* describes how Marpa died. First, he … transformed his consort Dagmema into light and dissolved her into his heart center. Straightening his body, he said, "Sons, if you do phowa, do it like this!" *Then a sphere of five-colored light the size of an egg ascended into the sky from a crack at the crown of his head.*[21] That is how Marpa passed away. Even though it appeared that he died while leaving a physical body, he attained what is called the unified level of a vajra holder.

The great Dzogchen master Melong Dorje also passed away in a special manner. He gathered all of his disciples around him, sang songs and gave his last teaching amid a feast gathering. Then he said, *…Now I will die. He …sent a white light the size of a cooking pot up into the air from the crown of his head. Growing bigger and bigger, it filled the sky with rainbow lights and circles.*[22] Although it appeared that both Marpa and Melong Dorje did phowa at the moment of death, there is actually no difference between what they manifested and the attainment of rainbow body. There have been many other such masters in the past.

The success of our practice depends mainly upon our faith and devotion and on maintaining pure samayas. With strong devotion, the practice of phowa is certain to be successful. The one thing that definitely hinders successful phowa is broken samayas.

We should train now, during this lifetime, in the practice of phowa until we develop signs of result. One special sign in particular assures us that at the moment of death we are prepared to perform phowa successfully. However, someone not very proficient in the practice of phowa can do the practice with the help of a lama at the moment of death. With this combined effort it is quite easy to accomplish phowa.

Phowa is defined as the ascent of the mind together with the prana principle. The combination of mind and prana are sent to a good and worthwhile place. Departing from here to the destined place is the practice of phowa.

A correspondence exists between the place of the next rebirth and the aperture in the body through which the consciousness leaves at the moment of death. For example, if the consciousness leaves through the body's lower openings one will be reborn in one of the lower realms as a hell being, hungry ghost, or animal. If the consciousness exits through the upper openings, such as the ears, eyes, nose, and so forth, one will be reborn in the higher realms of humans, asuras or gods, yet still within samsara. Therefore, during the practice of phowa, one must first block all the openings in a special way so that only the aperture at the crown of the head remains open. When the mind leaves the body through the crown of the head, one will be reborn in a pure land beyond samsaric existence where the conditions for practice are perfect.

Someone performing phowa on behalf of another person must be absolutely sure that the person is dead. Otherwise a great sin is committed. An advanced practitioner who knows the death signs will check the nadis, the movement of prana and the body heat to see that the person is actually dead and then perform phowa. It should never be done before the person has truly passed away.

Moreover, when doing phowa for oneself one must be sure that one is actually dying, that it is really the end. If the consciousness is shot up out of the body prematurely it may not be able to return. Therefore, be absolutely certain that the time of death has really come, that the situation is irreversible. The true measure for ascertaining the time of death is when the experiences of whiteness and redness have occured. At that time one can safely practice phowa.

There are different methods and levels of phowa. The dharmakaya phowa free from reference point is performed simply by resting in the nature of the view. In other words, it is without concepts of a self to be transferred and a place to which one can be transferred. The advanced Dzogchen practitioner simply rests in the view of Trekchö and attains the dharmakaya phowa. For someone with true confidence in Dzogchen or Mahamudra practice, the word phowa, meaning 'transferrence,' is really no longer applicable.

The second type of phowa, sambhogakaya phowa, is practiced when one has become adept in the development stage of visualizing oneself as a deity. Having perfected this practice, at the time of death one can manifest in the form of the deity and thereby attain the sambhogakaya phowa. In the terminology of the Six Doctrines, this is equivalent to having some degree of stability in the practice called illusory body. At the time of death one simply applies the practice and attains sambhogakaya.

The third kind, nirmanakaya phowa, means actually maintaining the concept of oneself as the traveler enroute to a pure abode, an unmistaken pure land. The key point in nirmanakaya phowa is to have complete devotion to one's teacher and compassion for all sentient beings. Then one focuses on the form of a seed syllable that shoots up the central channel. A certain sound accompanies the seed syllable, either hik or phat, depending on which practice one is doing. We need not have great realization or hold a high view to do this practice successfully. We simply need devotion, compassion and the ability to visualize the seed syllable.

There was another phowa tradition that was lost centuries ago. It was literally called 'transference of consciousness,' as opposed to 'ejection of consciousness,' phowa. Marpa Lotsawa received this practice in India. He passed it on to his son who died prematurely and was unfortunately unable to transmit the lineage to others.

A fourth kind of phowa is similar to the practice of guru yoga. In this phowa, instead of visualizing a deity or a buddha like Amitabha, Vajrasattva or Guru Rinpoche, we imagine our root guru at the crown of our head. Apart from this, the details are the same.

The fifth kind, khachö, phowa, is performed when one has stability in dream yoga, in conjuring up apparitions during the dream state.

It is not enough to learn phowa practice from a book. We must receive oral instructions from a spiritual teacher and then apply the practice. The first sign of a result in phowa practice is that a strong itch is felt at the top of the head. Later a tiny hole appears into which a straw of grass can actually be inserted. One should continue the practice under competent supervision until this sign manifests.

When we have received the teachings on phowa, trained and attained the signs, then we are somewhat independent. When in addition, we gain some mastery, we can then help others to practice phowa when they are dying. Moreover, we are always prepared to eject our own consciousness at the moment of death.

When the actual time for phowa arrives, we must one-pointedly concentrate on the practice and not be distracted by thoughts of taking care of relatives or making a last attack on our enemies. Focus your attention and be free from doubt. When doing phowa for the final time, eject the consciousness like a competent archer who shoots the arrow from his bow. It flies off beyond return and swiftly reaches the target.

The word phowa is used quite often, but in essence it means to prevent our awareness, which is wisdom inseparable from emptiness, from falling into further confusion. By means of techniques such as visualizing seed syllables, mingling our mind with the prana that shoots out and so forth, we dissolve conceptual mind into the sphere of dharmadhatu. The consciousness totally merges with the nature of dharmadhatu.

To sum up, be sure that you do not spend your whole life pursuing the eight worldly concerns. Do not let Dharma practice remain as mere words and theory. When the time to die comes, if you have not already gained the confidence of realization, then you should at least be able to perform the practice of phowa. In that way, your life will not have been wasted.

The Luminous Bardo of Dharmata

The third bardo, the luminous bardo of dharmata, is again described under three headings: definition, experience and how to deal with the experience. When describing the luminous bardo of dharmata quite a few complicated key terms specific to the teachings of Tantra are used, especially from the Mahamudra and Dzogchen systems. The two most important terms are ground of liberation and ground of confusion. The instructions on how to understand these two terms are crucial points, extremely pithy and profound. To understand what these words point to their vital meaning, we must understand what takes place during the luminous bardo of dharmata.

The luminous bardo of dharmata occurs after the outer elements, the sense faculties and sense bases as well as the inner gross and subtle thoughts have dissolved. It follows the completion of the three experiences of whiteness, redness, and blackness at the end of the painful bardo of dying. To reiterate, the white element descends from the crown of one's head and the red element ascends from one's navel. When these two elements meet at the heart center, consciousness and the prana principle melt together, causing the ordinary person to faint and remain in a state of mindless oblivion.[23]

Regardless of whether one has practiced or not or whether one is a human being or an insect, at the moment of the meeting of these two elements the ground luminosity of dharmakaya dawns. The one who recognizes this for what it is, is liberated. The one who falls under the power of ego-clinging and does not recognize this falls unconscious, oblivious. According to the general system of teachings this unconscious state lasts for three and a half days.[24]

The three experiences of whiteness, redness, and blackness are accompanied by the cessations of the three poisons, attachment, anger, and delusion. Whiteness is accompanied by the complete cessation of the forty thought states resulting from anger. Redness appears together with the cessation of the thirty-three thought states resulting from attachment. Blackness marks the cessation of the seven thought states resulting from delusion. What remains when all of these thought states have ceased is simply the unconstructed nature of mind called dharmakaya. In Dzogchen terminology, this is called basic wakefulness and is the naked awareness itself. The Mahamudra teachings name this state 'ordinary mind.' The experience happens for everyone, whoever they are; the only difference is the length of time this state last.

Someone who has received the pointing-out instruction from a qualified master and has been able to recognize the nature of mind must at this point sustain the continuity of that state and attain liberation. Anyone else will not recognize this basic state of mind and will return to being obscured by the different aspects of ignorance. Again, the effects of past karma will propel one towards a new rebirth.

When the three subtle dissolution stages are taking place, one must be alert because what happens immediately after is the ground luminosity. The general vehicles call this basic state ultimate truth or prajnaparamita, transcendent knowledge. In Buddhism, this is the ultimate 'thatness' to be realized. Different systems of teachings give this ground luminosity different names. According to Madhyamika, it is ultimate truth devoid of constructs, according to Mahamudra, recognition within nonthought and according to Dzogchen, awareness resuming its essence.

Prior to the bardo of dharmata various manifestations appear: mirages, five-colored lights, and experiences similar to sunlight, moonlight, the light of a butter lamp and darkness. When these have ceased, the ground luminosity that is beyond all of these displays dawns like a clear and cloudless sky. This ground luminosity is referred to as dharmakaya, the mind of the Buddha Samantabhadra, the wisdom beyond intellect or simply basic wakefulness. The practitioner who has received the pointing-out instruction during his lifetime and has recognized what is called the luminosity of the path, will immediately recognize the ground luminosity and thereby attain liberation. This moment is called the meeting of mother and child luminosity.[25]

In this case, the practitioner's former training makes liberation very easy. That is the whole reason why it is so essential to rest again and again in the natural state of ordinary mind during one's lifetime. By becoming familiar with the ground luminosity now, one can attain liberation into dharmakaya at the moment of death. The whole point of practice is simply to recognize the luminosity of path, the natural state of Mahamudra. This and only this is what is truly effective when we die. Many great scholars who failed to train in this recognition were not liberated at the time of death.

In essence the ground luminosity is empty, but in nature it is said to be luminous, which in this context means cognizant. These two qualities, emptiness and cognizance, are indivisible. During our studies we hear a lot about emptiness, the emptiness of this and the emptiness of that, but the actual, true emptiness is directly and nakedly present in the period immediately preceding the luminous bardo of dharmata. For all sentient beings this moment holds the possibility of being either the ground of liberation or the ground of confusion, leading to either enlightenment or further samsaric existence.

There are many reasons why it is beneficial for us to practice the Dharma right now, but the main reason is that it will help us attain liberation during the meeting of mother and child luminosity.

Why is the ground luminosity experienced at this point? It is simply because all sentient beings already possess an enlightened essence, the sugatagarbha. This essence is present and permeates anyone who has mind, just as oil completely permeates any sesame seed. So why don't we recognize the mother luminosity if it is present in ourselves as our true nature? We do not recognize it because our nature is obscured by coemergent ignorance and conceptual ignorance. Obscured by these two types of ignorance, we fail to recognize innate wakefulness, the wisdom inherent within ourselves. We wallow in delusion, mistaking what is impermanent to be permanent and holding that which is untrue to be true. These delusions perpetuate our wandering through the realms of samsaric existence.

However, the end of the dissolution stages of whiteness, redness and blackness is like a momentary lifting of the veil of delusion, leaving all obscurations temporarily yet totally absent. At this time the ground wisdom is vividly present; the natural state of Mahamudra is revealed bare and naked.

Ordinary people do not recognize this experience when it dawns upon them. Instead, old habitual tendencies reappear and carry them away into patterns of conceptual thinking. Thus, they return to the state of conditioned existence. Nevertheless, practitioners who have received the pointing-out instruction and made it their personal experience during this lifetime will at death, due to the power of that practice, be able to recognize their natural face, the primordial state of ground luminosity, and be liberated. *The Mirror of Mindfulness* describes this recognition: *... They meet as old friends, or like a river flowing into the ocean.*[26] At that point, all that is left is dharmadhatu, space that is totally free from mental constructs yet naturally endowed with cognizant wakefulness.

The Nyingma system gives this ground luminosity the name Samantabhadra with consort. It is the unity of emptiness and cognizance, the unity of prajna and upaya, and has no concrete existence because in essence it is primordially pure. Nonetheless, at the same time, it is not nonexistent because the five wisdoms as well as numerous other qualities are spontaneously present. Its very nature is spontaneous presence that is *...the utterly pure nature of space dwells as the indivisible great bliss, the essence of primordial purity in the unchanging fourth time of equality.*[27]

Although this primordial state appears to everyone, merely having recognized it in glimpses during our lifetime is not enough. We must become familiar with it and grow accustomed to it through training.

Due to our habitual tendencies and ignorance, this state of ground luminosity has not yet been fully acknowledged. However, based on the dissolution stages of appearance, increase, and attainment, all our disturbing emotions are for a moment totally cleared away, like a curtain being drawn aside. The sights, sounds, smells, tastes, and tactile sensations of the sense organs, and all dualistic grasping and fixation have disappeared. One arrives at the luminosity of the ground, the mother luminosity; therefore, the luminosity of the child, the path luminosity, is able to merge with the mother.

Because fixation on sense objects is absent, our innate wakefulness is able to manifest nakedly. This state of not fixating on anything whatsoever is wakefulness free from arising, dwelling, and ceasing; yet, all things can be cognized. It is not a total blackout but an experience of the natural wisdom beyond words, free from subject and object and concepts of this or that. In ordinary experience, the mind always fixates on the attributes of the sense objects that appear through the five senses. But here, since that kind of dualistic experience is absent, our innate wakefulness is experienced directly. Within the state of having recognized our nature, we reach enlightenment, described as self-occurring self-liberation. We realize that the source of whatever arises is the expanse of primordial purity.

If we fail to recognize the ground luminosity, we again commence the creation of karma through dualistic fixation. But if we have been introduced to the ground luminosity through the pointing-out instruction and have trained in the child luminosity of the path, we can be liberated. We can dissolve into the expanse of spontaneous presence. All hope and fear, all accepting and rejecting and all dualistic fixation has been destroyed. Simply by recognizing this ground luminosity, we are liberated and do not have to undergo any further bardos.

A distinction should be made here between the dharmakaya luminosity just explained and the sambhogakaya luminosity. If we do not recognize dharmakaya or ground luminosity at the close of the bardo of dying, the luminous bardo of dharmata offers us a second chance to attain liberation through the appearance of sambhogakaya luminosity.

Having entered the bardo of dharmata, unusual manifestations occur that are the displays of the body, speech, and mind aspects of our own buddha-nature: peaceful and wrathful deities appear, strange sounds are heard and different manifestations of mind are experienced. If we have gained stability in practice and have recognized emptiness, or if we have some strength in shamatha, or a degree of stability in the development stage so that we can visualize ourselves as a deity, then these appearances, the displays of dharmata, hold the possibility for attaining liberation.

Now the following question might arise: … "What about people who have never seen any pictures of peaceful and wrathful deities and who have never visualized them? Do they also experience these deities in the bardo?" We cannot really say what non-practitioners experience at this point, but they certainly experience very colorful and intense forms that can be as big as Mount Sumeru, the enormous mythical mountain, or as minute as a sesame seed. Images are extremely brilliant and colors are overwhelmingly clear. Incredibly loud noises resound like one hundred thousand simultaneous thunderclaps. The light can be so bright that we feel like we are being completely perforated by light rays. If someone has practiced there is a great chance of success, but someone who has absolutely no experience of Dharma practice might faint from sheer fright.

Many peaceful and wrathful appearances manifest. One might experience pure realms with divinities, not just small realms but the whole expanse of space filled with these manifold appearances. Why do manifestations such as the peaceful and wrathful deities and the sounds, colors and lights appear? They appear because all sentient beings possess the buddha nature. Based on that, what we at present perceive as the five aggregates, the five elements, our consciousness and the sense objects are in their pure aspects the display of this buddha nature, our innate wakefulness. They are already the pure mandala of deities. At the end of the dissolution stages, this manifestation of innate wakefulness simply appears in its pure form.

All sentient beings are buddhas, but this fact is veiled by our temporary obscurations. When these veils are removed, we are actual buddhas. When a gap occurs in our dualistic fixation during the process of death, then all these different manifestations of our buddha nature are experienced unveiled. Based on our stability or lack of stability in practice, that period might last for days or it might just flicker by. For someone who has no familiarity with spiritual practice this experience is very short and the tendency for confusion and ego-clinging, holding onto duality, will quickly cloud awareness, covering up these manifestations. Then the bardo of becoming begins.

The natural manifestations of dharmata, the pure aspects of the five aggregates and the five elements, are the five male and female buddhas, the male and female bodhisattvas, and so forth. In their totality, these are known as the one hundred peaceful and wrathful deities. Generally, it said that these one hundred peaceful and wrathful deities appear, but actually this depends very much upon the individual and his tendencies, as well as the kind of practice with which he is familiar. In short, what appears corresponds to the method used to purify oneself, and that which one has focused on as the object to be purified (i.e. one's yidam practice and what it is aimed at purifying).

In essence, our buddha nature is empty; in nature, it is cognizant; and, in manifestation or function, it is unobstructed. As a normal person, it is hidden by temporary obscurations. The moment our ego-clinging falls apart, then our innate wisdom, the luminosity of dharmata, will vividly, nakedly appear. This ground luminosity is not just empty; it is also luminous, aware. This aspect of luminosity and awareness can manifest in myriad ways. All the various manifestations appearing in the bardo of dharmata come from that. According to an individual's karmic tendencies, these manifestations may appear as terrifying. One may feel threatened and think, … "They have come to take me away! or …They are attacking me!" It all seems very real.

In short, the dead person experiences many pure and impure visions, vivid and brilliant, like a huge brocade suddenly unfurled in the sky. At this time, we acquire special qualities we never had during our lifetime, such as clairvoyance, perfect recall of the past, and other miraculous abilities. These are variously known as the five superknowledges, the six recollections, perfect recall, and continuous samadhi. Nevertheless, the bottom line here is whether or not we have trained during this lifetime. If we have and can recall the practice, liberation is possible. If not, we continue on to what is called the bardo of becoming as it dawns in our experience, flashing forth like in a dream.

Direct Instructions

We have already covered the first three bardos: the bardo of this life, the bardo of dying, and the bardo of dharmata. Now we will examine further the third heading in these categories—how to apply the instructions. The appearance of the ground luminosity of dharmakaya at the end of the bardo of dying and the appearance of the sambhogakaya luminosity in the bardo of dharmata both provide unique opportunities for the practitioner to attain liberation from samsaric existence. This point is crucial and should be closely examined.

Many things happen during the bardos of dying and dharmata, but for most people these bardos do not last long, not more than several moments. These moments are called 'moments of completed action,' the duration of which depends on whether the individual is a practitioner or not. For most non-practitioners it passes quickly, flickering by like a few snaps of the fingers. For practitioners it depends on one's physical constitution, how the subtle channels of one's body are structured, and also on the degree of stability in practice that one has attained. Among people with some stability, the unfolding of primordial purity at the end of the bardo of dying can last as long as it takes to eat a meal. In this case, the measurement of time is called a 'meditation day.' This 'day' is defined as the length of time one can sustain the natural state, the continuity of recognizing innate wakefulness, the nature of mind. A practitioner who possesses confidence in liberation can rest for as long as he or she desires in that state.

What does it mean to possess confidence in liberation? First, it is not enough to have merely recognized the nature of our mind; we must also have resolved this recognition beyond all doubts. But even that is not sufficient. We must acquire complete confidence in the liberation of thoughts, like the confidence that one can swim to the other side of a river. A practitioner with this kind of confidence will be able to rest in the ground luminosity at death for as long as he or she wishes. There are many instances of people whose bodies did not decompose for several days after passing away; during that time there was still slight warmth at the heart center. This happens in two cases. One case is that of someone who has recognized the view of the luminosity of path, the unconditioned nature, and simply rests in the realization of this nature. Another case of the body remaining without decomposing is that of someone who has attained stability in a certain type of mental concentration called supramundane shamatha.

There are two types of shamatha, mundane and supramundane. When an individual has reached a certain level of stability in supramundane shamatha, it is possible for the dead body to remain without decomposing for as long as several years. In Burma and Thailand, there are several practitioners whose bodies have not yet decomposed and who are still in that state. This has also happened in Tibet. Shamatha means abiding calmly: when this practice is perfected one overcomes negative emotions and thought activity. Like water that is undisturbed by the wind, one simply rests in a concentrated state without objective support, remaining totally undisturbed. For this reason, one can remain for a very long time. Actually, it is quite a good state and is a sign that one has some degree of mastery over one's mind. This enables the mind, indivisible from prana, to abide in the body without the body decomposing for as long as one wishes. At the end of that time, the consciousness does not leave the body through the inferior openings, such as the eyes, ears and so forth; it exits through the crown of the head.

I shall now describe how death occurs for someone who has gained stability in the path luminosity during the bardo of this life. At present the mind within the physical body is like space within a jar: inner space is still separated from the space outside. The moment the jar breaks, the space within and without merge and are indivisible. Likewise, at the time of death, the moment the physical body disintegrates, the advanced practitioner's consciousness merges with the primordially pure nature, the ground luminosity. At this point a sign that such a person has been liberated can be seen by others. A drop of red and white liquid, called the bodhichitta essence, is exuded from the left nostril or from the crown of the head. Why is that? Within the physical body there are certain energy currents called pranas: the wisdom pranas in the left side of the body, the karmic pranas in the right side of the body. Therefore, it is a very good sign after someone has passed away if the bodhichitta essence issues from the left nostril.

The consciousness may remain in the body while the practitioner is resting in the meditation state after death. A visible sign of resting in the meditation state is that the flesh remains supple and radiant. It seems almost impossible to ascertain whether or not the person has died. In this case the eyes have a loving, compassionate expression; warmth remains at the heart center and the body appears very fresh and glowing. On the other hand, if the consciousness remains due to strong attachment or resentment, the heart center might still be warm but the body will be as stiff as any other corpse, with the face contorted in an unpleasant expression. These different situations are both mentioned because instructions are meant to clear away doubt; otherwise one may conclude that whenever some heat remains at the heart after death, the person is resting in the state of meditation. This is not necessarily true.

Generally, most people consider the dividing line between life and death to be whether or not the body is still breathing. But, actually, if we examine these two situations mentioned, the mind is still in the body even though external breathing has stopped. The only sure sign of whether the mind has actually departed from the body is if the red and white essences have appeared at the bodily apertures, either at the lower openings or at the upper openings such as the nostrils or the crown of the head.[28]

According to Buddhist tradition, if that has not happened then it is improper to cremate or bury the body. For the practitioner who is quite stable in practice, it does not matter what is done with his body. It can be chopped up or burned immediately. But for a beginner or for one with only some degree of stability in practice, the body should be left completely at peace for as long as the mind remains in the body, usually three and a half days. There should be no shouting or talking. One should not even burn incense.

Although I have told this story in the past it deserves to be told once again. Around 1986 Lama Lobsang Tenpa, a Nepali practitioner, died. He was from northern Nepal but when he was young, he went to Tibet and received many teachings. Though not completely realized, he was a good practitioner and definitely not a beginner. He had fallen ill and knew that he was going to die. He had already resigned himself to this fact, but his benefactors, some businessmen in Kathmandu, said, … "We have to do whatever we can," so they flew him to Delhi and put him in a hospital. The doctors tried open-heart surgery, but because of a serious malfunction in his heart, it could not be repaired, and he died on the operating table. The sponsors and his disciples were outside in the waiting hall. What happened after he died was that the body started to sit up by itself in the meditation posture. The doctors put it back horizontally but again it sat upright. Unused to seeing such an event, they strapped him down, but still the body tried to sit up. Startled by this behavior, the doctors took his body into the cremation chamber where it was immediately burned. When the disciples finally knocked on the door and asked, … "What happened to our teacher?" the doctors said, "Something really bad happened! We had to burn him immediately. Here are the ashes!" and they handed over a vase. This ignorant action on their part was probably a slight obstacle to Lobsang Tenpa's realization. The mind is something quite amazing and this is a strange story.

How do we recognize the ground luminosity, our buddha nature, during the bardo of dying? What does this recognition depend on? It depends on one thing alone: our present practice. Without practicing now, it is extremely unlikely that we would recognize the ground luminosity during the bardo of dying.

During the bardo of dying, the dissolution stages of appearance, increase, and attainment occur. At their conclusion, if one fails to recognize the dharmakaya luminosity one may black out. When one suddenly awakens, it is to the sambhogakaya luminosity of the bardo of dharmata. This state is extremely clear, brilliant, open, and empty. The adept practitioner feels free and blissful. However, someone not familiar with this state through recognizing the path luminosity during this lifetime will find the luminosity of the bardo of dharmata painful and frightening. One will panic and after just a few seconds the tendency towards ego-clinging will reassert itself. One thinks, … "What happened! What is this! Where am I?" This ego-clinging, this desire to anchor the identity of 'I' and 'that' in dualistic experience is the very basis for our experience of a solid reality. Grasping at a self-entity is the direct cause for the vicious circle of samsaric existence to evolve once again.

During the bardo of dharmata a clear and open state happens by itself, unlike our daily life when usually we must push ourselves a little to be mindful of the meditation state. The naked meditation state arises naturally and effortlessly because the dharmata, our innate nature, is unconditioned; it is not produced or fabricated by our meditation practice and so this state is extremely simple. The experienced practitioner can simply relax into this state with full confidence, knowing, that this is what I am used to practicing. Now, without having to create anything, it occurs by itself. With this kind of confidence gained from everyday practice, attaining stability and liberation are easy. At this point of the bardo of dharmata, the practice is beyond effort and we realize a free, comfortable state of mind.

Why are such words as luminosity, suchness, naturalness, unfabricated state, or innate nature used? Because these words describe how our buddha-nature is when left alone. The key point is to grow accustomed to the state of luminosity right now. Almost half of our life may be over, and, assuming that we still have half left, we should try to use the rest of our life to become genuinely acquainted with this state of innate luminosity. Then, liberation will occur at death, and we need not undergo any of the following bardos or take another rebirth. The compassionate, skillful Buddha gave many extensive and profound teachings, but they can be condensed into a single sentence: "Train right now in the path luminosity so that at the moment of dying you can dissolve confusion into the ground luminosity."

Once we become interested in gaining personal experience of the Dharma, we must try to apply a teacher's instruction on meditation practice. There are many different techniques: some suggest concentrating on a mental object, some advice simply resting without a focal point; some techniques utilize certain concepts, some are nonconceptual; some practices are very simple, some are elaborate. Nonetheless, understand that basically there are two states of mind. I will use the Tibetan words for them so that we can remember them later on. One state is called *sems* and the other *rigpa*. Sems refers to the state of conceptual thinking, involving fixation on some 'thing.' It is a mistaken way of perceiving. Rigpa means free from fixation. It refers to a state of natural wakefulness that is without dualistic thinking. It is extremely important to be clear right now about the difference between these two states of mind. Through studying the teachings, receiving oral instructions and clearing away doubts, we can recognize the genuine, authentic way of spiritual practice. When our practice is genuine, the time spent in rigpa may be very short, but repeating that authentic state many times is extremely effective at quickly clearing away confusion and disturbing emotions. We rapidly realize what should be realized and develop the enlightened qualities. On the other hand, without knowing genuine rigpa, to practice a state of mind that is undecided about what is rigpa and what is sems, does not hit the vital point, and progress is much slower. Above all, we must distinguish between sems and rigpa.

The teachings of the Buddha describe reality in two ways: the seeming and the real, the superficial and the absolute, the relative and the ultimate, how things appear and how things truly are. Whatever is experienced in the state of sems or conceptual mind is always just the superficial, the seeming; relative truth or things as they appear. But, whatever is experienced in the state of rigpa, nonconceptual wakefulness, is always the genuine, the real; things as they are. What the Buddha calls the path luminosity is simply the nature of things. It is not discovered simply by adopting a set of philosophical ideas, be they Buddhist or whatever. Moreover, path luminosity is not something one discovers through clever thinking, by trying to figure out a reasonable version of reality. Neither is it some new state that the Buddha invented. It is just the nature of things as they are.

In the past, a man dressed in yellow robes called Buddha Shakyamuni spoke. His teachings were collected and were later given the label Buddhism. But actually, he simply pointed out the nature of things, the innate wakefulness that is primordially present in us and which did not suddenly appear at the time of the Buddha. This true state of innate wakefulness, the ultimate nature called ordinary mind is the ground luminosity. This is something that we all experience briefly from time to time, but in reality, we are never separate from it. Innate wakefulness is not something that only the buddhas experience in some extraordinary place far away. We also experience it, but we fail to acknowledge it. Because of not recognizing the ground luminosity, we do not train ourselves in it. Even if we have recognized this innate wakefulness, because of instability in the recognition, we always lose track of it and continue in samsaric existence. On the other hand, 'buddha' means someone who recognized innate wakefulness or ground luminosity, trained in it as path and attained stability in that recognition. He discarded all falsehood, attained liberation, and actualized all the enlightened qualities. That is the meaning of buddhahood.

The different levels of Buddhist teaching contained in the nine vehicles use different terminology to describe this natural state of being. The terminology depends on how direct the teachings are, but what they all actually point to is the same; it is simply the path luminosity.

How should we personally practice the path luminosity? We must depend on some technique, some method. First, we see a teacher and ask what to do. He or she says, … "Meditate," and we think, … "All right, I will practice meditation." Then what happens? What is meditation? Usually, we think it means sitting with something held in mind, either a concrete object or something abstract. We think that by keeping that mental focal point we are practicing meditation. But the actual state of path luminosity is not a meditation on some 'thing;' neither is it a state of distraction, following old thought patterns. Luminosity refers to what is actual; simply that which is naturally present. We use the term path luminosity when talking about it, but training in it means simply maintaining a continuity of wakefulness without words, without meditating on a particular object. As long as we think there is some object upon which we should fix our mind, innate wakefulness eludes us. Regardless of whether we are keeping an abstract or a concrete thing in mind, it misses the point, obscuring the path luminosity.

Upon hearing this, we might frown upon the practice of meditating on conditioned phenomena, regarding it as not very advanced. We think, … "Now, I will go a step further and meditate on that which is unconditioned. I will keep nothing in mind!" but we retain a conceptual reference point in that we fixate on something unconditioned. This is still conditioned in the sense that some dualistic setup lingers in our mind. It is not the real meditation practice of path luminosity.

Another thing that can happen is that we want to gain a thorough comprehension of the philosophy of Buddhism. We hear the teachings, … "All phenomena are empty. The ego is devoid of true existence," and we start to think about that… "Oh, what I usually believe to be the real world, what I experience through my five senses as the sights, sounds, smells, tastes and tangible things, when examined closely possess no true independent existence. Although I experience them while they appear, they are actually empty of any self-entity." At some point we feel understanding this theory of emptiness is not difficult. Moreover, that which discriminates, thinking … this is right, this is wrong, the 'me' who is trying to find itself or track down the ego, is also not a tangible thing that can be pinpointed. The self only seems to exist. It appears as though there is a self, but at the same time this so-called 'I' is actually impossible to find. Now we got the idea that there is also no real ego. That is all right in itself. We have a theoretical understanding of emptiness, but we might mistake it for genuine realization when it is nothing more than theory, just the thought of emptiness. We practice this idea in our meditation, solidifying the theories, and nothing much happens. Years can go by. We find it very hard to progress beyond this theoretical understanding and become depressed. We think … "I did all this practice and nothing has happened. I am useless!" Or we get angry and resent our teacher, thinking, … "He did not give me the right teachings. He fooled me! I wasted my time!" This is quite a serious problem, quite a big obstacle. In fact, it is the biggest mistake we could make. That is why I place so much emphasis on the fact that it is extremely important right now to gain some personal certainty, some practical confidence in the view, in wakefulness free from mental constructs. This is what really counts. Yet, it may take some preparation.

Often the teachings make use of difficult terminology such as dharmakaya or the luminosity of dharmata to refer to the ultimate view. But actually, the real meaning is our present state of mind when it is not distracted for even a second and at the same time not meditating upon anything. At this point nondistraction means not slipping away or straying from the continuity of our innate nature. It means nothing other than this. We can use the word meditation, but as long as an object is held in mind, whether it is sublime or ordinary, there is always dualistic fixation. The phrase 'luminosity of dharmata' means that dharmata, our innate nature, while empty, is at the same time naturally cognizant. It is like space. Space is empty, but we can still talk about space. Space simply is. When we talk about the elements earth, water, fire and wind, they are easy to understand because we can actually see and take hold of them, even measure them. There is no question about the presence of the first four elements. We also must say that the element space exists. But while space does not actually exist concretely, it still functions. Space accommodates. In the same way, the luminosity of dharmata is extremely basic.

Dharmata literally means 'nature,' that which is not manufactured, that which is simply natural. It is not produced by a creator; it is uncompounded; it is empty. But at the same time, just as space, though empty, can accommodate things, dharmata, though empty, accommodates the arising or manifestation of all things. Unlike space, dharmata has many other qualities.

In order to take full advantage of the bardo of dharmata, we must recognize the correct view right now. Next, we must know how to sustain the continuity of that view; in other words, how not to spoil it. Whenever we try to remain mindful of it as a thing or to meditate upon it as an object of mental focus, it is spoiled.

Among all the 84,000 different teachings given by the Buddha, the extensive Sutra, the profound Tantra, and the essential oral instructions, among all the different categories, such as Dzogchen or Mahamudra, the key point is, in essence, identical with what is experienced at the moment the luminous bardo of dharmata dawns.

Because the three kayas are automatically present in the luminous bardo of dharmata, it is the state of Mahamudra. Do not think of the three kayas as physical deities with various colors and attributes. The three kayas are simply words used to describe different aspects or facets of the naked state of this luminous bardo of dharmata. It is taught that dharmakaya is empty in essence and the sambhogakaya quality is naturally luminous or cognizant, while the nirmanakaya aspect is the unity of these two, emptiness and cognizance. Because this state is free from any mental effort of fixating upon a certain object or idea, we can call it prajnaparamita, transcendent knowledge. Before, while involved in conceptual thinking, one never truly realized what prajnaparamita was.

Madhyamika, the Middle Way, is defined as the absence of extremes. A good khenpo who knows not only the words of the scriptures but also has some experience in practice can explain the Madhyamika view as being in perfect harmony with all of the other teachings. This is difficult for someone who has only studied scriptures but lacks practical experience. Statements made from different perspectives often seem to contradict each other. In Tibet, there were many arguments between two schools called *Rangtong* and *Shentong*. A teacher who has the confidence of the view, meaning direct experience, is able to establish the Rangtong view very precisely and without any conflict. It will make perfect sense. Furthermore, such a teacher is also able to establish the Shentong view without stating any contradictions. It too will make perfect sense. But when a scholar bases his exposition only on the scriptures and mere theoretical understanding, and says, … "Everything, all phenomena from the aggregate of form to the state of omniscient enlightenment, is totally empty, like space," it sounds a little too nihilistic. It sounds as though no matter how much one practices, the results will be empty. What is the point then? One can become discouraged. Alternately, when an inexperienced teacher expounds the Shentong view that the kayas and wisdoms are truly self-existing and that the state of enlightenment is changeless and eternal, it sounds a little too eternalistic, as though it is a non-Buddhist view. That can also be confusing. Therefore, the main point in practice is to arrive at the view free from mental constructs. To think that things are nonexistent is just a type of mental construct; and to hold the other extreme that something ultimately exists is also a type of mental construct. The real view is free from holding onto any such ideas. That is why it is said that the true view of Madhyamika is free from the confines of mental constructs.

Other practice traditions in Tibet arrive at the same end. The main practice of the Sakya lineage is the *Lamdrey* system. Lamdrey means path and result. Path refers to the teachings that are applied during practice; by combining these with the view of the result one takes the end result as the path right from the very beginning. How does one do this? Ground luminosity, the unconditioned nature, is possible to realize directly, right now. It must be mingled with our experience along the path. Since in essence ground luminosity and path luminosity are identical, we realize the ultimate result during the bardo of dharmata by growing used to the path luminosity right now.

Why are there so many different teachings; why not just one? What is the use of having all these different names and different approaches? People have diverse interests. We have different ideas about how to drink a cup of tea. Some people must have a spoonful of sugar or their tea is undrinkable, while other people only drink tea without sugar. Everyone has their own idea about how a meal should be, whether it should have a lot of salt, no salt or just a little bit. Some like Nepali food, some like only Western food, or especially French food, even though food is basically the same, it goes in the mouth and comes out the other end and it keeps us alive. Still, according to our habits and inclinations we maintain different ideas about how food should be prepared and how it should be eaten. The same principle holds true for the Buddhist teachings; they are easily adapted to suit the varying dispositions of different people. That is why Buddhism has different lineages and different approaches.

The Buddha very kindly gave many different teachings and methods of practicing, but all these different systems converge at one point: right now, while you are alive, get used to the nonconceptual wakefulness called luminous dharmata, the state free from concepts, beyond a meditation of mental fabrication. This is what it all comes down to. Accustom yourself to nonconceptual wakefulness now, so at the time of death you will not have to go through the remaining bardos to a new rebirth. Resting in nonconceptual wakefulness is enough to cover all aspects of practice. We call this by so many different names, but once we realize it, buddhahood will no longer be a mere concept, it is a direct experience. The highest yoga is to be attained right now. Rest in nonconceptual wakefulness and you are a genuine yogi, a truly qualified practitioner.

Sadly, when information is given directly to some people, no matter how clearly it is explained, if the listener does not have the karmic aptitude for the teaching it doesn't really penetrate. The numerous teachings given by the Buddha describe how all phenomena included in samsara, nirvana and the path appear. There is their 'seeming mode,' the relative truth, and their 'actual nature,' the ultimate truth. What occurs during the bardo of dharmata is the ultimate nature of things. Dharmata means true nature, a wakefulness beyond concepts, free from acceptance or rejection or artificial constructions. To ensure liberation at that point we must train right now in nonconceptual wakefulness.

The Dzogchen teachings contain certain practices that relate directly to the experiences that arise during the bardo of dharmata. The Mahamudra system includes teachings called *the Six Doctrines of*

Naropa, with practices such as illusory body, dream yoga, and bardo practice. If we train in these and combine them with the meditation practice during the waking state, called the bardo of meditation, and the sleeping practice, called the bardo of dream, we can recognize the luminosity of deep sleep. By that we will be able to recognize luminosity and attain liberation during the bardo of dharmata. A practitioner of the path of means, the Six Doctrines, should after recognizing the different signs of apparent luminosity such as the mirage, the whiteness, and so forth, simply rest in self-cognizance, nonconceptual wakefulness or ordinary mind, and realize that all these appearances are manifestations of dharmakaya. For someone who has mainly practiced Dzogchen's Tögal it is essential to trust that all the various experiences, the sounds, colors, and lights, the peaceful and wrathful deities and so forth, are all the natural manifestation of one's own nature. Having attained that confidence, liberation is assured.

The vital issue here is to recognize the correct view, whether it is Dzogchen, Madhyamika, or Mahamudra. First, recognize the view. Then, in order to enhance your experience of the view and attain stability, utilize a practice such as yidam deity, the Six Doctrines, Tögal and so forth. The Dzogchen system recommends Tögal practice, in which our realization of the view progresses by means of various manifestations and experiences. In the same way, whatever occurs in the bardos, all the apparent experiences, displays and manifestations, will further enhance our realization. Whatever arises actually becomes a display or adornment of our innate wakefulness, and in no way becomes an obstacle.

Tsele Rinpoche mentions Garab Dorje's *Three Words Striking the Vital Point.* These three sentences condense all the teachings of the Buddha to the quintessential meaning: recognize your essence, decide on one point, and gain confidence in liberation. First, recognize your essence. That is the primary root, the starting point. Without having first recognized your essence, you cannot decide or resolve on it without a doubt. If one is unable to decide upon that as the ultimate, one can never gain confidence in liberation.

The first thing to really focus all our actions of body, speech and mind on, is recognizing the essence of our mind. That is the starting point. The sentence "Recognize the essence of your own mind" is an extremely important point. It simply means recognizing that what you already have, your innate, nonconceptual wakefulness, is already a part of yourself and is not something new. The word 'recognize' literally means to arrive at some understanding that we did not have earlier. Do not mistake it to mean discovering something that you did not already possess.

Up until now we have studied and learned and our understanding may have remained an idea, a separate object held in mind. But the natural state of dharmata, the luminosity of wisdom as it is, is not a physical object composed of matter nor a shape with a certain color that we can see. It is not like that at all. Moreover, it is not as though we, as one entity, are supposed to look at the essence of our mind as another entity. We do not recognize our essence through the dualistic act of one thing looking at another. Recognizing the basic state is not like that.

What is really meant here? Innate wakefulness, the luminosity of dharmata, is the very essence of the mind that fixates or thinks of something. Yet our dualistic fixation and thinking is like a veil that covers and obscures this luminosity.

In short, what is recognized is not a 'thing.' Then what do we recognize? We must experience naked wakefulness directly, and this occurs the instant that our mind is stripped bare of conceptual thinking. That experience, therefore, is not a product of our fabrication. It simply is. The problem is that it is too near to us just like something held so close to our eyes that it is difficult to see. Moreover, it is too easy. We like something more difficult. Simply remaining free from concepts is extremely easy. The only difficulty is it goes against our tendencies, we enjoy conceptual activity, we like to have something to take hold of. So, although it is easy to remain freely, our habitual tendencies pull us away from that state.

The Buddhist teachings are structured according to levels, one above the other, and people with sharp minds will compare the lower teachings to the higher and find that the lower philosophical schools have some defect, some shortcoming. Yet all philosophical ideas are established intellectually, through concepts. As opposed to intellectual reasoning or conceptual insight, the view of Trekchö is nonfabrication, nonmeditation and nondistraction. It is beyond theoretical philosophies.

The Buddha said, … "I have taught you the path to liberation but know that liberation depends on yourself." The Buddha described how to realize the ultimate truth, but he could not make us realize it, we have to do this ourselves. We are like a person with a cataract; people may show us an apple and say, … "Look at this. See how clear it is!" but unless the cataract is removed, we cannot see clearly. Likewise, in order to directly perceive and sustain the natural state, the ultimate nature of things, the obscurations of dualistic knowledge and habitual tendencies must be removed. The most efficient way of quickly removing these subtle obscurations is, after having been introduced to innate wakefulness by a qualified master, to simply rest in the continuity of the natural state. However, unless our obscurations have already thinned out to a certain degree and become very shallow, it is impossible to simply cut through them. That is why all the teachings with a conceptual reference have been given, to reduce our obscurations. We must therefore gather the accumulations of merit and do purification practice. That is the whole point of all the teachings, to advance step by step until it is possible to cut through even subtle obscurations.

All things arise due to causes and circumstances coming together. For example, being born with a beautiful appearance is not necessarily due to one's mother and father being beautiful, since beautiful parents can also have ugly children. A few other causes are necessary. Beauty mainly results from having done something by way of one's body, speech or mind that benefited the physical body of other sentient beings at some point in the past. We can right now directly establish how our mental attitude affects things, without getting into long explanations. A calm, gentle and disciplined person is more capable of doing things in a proper, agreeable way than someone whose mind is disturbed by aggression or a sense of competitiveness. When a disturbed person does physical work, the outcome is somehow distorted. Our actions create habitual tendencies that then reoccur within our mind. Conversely, when we realize the nature as it is, the three poisons and the various negative thought patterns begin to disappear, the obscurations start to diminish. Once the obscurations diminish, realization of the view is easy. Therefore, the whole basis of Dharma practice is very direct and related to our present state of mind. Practice is not based on old stories and romantic narrations from the past.

When an architect, doctor or artist becomes very agitated by negative emotions due to, say, a problem with his mate or money, he cannot possibly do his job properly. It even is difficult for a doctor to take the pulse of a patient. For an artist, it is difficult to draw a straight line. Why is that? It is because his mind is disturbed. If one is on the verge of a nervous breakdown, deeply depressed or worried, one cannot do anything in the usual way.

When some people get really angry, they cease to see clearly. Even the ordinary perceptions of the five senses are obscured; they are certainly unable to recognize the innate wisdom. On the other hand, when our mind is relaxed and we feel free and easy, everything is beautiful. This whole world is nice and pleasant. Flowers look pretty, it is feels good to be with friends and food tastes delicious. But when our mind is agitated and disturbed, everything feels wrong. Our best friend is annoying, beautiful things look ugly, and we have no appetite. If sitting, we want to be somewhere else. When going somewhere else, we want to sit down quietly. At night we cannot sleep. At that point, we are actually a little crazy. This is a mild form of insanity. What is making us crazy? It is the manifestations of our own disturbing emotions, karma and obscurations. Wouldn't it be better to just rest in the natural state in which emptiness and cognizance are a unity?

We must "Decide on one point." The natural state is totally free from any mental constructs, whether good or bad, special or ordinary; it is perfectly empty. Although empty, it is not blank. It is naturally cognizant, aware. This state of emptiness and awareness as unity is the natural state of the ground luminosity. It is called luminosity of dharmata in this context and is what is shown by a qualified master during the pointing-out instruction. She says, … "That's it!" and we may recognize it. But simply having recognized it is not sufficient. We must be totally free from doubt about it. That is what is meant by 'deciding on one point.' Having resolved your experience to be the innate wakefulness beyond a shadow of doubt, train then to "Gain confidence in liberation.." Once you possess the confidence of the view then no matter what scholars or other people say, even if the buddhas and bodhisattvas appear and say, … "You are wrong, you are confused, you are still mistaken," because you already experience the natural state of things, the ultimate truth right at that moment, there will be no basis for bewilderment. You have gained total confidence.

Based on our confidence in liberation, we progress towards true realization. Passing away is then like a vase breaking: the space within and the space without mingle together without the slightest division. It is like the birth of a baby snow lion who immediately has the strength to walk and jump. Or like a baby garuda bird; the moment it hatches from the egg it is able to fly. Likewise, for the practitioner who has confidence in the view, death, and liberation are simultaneous. Our experience of the path luminosity during this life and the experience of ground luminosity that happens at the moment of death mingle and blend into one experience. They are not two different luminosities, but just one that is inseparably mingled with dharmakaya.

We may be the type of person who need not depend on elaborate practices in order to stabilize rigpa, nonconceptual wakefulness. On the other hand, we may really need to make use of other practices to stabilize our understanding. If stabilizing rigpa were easy for everybody and they only had to do that and nothing else, then there would not have been much point in Marpa making Milarepa go through all the various trials and tribulations that he underwent. The key point here is that if one can recognize rigpa directly, it is fine. But if this is difficult, then engage in the practices to gather accumulations and purify the obscurations in order to facilitate recognition of your buddha nature.

...Like the confusion in the dreams of one's sleep last night...Later on it will be difficult to practice in the bardo.[29] We may have recognized the nature of mind when it was pointed out, but if we just leave it with that and think, ... "Last year I received the pointing-out instruction, the transmission of mind nature. That is enough. I've got it now," it is actually not enough. Why? Even though we may have recognized mind essence, aren't we still completely deluded at night while sleeping? When pleasant and unpleasant events occur in dreams, we either accept or reject, feel happy or afraid and so forth; in other words, we are totally deluded. If that is the case right now, what will happen when we arrive at the bardo of dharmata? As in our present dream state, we will not even remember the teachings, let alone remember to recognize mind essence. So, there is not much chance for an unskilled practitioner to attain liberation during the bardo of dharmata. It is not enough merely to recognize mind essence once or twice; we need to train in it again and again and become so thoroughly acquainted with it that we do not fall into confusion when meeting different kinds of experiences, even in the dream state.

Tsele Natsok Rangdröl states: *...Passing one's days and nights in confusion and tenaciously clinging to a solid reality now, while one's body, speech, and mind are together and one has some freedom, will disappoint one's hopes of being able to rest in meditation during the intense pain at the moment of death, or when fears and delusions are swirling like a tornado in the bardo of dharmata. I think therefore that one must prepare oneself for the great and permanent goal.*[30]

At present, our days and nights are for the most part spent holding onto a sense of solid reality. We think that things are permanent when they are not; that conditioned existence is happiness when it is not; that impure phenomena are pure when they are not; that there is a true ego when actually there is not. Deluded by fixation on a solid reality, we spend our whole life on pointless pursuits, thinking that an instant of recognition is sufficient and that later on we will definitely recognize and become liberated in the bardo of dharmata. This is extremely foolish.

Right now, while the mind is in the body, we have the freedom to choose what to do. Wouldn't it be better to spend our time preparing for the after-death state? The final goal, realizing the natural state of the luminous dharmata, innate wakefulness, is made possible by the power of your present practice. That is what is really important.

The Karmic Bardo of Becoming

The first three bardos have now been covered and we arrive at the fourth, the karmic bardo of becoming. Why is it called the karmic bardo of becoming? After death, our minds are dominated by the results of our karmic actions, combined with the twelve links of dependent origination such as ignorance, consciousness, formation and so forth. Due mainly to the accumulation of past karma, we succumb to our next rebirth. Like the others, this bardo is explained under three headings: first, how to identify it, second, how it is experienced, and finally, how to apply the instructions.

It is imperative to understand that the karmic bardo of becoming does not happen for everyone. Advanced practitioners will already have been liberated and need not undergo this bardo. It is not necessary to mention realized practitioners here. This teaching is for the yogin practitioner of lesser capacity who has been unable to attain liberation during his lifetime, at the moment of death or in the luminous bardo of dharmata. The Tibetan word used here for yogin practitioner is *naljorpa*. Nal means the natural state and jor means to unite oneself with that, to rest in it. A person who adheres to the natural state is called a yogin practitioner.

We may have received the pointing-out instruction and practiced a little during our lifetime, but we didn't attain real stability or progress very far. Therefore, while dying or in the bardo of dharmata we will not be liberated. There is, however, one last chance for liberation in the karmic bardo of becoming.

To attain liberation in this bardo we need to have the habit of former practice. It is not enough just to have heard teachings; we must have personally practiced them to some extent, even a very slight degree. We should at least be able to recall the instructions we received during our lifetime. To apply whatever teachings one has received, whether they are teachings on Mahamudra, Dzogchen, or Madhyamika, will be very helpful in the karmic bardo of becoming. At least, we should be able to recall having recognized the path luminosity in our lifetime, the innate wakefulness free from mental constructs and beyond arising, dwelling, and ceasing.

The karmic bardo of becoming is like a dream; it seems to last for only a short period. At this time, we should try to be free from fear and attachment and instead remember the precious Dharma teachings and supplicate our root guru. The power of our devotion will ensure that we receive his blessings. Due to the coincidence of three factors, the blessings of our teacher, our recollection and practice of the instructions, and the power of the nature of things, it is possible for us to be reborn in a natural nirmanakaya realm, one of the realms of the five buddhas, just like awakening from a dream.

...*As when awakening from a dream, they will achieve the samadhi of awareness.*[31] The samadhi of awareness at this time is exactly the same as what is realized in Mahamudra practice or the practice of Trekchö in Dzogchen. It is the path luminosity as described in the Madhyamika teachings: free from the four extremes and the eight constructs, not existent and not nonexistent; not both, not either; not arising, not ceasing, not singular, not plural, not permanent, not interrupted, not coming and not going. Many other teachings explain path luminosity and they all point to the same thing.

The samadhi of awareness is what enables us to take rebirth in a pure realm. What does that mean? It means that the obscuration of disturbing emotions is purified, but not the obscuration of dualistic knowledge or that of habitual tendencies. In this situation, taking rebirth in a pure realm of one of the five buddhas, we still have to progress through the last stages of the path. *The Mirror of Mindfulness* mentions that, figuratively speaking, it takes five hundred years of practice in such a place to attain liberation. In a natural nirmanakaya realm we continue the practice of recognizing mind essence, training in that and perfecting it. Finally, we arrive at the state of Buddhahood called the great primordial purity. Through that we can manifest the two forms of rupakaya, sambhogakaya and nirmanakaya for the benefit of sentient beings.

A practitioner who has attained a certain degree of stability in practice, who is not a complete beginner, who has not broken the tantric commitments or samayas with the teacher and vajra friends, and who has some power resulting from past practice will experience the bardo of becoming for only a fleeting moment, like awakening after a short dream. Actually, such a person does not really undergo the bardo of becoming because she is liberated into a pure realm very quickly, but has a short experience of it and so it must be included here. Such a person will not have to enter a new womb and take rebirth.

Right now, we have a physical body composed of flesh and blood, the elements, aggregates, and mind. We understand, perceive and experience, and are called a living human being. When these constituents separate, we are a dead person, a disembodied consciousness. The only difference from the experience of this life is that body and mind have separated.

Earlier I explained what we experience when the external breath ceases and the experience that arises after the inner breath has ceased. At this point one experiences the luminosity of dharmata with its accompanying manifestations of colors, sounds and lights. Unable to remain stable in innate wakefulness, our habitual tendencies cause our consciousness to assume the form of a mental body and continue to the bardo of becoming. The actual bardo of becoming is defined as …*The period beginning from the arising of the confused tendencies up until one enters the womb of the next life.*[32] While the mental body travels through the bardo of becoming seeking a place to be reborn, one is frightened, filled with despair. One experiences incredible suffering during this state.

What appears, what is experienced during the bardo of becoming? An ordinary person is someone who has not received the oral teachings and has therefore not been able to put them into practice. …*In addition, their predominant karmic obscuration makes it difficult to form the right frame of mind or to arrange an auspicious coincidence through an instruction such as phowa.*[33] It is difficult for people at the moment of death to practice phowa if they lack the power of practice or have obscured their minds by breaking tantric commitments. One's consciousness roams through the bardo state like a leaf blown by the wind. It is of great benefit at this point to have some accumulation of merit and have purified negative actions, or to have a link with a spiritual teacher, whether positive or negative.

All the problems experienced in the bardo of becoming and afterwards, in the next life, spring from one cause: the fact that during this lifetime we did not acknowledge our inherent nature, the enlightened essence. Not having recognized our basic nature when it was laid bare in the luminous bardo of dharmata with its manifestations of sounds, colors, lights, peaceful, and wrathful deities, we became terrified and fainted. Trying to escape these overwhelming and formidable pure appearances we finally arrived at the karmic bardo of becoming. This tendency to avoid recognizing the nature of mind and to escape from the pure appearances back into a dualistic setup is the very cause that propels us to a new rebirth in one of the six realms of samsara.

Exiting the unconditioned bardo of dharmata, we again mount the wheel of the twelve links of dependent origination, spinning through the links of ignorance, formation, consciousness and further into the aggregates of name-and-form, and so forth, endlessly. Some of these twelve links are disturbing emotions, some are sufferings, and some are the creation of karma. For example, ignorance is a disturbing emotion, formation is karma, and so forth. But in fact, each following link depends upon the former. As this wheel continues to spin, it carries one to the next rebirth.

Ignorance, the first link, is the fact of failing to recognize ground luminosity, our basic buddha nature. Out of confusion and ignorance, thoughts arise in our mind in the form of attraction towards one thing, aversion towards another, or simply a feeling of indifference. These thoughts become more and more solidified so that we start to grasp, and increasingly stronger fixation results.

At this time, we possess a so-called mental body that is not composed of physical substance like the body we have right now. It seems to be solid because it is composed of the essences of the five elements, and so we still feel hungry and so forth. Although we cannot eat material food at this time, we do feel the need for sustenance.

It is said that the mental body in the bardo state lives on smells. However, the deceased person can only partake of these smells in the form of burnt offerings that are especially dedicated to that purpose.

Furthermore, at this time we have some level of clairvoyance and can perceive the thoughts of others. Because the white and red elements from one's father and mother are absent in this mental body, we do not perceive an external sun and moon. But the mental body is somewhat luminous so that wherever we go is lit up by our own radiance. When returning to our home we see our relatives and try to talk to them, but they cannot perceive our mental body and therefore do not respond. We see that they have started to spend our money and to use our belongings so we may feel angry and upset, as well as very attached to our former possessions.

The deceased person can instantly travel anywhere except for two places. One cannot go to the womb of a new mother nor to the Vajra Seat at Bodhgaya in India.[34] We arrive at a new place, simultaneously with the intention to be there. The realization that we are dead can suddenly strike us when we notice that our feet make no imprint on the ground and our body is not reflected in a mirror. Now we begin to feel very afraid, thinking, … "Could it be that I am dead?" Slowly we discover that this is in fact true.

The experiences of the bardo of becoming are exclusively the product of our personal karma. For some it may be briefly very pleasant and then change to being intensely dreadful. It is said that the five elements arise as enemies; some beings may feel burned, flushed away or blown apart. But again, that is due to one's individual karmic phenomena. Some people who have killed insects and animals may experience such animals and insects chasing them, trying to eat them or rip them into pieces.

There have been rare cases where the consciousness, having left the body, actually returns to the corpse, revives it and continues to live. In Tibetan this is called returning from the dead. Although the spirit of the deceased cannot be seen by ordinary human beings, it is perceived by people who are clairvoyant or have a high level of realization. But spirits can see each other because they share the same status; they are the same class of beings. One story refers to a man who passed away and in the bardo of becoming met someone else who had also died. The second deceased person said, … "This is dreadful. When alive, I hid a lot of gold inside the wall of my house and I am really attached to it. Unless somebody can take it out and use it, I will be stuck here for a very long time." In the bardo of becoming, the spirit of the dead person has clairvoyance and can foresee the future. He said, … "You are going to return and live again. Please go and tell my family who live in such-and-such a place that gold is concealed in the wall of such-and-such room. Please tell them to take it out, spend it virtuously and dedicate the merit on my behalf." The first person did indeed revive again. He acted as requested by the dead person and, just as specified, the relatives found the gold and spent it on his behalf.

There are only two types of people who do not enter the bardo of becoming. One type is advanced practitioners who are immediately liberated at death or in the bardo of dharmata. The other is extremely evil people who out of hate and spite have killed many, many people: they go straight to the hell realms. Apart from these two cases, all living beings experience the bardo of becoming after death for approximately forty-nine days, but this is only an average, not fixed. In some cases, people can remain in the bardo of becoming for months or years. During these seven weeks the deceased spirit re-experiences dying and reviving in the bardo state once every seven days.

Immense benefit results if other people do spiritual practice on behalf of a person who has passed away, especially during the first four days after death. Furthermore, at this time there is tremendous effect when a close Dharma friend reads aloud the teachings called *Liberation through Hearing in the Bardo*. Someone who has attained powers through the practice of the three samadhis can summon the consciousness of the deceased person. It is the nature of things that the powerless consciousness of the dead person will appear before such a practitioner. She can then expound the Dharma and give final instructions such as, … "Now this is happening to you. Do not be afraid. Do not be distracted! This is how to practice. Do such and such." There are many stories from the past about how extremely effective and beneficial such instruction can be for the deceased.

There is great benefit when other people do spiritual practice on behalf of the deceased during the forty-nine days of the bardo of becoming. The greatest chance for the deceased person to attain liberation occurs every seven days, i.e., on the seventh and then on the fourteenth day after passing away, etc. That is why special ceremonies for the deceased person are often done on those days.

It is best if a spiritual master is requested to do something for the person who has passed away. In this case, …'master' means someone who has understanding of emptiness and possesses the confidence of realization. Therefore, any virtuous act she performs, such as a feast offering or ceremonial ritual that accumulates merit, becomes the combination of conditioned and unconditional virtue. If a great living master cannot be reached, someone with pure motivation can at least chant the sutras etc., or make offerings to the enlightened beings and dedicate the merit to the person who has passed away. Great benefit also results from that.

Halfway through these seven weeks a dividing point emerges. The first half of the bardo of becoming is dominated by the experiences and habitual way of perceiving things that belonged to one's former life. The second half is dominated in a progressively stronger way by the character of the next rebirth one is about to take. Our next rebirth depends in part on which of the six disturbing emotions is strongest in our mind. This does not mean that we lack the other five poisons, but that the most dominant of the six emotions of attachment, anger, delusion, pride, envy or avarice, determines in which of the six realms we will take rebirth.

Because the essence of these disturbing emotions is wisdom, it is possible to be liberated by recognizing their nature. Due to not recognizing that nature, we ended up in the bardo of becoming and continue to wander in samsara.

Different colors appear in the bardo of becoming, pale lackluster colors that represent each of the six realms. White light appears if one is to be born as a deva in the realm of the gods, red appears for the demigod realm, blue for human beings, green for animals, pale yellow for hungry ghosts, and grey or black if one is to be born in a hell realm.[35]

If you are to be reborn in our world as a human being in one of the unfree states you will have the experience of entering a mist. If you, on the other hand, are about to obtain a precious human body in which you can practice the Dharma, then you experience entering a beautiful city.

When taking rebirth as a human being, the consciousness enters the womb of the mother. There is an indication as to whether one will be born male or female: when strongly attracted to one's future father, one will be born a female; if strongly attracted to one's future mother, one will be born a male. One also feels aggression towards the parent of the same sex. Even if one is not born through a womb but is instantly reborn through what is called miraculous birth, aversion and attachment are still manifest. One is always born with a combination of these two emotions.

Tsele Rinpoche states that it is easier to recognize our nature, the ground luminosity, during the bardo of dharmata and the bardo of becoming than in the bardo of this life. Even if we do recognize it now, it is difficult to train and progress. Even if we attain some degree of stability it is difficult to become totally liberated. Nevertheless, *The Mirror of Mindfulness* and other meditation manuals state that liberation is quite easy during the bardo of dharmata and the bardo of becoming. Why is that?

At present our consciousness, which is called 'prana-and-mind-indivisible,' is encased in a physical body. When imprisoned in a material body the mind is not really free. But in the bardo states of dharmata and becoming, the mind and body are separate until we enter the womb of the next life. During this time the mind is ungrounded and unfettered by an 'encasement;' thus it is easy to recognize, train and attain stability in those two bardos.

The possibility of liberation all comes down to this: during the bardo of this life, we must train and become acquainted with the path luminosity. If we are totally acquainted with this luminosity, meaning stable in that experience, then at best we will not have to undergo the bardos at all. According to the degree of stability we will definitely attain enlightenment either at the moment of death, in the luminous bardo of dharmata or in the bardo of becoming. There is no doubt about this.

Certain practices done now will facilitate recognition of mind essence during the after-death experience. In dream yoga and the practice of illusory body, we try now to get used to this idea, … "This is just a dream. Everything is illusory and dream-like. I am already dead. Nothing is real. All these appearances I perceive are unreal and insubstantial." To have this habit imprinted in our mind makes much it much easier when we actually are dead to recognize that fact, apply the oral instructions and attain liberation.

Tilopa told Naropa, … "One is not fettered by appearances but by attachment. So cut your attachment, Naropa!" In all the different teachings, the main thing that must be cut is not our experience but our attachment, fixation, and clinging to these experiences. That is the main objective.

The primary obstacle to liberation in the bardo of becoming is lack of confidence in the view. We may have recognized the view but unfortunately failed to gain stability in that recognition. Another thing that really creates a great hindrance in the bardo state is attachment to our former possessions or strong resentment. Before passing away or while dying it is therefore extremely important to totally give up the thought of anything or anyone towards which we can be either angry or attached. Otherwise, if these negative thought states recur during the bardo state, they make liberation very difficult.

The Mirror of Mindfulness and *Liberation Through Hearing in the Bardo* give instructions on how to block the gate to rebirth when about to enter the mother's womb. It is possible to avoid rebirth and instead attain liberation. The best means is simply to rest in the view of Mahamudra, Dzogchen, or Madhyamika. If we cannot do that, then we should visualize the father and mother as the deity with consort and avoid taking rebirth at this point. Otherwise, our desire and aversion helplessly drag us into another life. It is important to take care not to let that happen.

When about to take rebirth the best means to apply is the completion stage; next best is the development stage. Through these methods we can quickly perfect the practice of recognizing mind essence and attaining liberation. But if we are completely unable to do either and have no control over our state of mind, then we should form a strong aspiration and supplicate our root guru, saying, … "I have no power to choose, so please bestow your blessings that I may be born in a situation where I can connect with the teachings, receive the oral instructions, and quickly progress along the paths and stages toward enlightenment. Please make sure that I am not born as an ordinary person; let me attain a precious human body!" Due to the coincidence of the blessings of the buddhas and bodhisattvas, the nature of things and the power of such an aspiration, it is possible to be born in a situation in which one can reconnect with the teachings.

What can others do for someone who has passed away? Many things can be done to help the dying person: different rituals can be performed, certain sacred substances can be put into the mouth of the dying person, *the Liberation Through Hearing in the Bardo* can be recited and a sacred image called 'liberation through wearing' can be attached to the body. It is especially effective when a realized master performs a ritual in which he summons the consciousness of the deceased person to come before him, and then dissolves it into a certain image upon which he then confers the four empowerments. At each initiation he gives a clear introduction to mind essence. This ritual, called name-burning, is extremely beneficial in aiding the dead person.

I would like to tell the following story. Dilgo Khyentse Rinpoche was one of three brothers. One brother was Sangye Nyenpa Rinpoche who was a great lama. The other was not an advanced practitioner but had met His Holiness the 16th Karmapa several times. The Karmapa liked him a lot and they always bantered together. Karmapa would call him a joker and play around with him.

While Dilgo Khyentse Rinpoche and his brothers were travelling from Eastern to Central Tibet, this third brother died. Before dying he had fallen, hit his front tooth and broken it off. Although this brother died enroute, Khyentse Rinpoche and his brother Sangye Nyenpa continued to Central Tibet where they met His Holiness the Karmapa, who said, … "I have already met your brother. He came by some time ago. He had broken his tooth but seemed to be doing quite well."

There was no way Karmapa could have heard that Khyentse Rinpoche's brother had died during the journey and even if he had heard, it was extremely unlikely that he would know that the tooth was broken. But somehow, he knew. Khyentse Rinpoche was astounded and said, … "How can you know these things? This is really amazing." Karmapa said, … "There is not much point in talking about this. I am a Karmapa. Certain qualities have developed due to past aspirations and practice, but there is no need to mention them. But one thing always happens: all those whom I have met during this lifetime, whether we have a good or bad connection, always come and visit me after they die before continuing on. I can help some, but not everybody. Anyway, your brother did not seem to have any problem."

There is another story about my grandfather, Chimey Dorje, who seems to have been quite an advanced practitioner. He was in retreat and my father, Kyabje Tulku Urgyen Rinpoche, was his attendant. While he was in retreat, many of Chimey Dorje's disciples lived near him. One of them, a nun, suddenly heard that her father had died and was filled with sadness and despair. She ran straight to Chimey Dorje's retreat hut and knocked on his door, shouting, … "Please, please you must do something quickly! My father has died!" Referring to the ritual for summoning the deceased consciousness, the nun pleaded, … "Please do the name-burning immediately so that my father does not have time to take a bad rebirth." She was so insistent that Chimey Dorje told Kyabje Tulku Urgyen Rinpoche, … "Arrange the ritual objects." Everything necessary was laid before Chimey Dorje and the dead man's name was written on a piece of paper mounted on a stick. Then Chimey Dorje started summoning the consciousness. He did so once, twice, and then suddenly said, …

"This is pointless!" He put his vajra and bell down and said, …Pack these things up. There is no reason to continue. The nun's father is not dead. Kyabje Tulku Urgyen Rinpoche said, … "But please, the nun has said that he is dead. He has stopped breathing and is already taken to the charnel ground. The only thing that remains to be done is to chop up the body and feed it to the birds." Chimey Dorje said, … "No, no! At least I know whether a person is dead or not, whether the consciousness arrives. I might not be completely enlightened, but I do know this much." The next day a man arrived on horseback and said that the nun's father had been carried off to the cemetery, but while he was lying there he actually woke up again and so they took him home. He was not dead.

The name-burning ritual for a dead person is best performed by a master who has the confidence of realization. Then there is no question about the benefit. Any lama or Buddhist priest can of course read the ritual aloud, but that is not enough. Moreover, it has to be performed with the pure motivation of truly wanting to help. Even if a practitioner is not realized and doesn't possess the power to summon the consciousness, if his motivation is pure there will still be some benefit for the dead person.

Furthermore, there is the tradition of performing virtuous deeds and dedicating their merit to the person who has passed away. This should be done in a proper way because the deceased person has the ability to perceive the participant's frame of mind and to know the effect of what has been done. Never slaughter animals to celebrate someone's death. It is important that anything that is done be done in a pure way. If a great practitioner has died, he or she is already liberated and does not need any further help. But if the deceased is not an advanced practitioner, rituals and meritorious actions are of great benefit.

Nevertheless, to ensure liberation it is not sufficient just to have someone else do rituals or good deeds for you after you die. You must acquaint yourself with practice right now while you are still alive. Someone who has realized the ultimate truth of the natural state, totally beyond mental constructs, does not have to undergo these bardos. The bardo states are only experienced by people who have not recognized the ultimate truth and actualized it.

This concludes the teachings on the four bardos. Some people may think that bardo teachings are a specialty and not of chief importance in Buddhist studies. They may think that these teachings are something that one might study on the side, that they are not really the main point. That attitude shows a lack of understanding. Everything that we experience in life and death takes place during one of the four bardo states and all the Buddhist teachings are given to enable the individual to deal with those states and attain liberation.

Afterword[36]

My mother Kunsang Dechen passed away on April 24, 1991. Though she had suffered from the painful disease of pancreatic cancer for months, she never uttered one word of complaint. Asked to write a eulogy relating her life and death to the teachings expressed in this book, I feel this is best said in her own words: … "Now that my time to die has come I have no attachments whatsoever. When I was young, I was afraid of death. For that reason, I practiced diligently my whole life. Now I have arrived at the brink of death. I have heard that the best practitioner is happy to die. The next best is fearless and the lowest has no regrets. I do not have any fears or regrets. The moment this trap of my material body falls apart, I will fly off like a bird escaping from a snare. My prayer now is a request that the lineage holders have long lives in order to benefit all beings. It is my wish that I can take upon myself whatever physical obstacle any of the lineage holders may experience so that they can be free of them. That is my aspiration."

Notes

1. The Mirror of Mindfulness, page 19.
2. Ibid., 20
3. This quotation is the first of four lines of teaching given to Sakya Pandita in a vision of Manjushri. The others are: ...*If you cling to samsaric existence, you have no renunciation. If you cling to self-interest, you have no bodhichitta. If you have any clinging, you don't have the view.*
4. Op cit., page 20
5. Ibid., 21.
6. Ibid., 21
7. Ibid., 21
8. Ibid., 22
9. Ibid., 22
10. More information about this story is found in *The Practice of Dzogchen* by Tulku Thondrup Rinpoche, Snow Lion Publications, Ithaca, N.Y. 1989 p. 127–128: Tulku Thondrup translates the khenpo's own words on this story: ... "At that moment I arrived at a certainty (of realization) from within. I had been liberated from the fetters of 'it is' and 'it is not.' I had realized the primordial wisdom, . emptiness and intrinsic awareness [united]. I was introduced to this realization by his blessing. As Saraha said: ... "He in whose heart the words of the master have entered sees (truth) like a treasure in his own palm." Tulku Thondrup's own commentary continues: ...Afterward, when the words of (Paltrul Rinpoche) were (intellectually) examined, there was nothing much, but just his having said that the eye-consciousness and ear-consciousness are the intrinsic awareness. However, it should be understood that the introduction [pointing-out instruction] (to Dzogchen) took place (through these words) because of the transmission of blessing, the realization of the meaning of *The Heart Essence*.
11. Opcit., 27
12. Ibid., 27
13. Ibid., 28
14. Ibid. 28
15. Ibid., 29
16. Ibid., 29
17. Ibid. 30
18. Kyabje Tulku Urgyen Rinpoche, *Repeating the Words of the Buddha,* trans. Erik Pema Kunsang, Rangjung Yeshe Publications. The dissolution of the elements

is before the real death takes place. There are gross, subtle and very subtle dissolution stages. The gross ones are felt by everybody. It is before the breathing stops, the dissolution of the five elements. First the earth element starts to disintegrate. One feels very heavy. That's when people say … "Please lift me up, raise me up. I feel like I'm sinking." When the water element dissolves then one feels very cold and says … "Please warm me up. It's too cold in here." When the fire element dissolves one feels very thirsty and wants water, one's lips are drying up. When the wind element dissolves one feels as if one is floating at the brink of an abyss, not anchored anywhere. When consciousness dissolves into space it means that everything grows very big and completely ungrounded. The outer breath has stopped but the inner breathing is still taking place.

The subtle dissolution stage is the three experiences of appearance, increase and attainment. They occur after the outer breathing stops. The inner breathing, the inner circulation of prana hasn't ceased yet. For most people it doesn't take very long; it's just one, two, three. The redness experience is like the redness of a setting sun spreading throughout one's vision. The whiteness is like moonlight and the blackness is like everything going completely dark. At the moment when the white and red elements converge in the heart center, the unity of bliss and emptiness, either one goes unconscious, or if one is a practitioner who has familiarity with the state of rigpa, there is the fourth moment of the ground luminosity of full attainment which is the same as primordial purity. The rigpa is not unconscious, but for people not familiar with the state of rigpa then there is nothing but a blackout. For the yogi who has some stability in rigpa there is the great possibility of enlightenment right there. The fourth moment, the ground luminosity, is the same as primordial purity, dharmakaya. Attaining stability in that very moment is complete enlightenment.

19 Kyabje Tulku Urgyen Rinpoche continues: …The crucial point in the context of the two elements converging in the heart center, is the experience of the fourth moment, rigpa. The experience of the white and red elements joining together is the same experience that grabbed the consciousness out of the bardo and into this life to begin with. It occurred when one was conceived into the womb at the time that the mother's and father's red and white elements joined together. In that moment of bliss-emptiness the consciousness faints and is then conceived. Therefore, it's extremely important to not fall oblivious and to remain detached. (From *Repeating the Words of the Buddha*.)

20 Tsele Natsok Rangdröl, trans. Erik Pema Kunsang. *The Mirror of Mindfulness*, (Rangjung Yeshe Publications), 36.

21 Ibid, page 38.

22 Ibid, page 38

23 Kyabje Tulku Urgyen Rinpoche, trans. Erik Pema Kunsang. Normal people

simply fall unconscious. On the other hand, we can never say for sure whether someone remains for a short time in meditation after the outer breath expires. If someone practiced shamatha or dhyana, the after-death meditation state will last for as long as the individual's ability to remain in one-pointed attention. For a person who never practiced meditation there is of course no state of samadhi. A great sinner experiences what is called the 'downward directness;' he goes directly to the hell realms without any bardo.

24 Kyabje Tulku Urgyen Rinpoche continues, …There are two aspects: primordial purity and spontaneous presence. At first, primordial purity manifests at the end of the bardo of dying. The practitioner who has trained on the path will recognize this and be liberated into dharmakaya. Ordinary people will faint for a period of approximately three days. When awakening the deceased will then experience the unfolding of spontaneous presence with its lights, sounds, light rays, and deities in the bardo of dharmata.

The ground luminosity or the unfolding of primordial purity belongs to the end of the bardo of dying. The practitioner can attain enlightenment in the state of dharmakaya only at that point. Similarly, the practitioner can attain enlightenment in the state of sambhogakaya during the bardo of dharmata and nirmanakaya in the bardo of becoming.

25 Kyabje Tulku Urgyen Rinpoche. The luminosity of ground is the buddha nature, the sugatagarbha. The luminosity of path is the natural face pointed out by your master, the state of rigpa that we can recognize. The luminosity of fruition is stability in rigpa. This can be attained at the time of death after the experiences of appearance, increase, and attainment. The experienced practitioner unifies the luminosity of mother and child. This means the ground luminosity that is like a mother and the path luminosity that is like her child meet together and, just like the child jumping up on the mother's lap, we capture the stronghold of rigpa. That is called the luminosity of fruition. (Also see the Foreword by Kyabje Tulku Urgyen Rinpoche).

26 *The Mirror of Mindfulness,* 47
27 Ibid., 47
28 Kyabje Tulku Urgyen Rinpoche: The moment the white and red elements converge at the heart center essential liquid slips out. This is accompanied by an intense feeling of fear, so strong that tears involuntarily flow forth from one's eyes and one falls unconscious. Normal people don't recognize the ground luminosity of full attainment that occurs at this point. The moment the essences fall, they faint. That is the very point at which the inner breath ceases, instantaneously and totally.

When the consciousness does not faint but remains within the state of the ground luminosity of full attainment, that means that rigpa has been recognized. As the sign of that, when this state of samadhi is relinquished a drop of bodhichitta nectar appears from the nostrils. We cannot claim that normal people do not shed the drop of bodhichitta, because what appears is simply the white and red elements from one's father and mother. But, in the case of normal people, these drops appear right away. If someone remains in the 'after-death meditation state' then the white and red bodhichitta drops appear as the sign that this state is over.

29 Ibid., 63
30 Ibid., 63
31 Ibid., 65.
32 Ibid., 66
33 Ibid., 66
34 Sometimes the Vajra Seat refers to the indestructible state of enlightenment.
35 Opcit., 70
36 Many thanks got to the proofreaders, Lynn and Michael who have made this version possible as well as to Joan Olson who diligently typeset the combined manuscripts.K

Activities of Chökyi Nyima Rinpoche

www.shedrub.org

DharmaSun.org

ryi.org

MonksAndNuns.org

Monlam.org

www.ingramcontent.com/pod-product-compliance
Lightning Source LLC
Chambersburg PA
CBHW050428240426
43661CB00055B/2306